Taxes
39%
Cash
Donations
1%
Book
Donations
60%

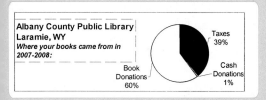

"YOU'LL NEVER KNOW"

by C. Tyler

BOOK I

"A GOOD and DECENT MAN"

OTHER BOOKS BY C. TYLER

THE JOB THING (FANTAGRAPHICS BOOKS, 1993)
LATE BLOOMER (FANTAGRAPHICS BOOKS, 2005)

FANTAGRAPHICS BOOKS
7563 LAKE CITY WAY NE
SEATTLE, WA 98115

DESIGNED BY C. TYLER
PRODUCTION BY PAUL BARESH
EDITED BY KIM THOMPSON
PROMOTION BY ERIC REYNOLDS
PUBLISHED BY GARY GROTH AND KIM THOMPSON

TO RECEIVE A FREE CATALOGUE OF COMICS, CALL 1-800-657-1100, OR
VISIT THE FANTAGRAPHICS WEBSITE: www.fantagraphics.com.

DISTRIBUTED IN THE U.S. BY W.W. NORTON AND COMPANY, INC. (212-354-5500)
DISTRIBUTED IN CANADA BY CANADIAN MANDA GROUP (416-516-0911)
DISTRIBUTED IN THE UNITED KINGDOM BY TURNAROUND DISTRIBUTION (208-829-3009)

FANTAGRAPHICS WEBSITE: www.fantagraphics.com
C. TYLER WEBSITE: www.bloomerland.com

FIRST PRINTING: March 2009

ISBN: 978-1-56097-144-2

PRINTED IN SINGAPORE

C. TYLER PERSONAL THANKS TO:
MARIANA WELFEN AND VIRGINIA UNVERZAGT FOR PRODUCTION ASSISTANCE. FRIENDS AND
ASSOCIATES AT UC'S DAAP SCHOOL OF ART AND THE CGC. JUSTIN AND JULIA GREEN FOR
SUPPORT AND FOR KEEPING IT INTERESTING. BABY AND TIFFANY, TOO. ALL OTHER FAMILY
MEMBERS (AND PETS, ESPECIALLY SARRAH). KIM AND THE FANTA TEAM AND EVERYONE
ELSE WHO KEEPS ME GOING. GRATEFUL, LOVING THANKS TO MY MOTHER FOR HER
ENTHUSIASM AND UNWAVERING SUPPORT. SHE STARTED THE TALKING PARTY WHICH
LED TO THESE STORIES. AND TO MY TWIRL SISTER FOR STAYING ON ME: GINIA IS THE
BEST. BUT THE BIGGEST THANKS OF ALL GOES TO MR. C.W. TYLER HIMSELF, WHO ONE
NIGHT DECIDED TO PICK UP THE PHONE...

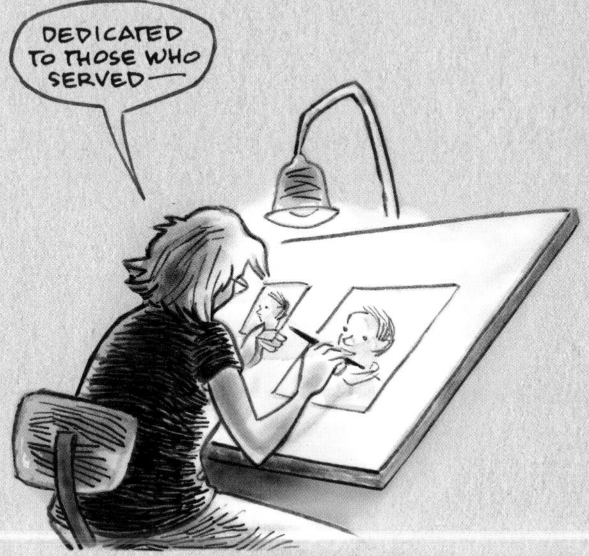
DEDICATED TO THOSE WHO SERVED—

WORLD WAR II

A catastrophic 6 year long global wave of aggression instigated by delusional, charismatic criminal leaders intent on incurring death, destruction and domination over nations, cultures and individuals through the use of bombs, guns, tanks, explosives and poison.

1939-1945

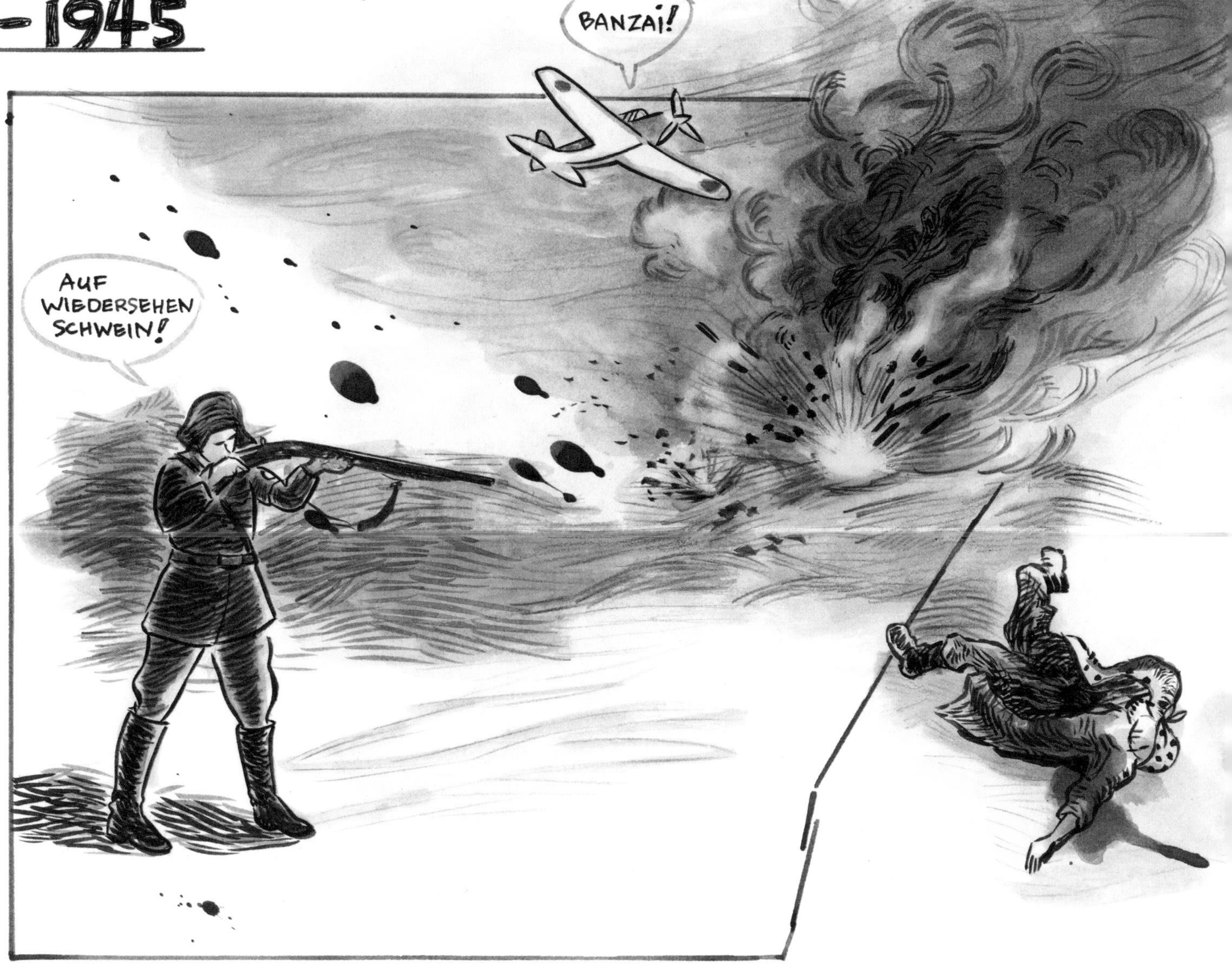
BANZAI!
AUF WIEDERSEHEN SCHWEIN!

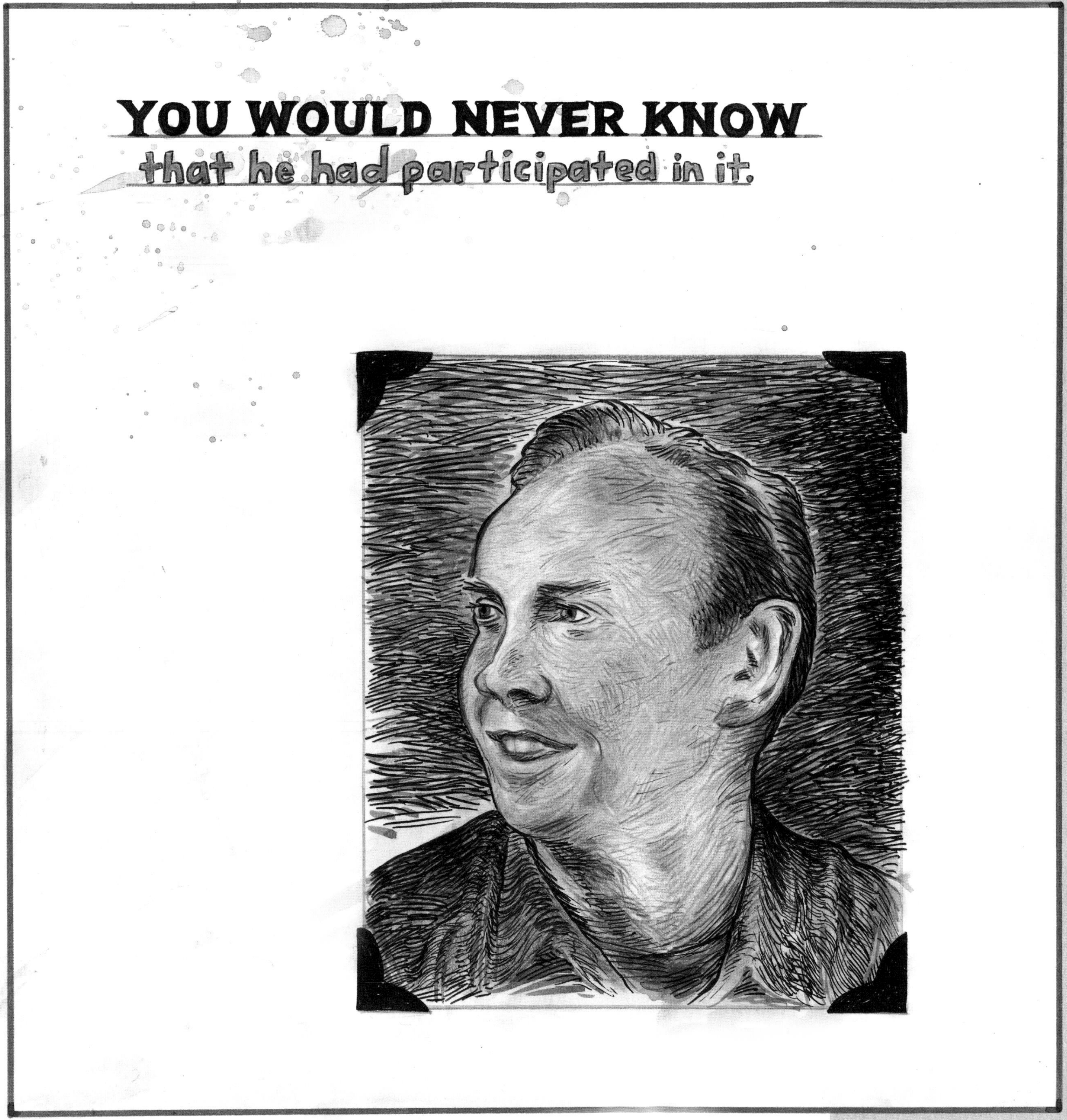
YOU WOULD NEVER KNOW
that he had participated in it.

You'd never know by looking at him in the 1950s...
1950
Fishin' in Wisc.
WITH HIS DAD
or the 60s... That swingin' decade!
1968
WITH HIS WIFE
25th anniv.
Playboy Club Key Holder Sporting the "RAT PACK" look!
or 70s. Nothing to indicate he was in it.
1974
Man with a Bra descending a fancy staircase he made from scratch
WITH HIS PALS
The 80s, 90s... ehh
NEW CENTURY
WHO GIVES A DAMN ABOUT Y2K.
YEAH, WHO CARES.
WITH ME, ONE OF HIS KIDS

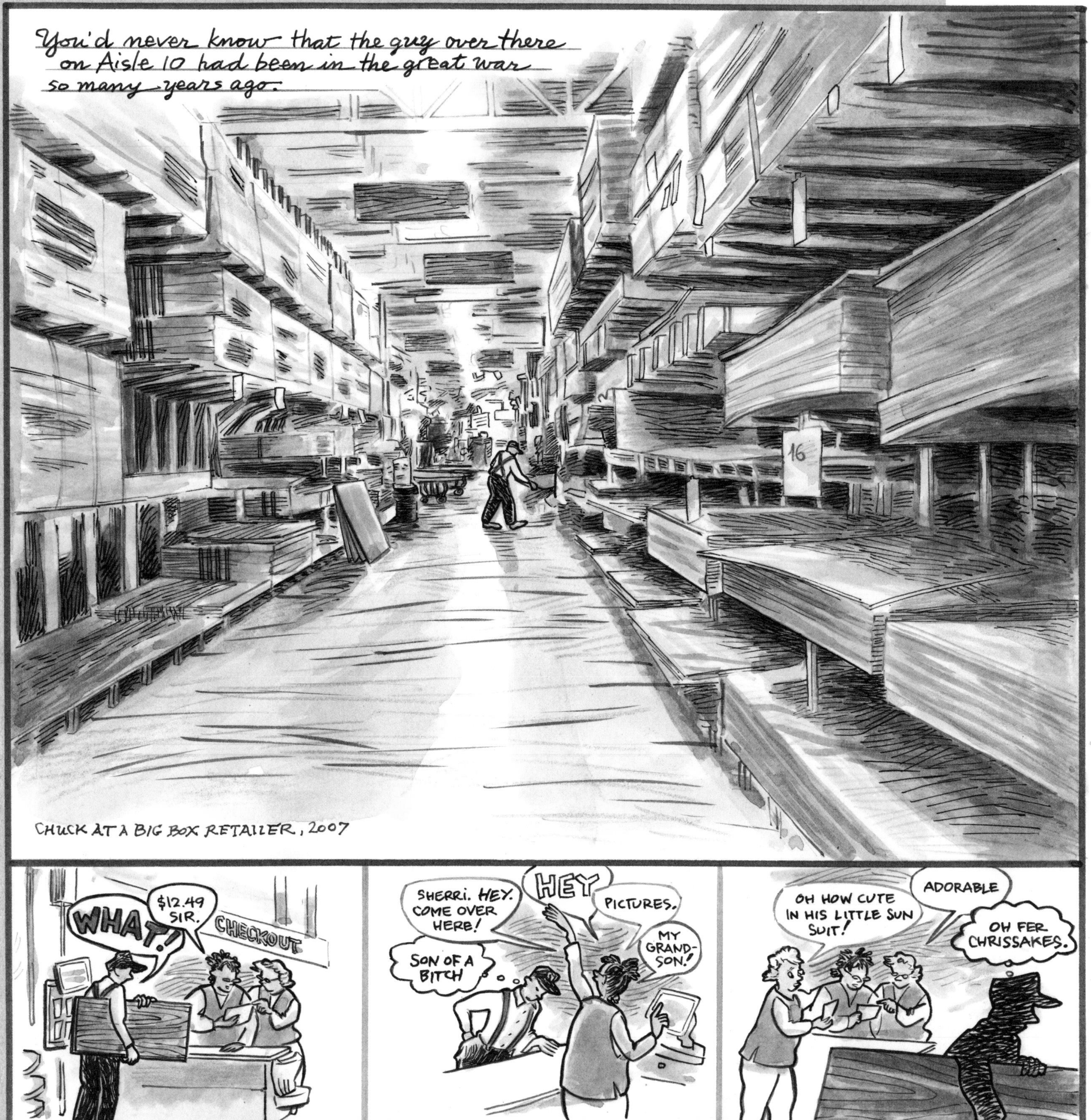
You'd never know that the guy over there on Aisle 10 had been in the great war so many years ago.
16
CHUCK AT A BIG BOX RETAILER, 2007
WHAT!
$12.49 SIR.
CHECKOUT
SHERRI. HEY. COME OVER HERE!
HEY
PICTURES.
MY GRAND-SON!
SON OF A BITCH
OH HOW CUTE IN HIS LITTLE SUN SUIT!
ADORABLE
OH FER CHRISSAKES.

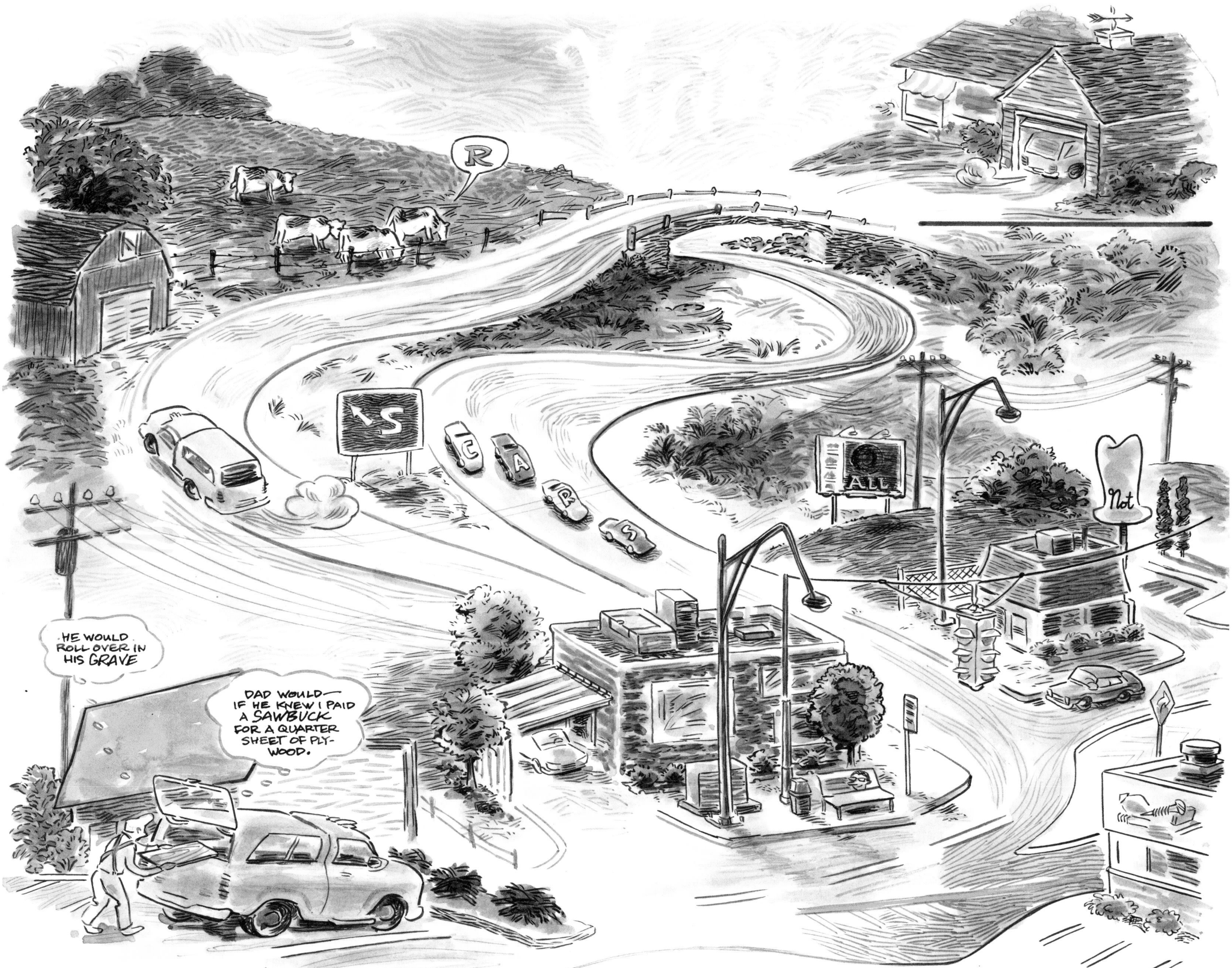
R
S
C
A
R
S
ALL
Not
HE WOULD ROLL OVER IN HIS GRAVE
DAD WOULD— IF HE KNEW I PAID A SAWBUCK FOR A QUARTER SHEET OF PLY-WOOD.

Not-all-scars R....

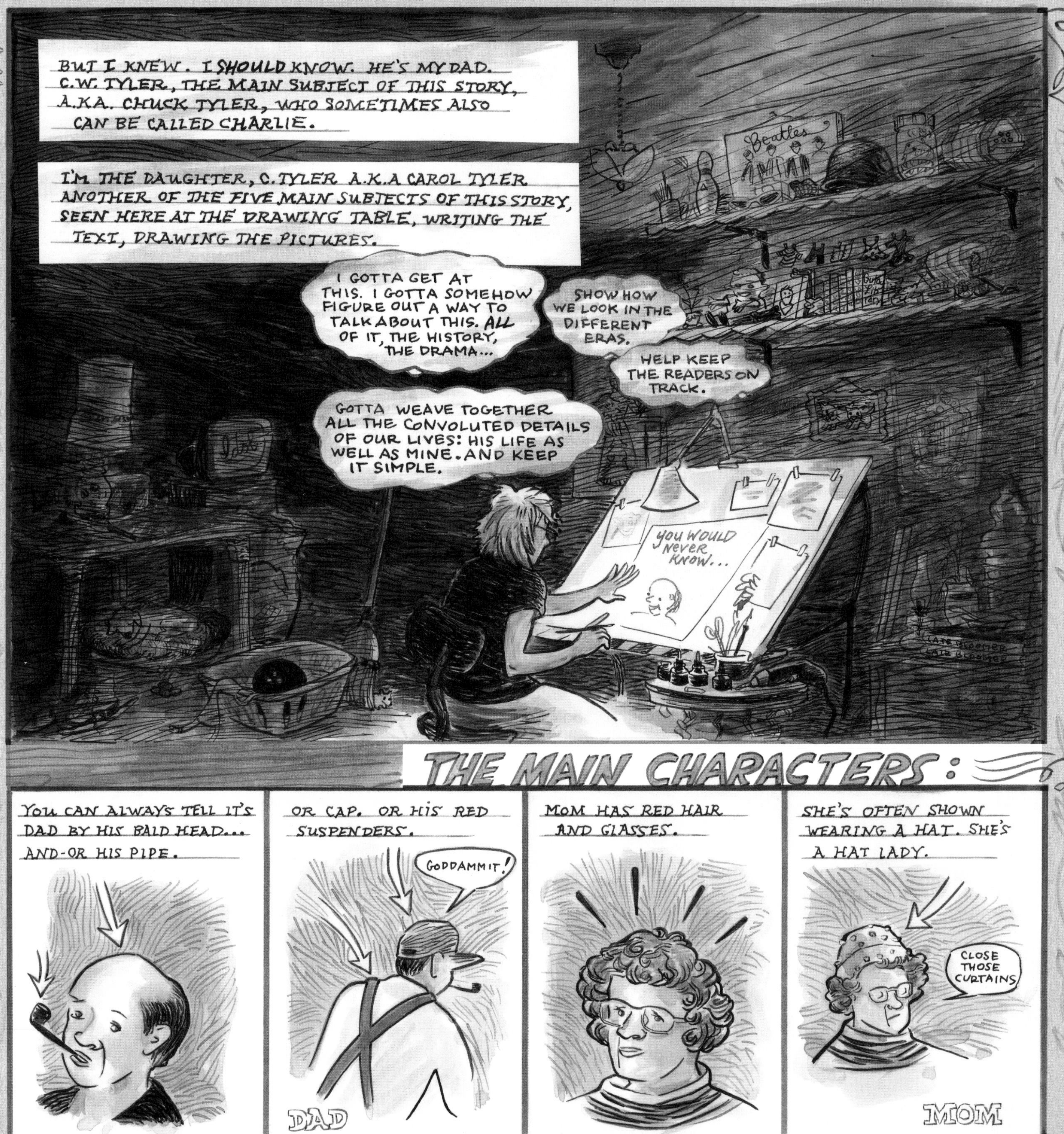
BUT I KNEW. I SHOULD KNOW. HE'S MY DAD. C.W. TYLER, THE MAIN SUBJECT OF THIS STORY, A.KA. CHUCK TYLER, WHO SOMETIMES ALSO CAN BE CALLED CHARLIE.
I'M THE DAUGHTER, C. TYLER A.K.A CAROL TYLER ANOTHER OF THE FIVE MAIN SUBJECTS OF THIS STORY, SEEN HERE AT THE DRAWING TABLE, WRITING THE TEXT, DRAWING THE PICTURES.
I GOTTA GET AT THIS. I GOTTA SOMEHOW FIGURE OUT A WAY TO TALK ABOUT THIS. ALL OF IT, THE HISTORY, THE DRAMA...
SHOW HOW WE LOOK IN THE DIFFERENT ERAS.
HELP KEEP THE READERS ON TRACK.
GOTTA WEAVE TOGETHER ALL THE CONVOLUTED DETAILS OF OUR LIVES: HIS LIFE AS WELL AS MINE. AND KEEP IT SIMPLE.
Beatles
YOU WOULD NEVER KNOW...
THE MAIN CHARACTERS:
YOU CAN ALWAYS TELL IT'S DAD BY HIS BALD HEAD... AND-OR HIS PIPE.
OR CAP. OR HIS RED SUSPENDERS.
GODDAMMIT!
DAD
MOM HAS RED HAIR AND GLASSES.
SHE'S OFTEN SHOWN WEARING A HAT. SHE'S A HAT LADY.
CLOSE THOSE CURTAINS
MOM

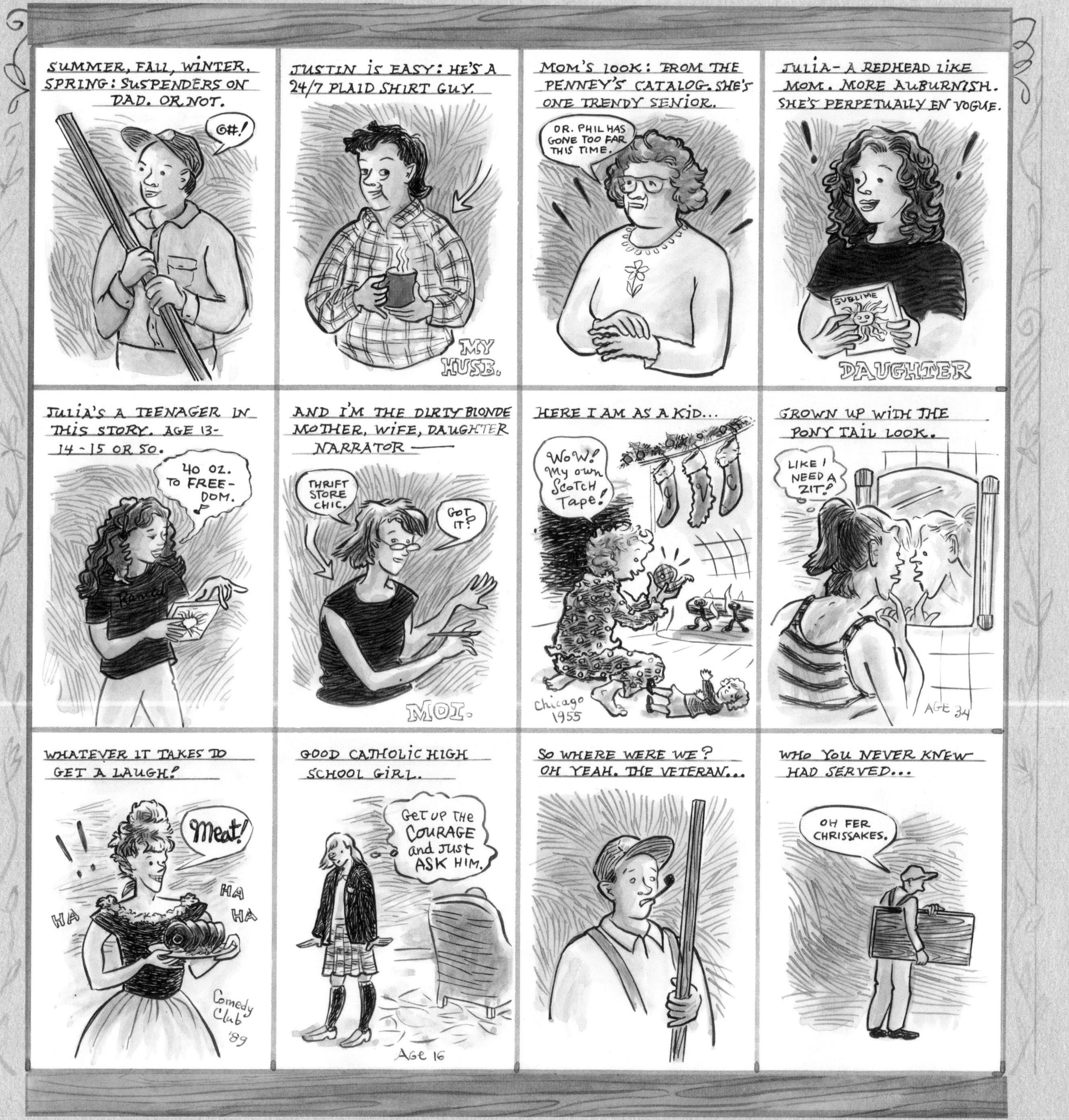
SUMMER, FALL, WINTER, SPRING: SUSPENDERS ON DAD. OR NOT.
@#!
JUSTIN IS EASY: HE'S A 24/7 PLAID SHIRT GUY.
MY HUSB.
MOM'S LOOK: FROM THE PENNEY'S CATALOG. SHE'S ONE TRENDY SENIOR.
DR. PHIL HAS GONE TOO FAR THIS TIME.
JULIA– A REDHEAD LIKE MOM. MORE AUBURNISH. SHE'S PERPETUALLY EN VOGUE.
SUBLIME
DAUGHTER
JULIA'S A TEENAGER IN THIS STORY. AGE 13-14-15 OR SO.
40 OZ. TO FREE-DOM.
AND I'M THE DIRTY BLONDE MOTHER, WIFE, DAUGHTER NARRATOR —
THRIFT STORE CHIC.
GOT IT?
MOI.
HERE I AM AS A KID...
WoW! My own SCOTCH Tape!
Chicago 1955
GROWN UP WITH THE PONY TAIL LOOK.
LIKE I NEED A ZIT?
AGE 34
WHATEVER IT TAKES TO GET A LAUGH!
Meat!
HA HA HA HA
Comedy Club '89
GOOD CATHOLIC HIGH SCHOOL GIRL.
Get up the COURAGE and Just ASK HIM.
Age 16
SO WHERE WERE WE? OH YEAH. THE VETERAN...
WHO YOU NEVER KNEW HAD SERVED...
OH FER CHRISSAKES.

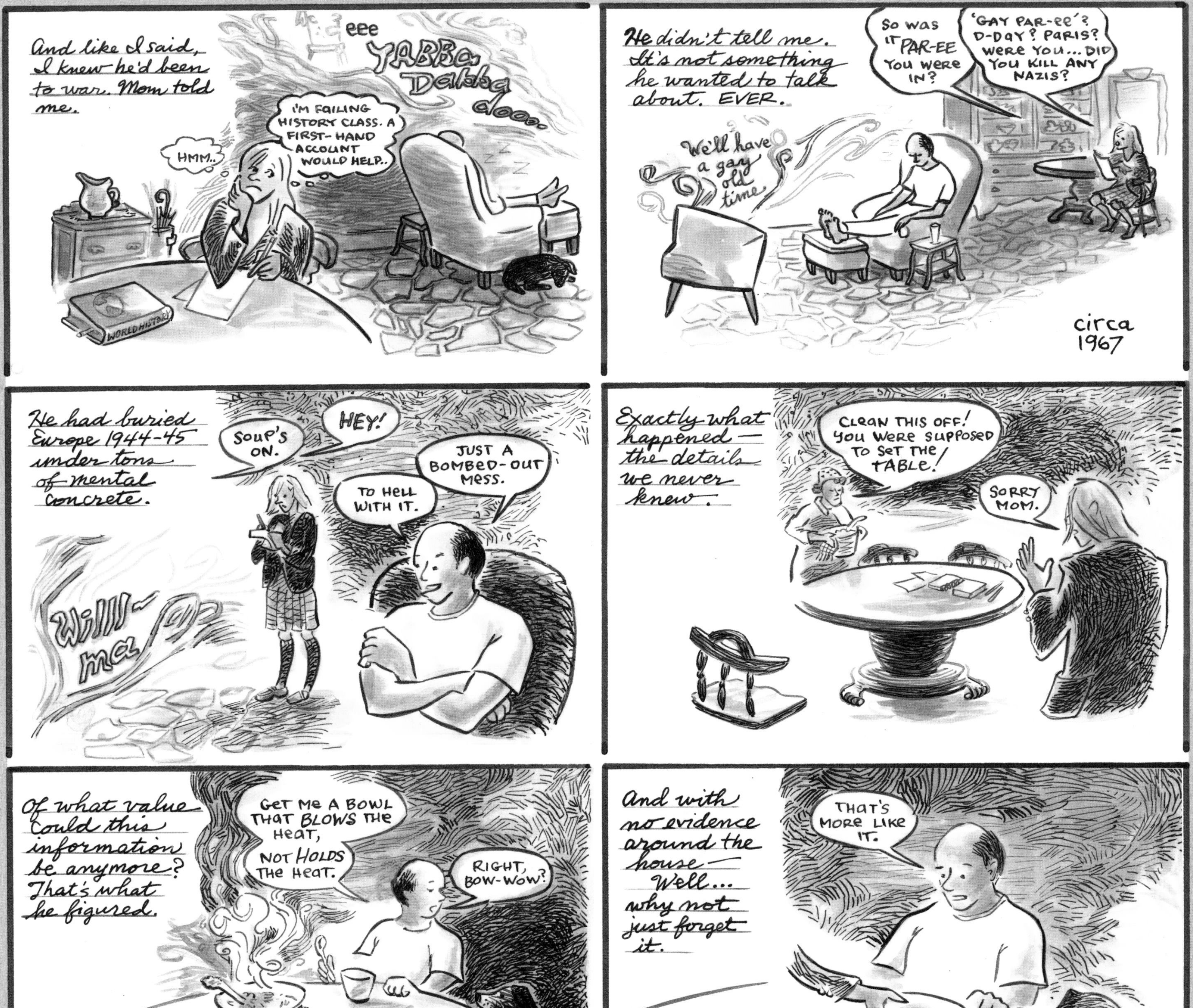
And like I said, I knew he'd been to war. Mom told me.
eee YABBA Dabba dooo..
HMM..
I'M FAILING HISTORY CLASS. A FIRST-HAND ACCOUNT WOULD HELP..
WORLD HISTORY
He didn't tell me. It's not something he wanted to talk about. EVER.
So was it PAR-EE you were in?
'GAY PAR-EE'? D-DAY? PARIS? WERE YOU... DID YOU KILL ANY NAZIS?
We'll have a gay old time.
circa 1967
He had buried Europe 1944-45 under tons of mental concrete.
SOUP'S ON.
HEY!
JUST A BOMBED-OUT MESS.
TO HELL WITH IT.
Willl-ma
Exactly what happened — the details we never knew.
CLEAN THIS OFF! YOU WERE SUPPOSED TO SET THE TABLE!
SORRY MOM.
Of what value could this information be anymore? That's what he figured.
GET ME A BOWL THAT BLOWS THE HEAT, NOT HOLDS THE HEAT.
RIGHT, BOW-WOW?
ALWAYS TALKS TO THE DOG
And with no evidence around the house — Well... why not just forget it.
THAT'S MORE LIKE IT.
Like it never happened!

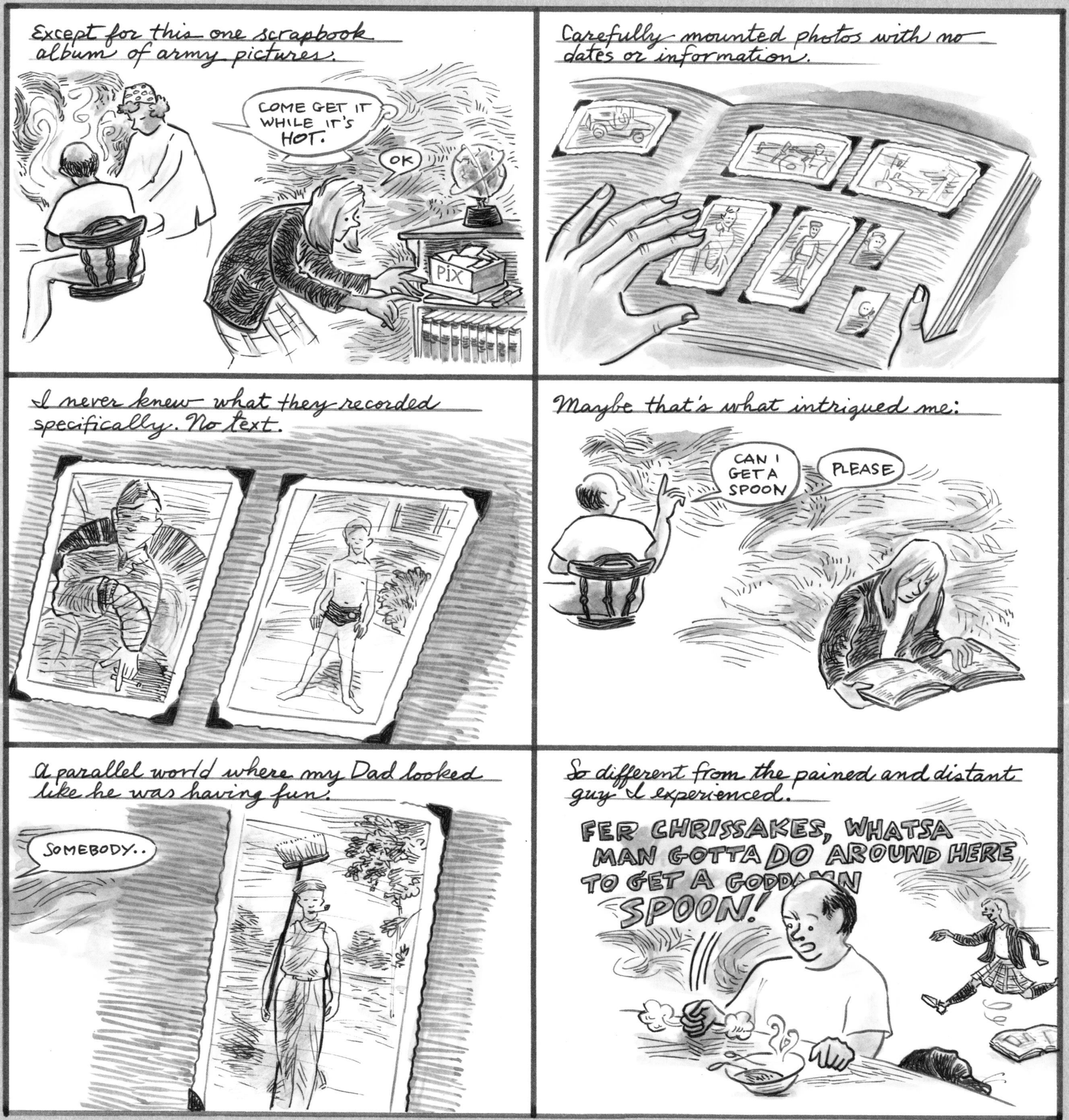
Except for this one scrapbook album of army pictures.
COME GET IT WHILE IT'S HOT.
OK
PIX
Carefully mounted photos with no dates or information.
I never knew what they recorded specifically. No text.
Maybe that's what intrigued me:
CAN I GET A SPOON
PLEASE
A parallel world where my Dad looked like he was having fun.
SOMEBODY..
So different from the pained and distant guy I experienced.
FER CHRISSAKES, WHATSA MAN GOTTA DO AROUND HERE TO GET A GODDAMN SPOON!

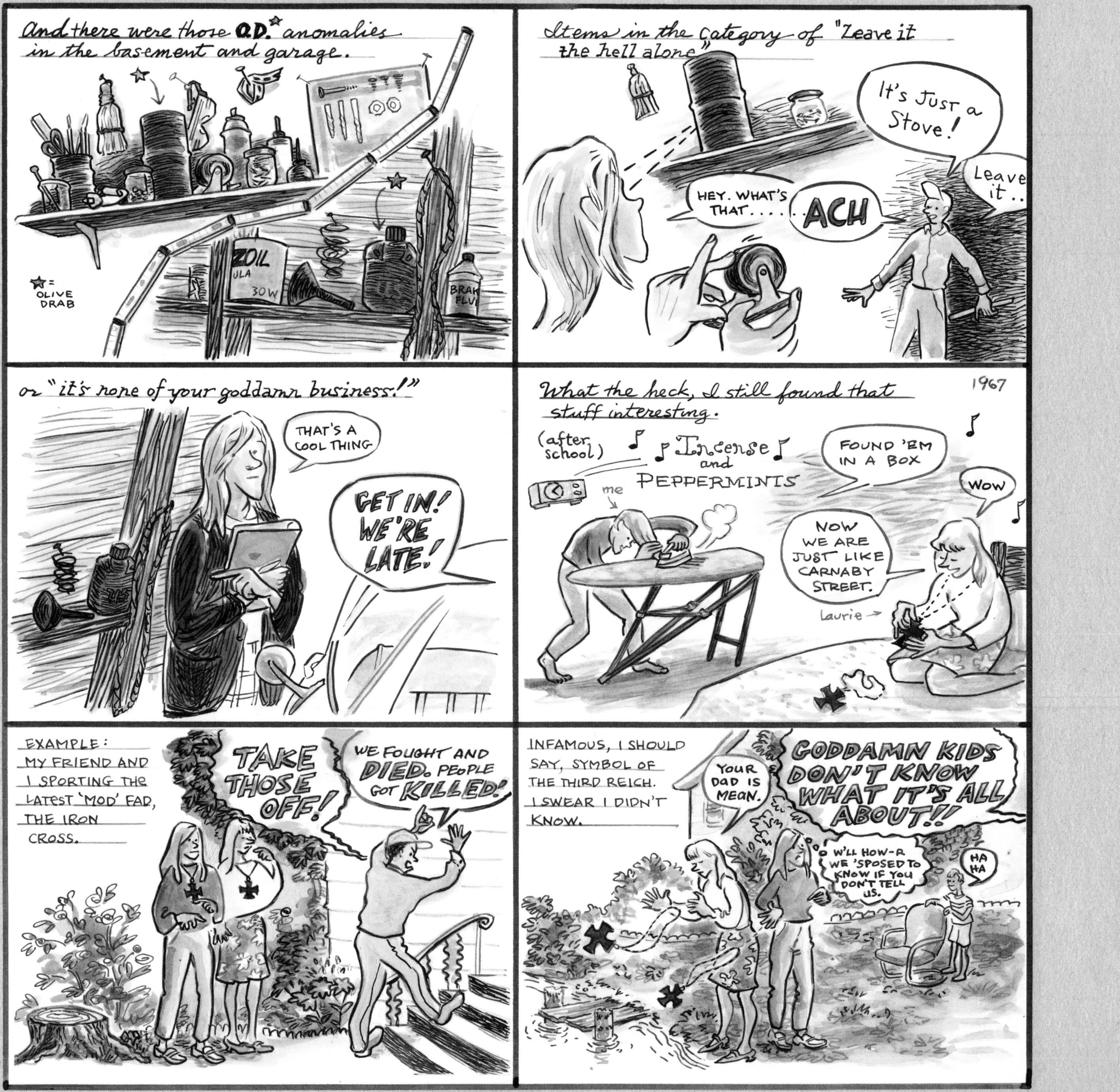
And there were those O.D.* anomalies in the basement and garage.
* = OLIVE DRAB
ZOIL
30W
Items in the category of "Leave it the hell alone"
HEY. WHAT'S THAT......
ACH
It's Just a Stove!
Leave it...
or "it's none of your goddamn business!"
THAT'S A COOL THING
GET IN! WE'RE LATE!
What the heck, I still found that stuff interesting.
1967
(after school)
Incense and PEPPERMINTS
me
FOUND 'EM IN A BOX
WOW
NOW WE ARE JUST LIKE CARNABY STREET.
Laurie →
EXAMPLE: MY FRIEND AND I SPORTING THE LATEST 'MOD' FAD, THE IRON CROSS.
TAKE THOSE OFF!
WE FOUGHT AND DIED. PEOPLE GOT KILLED!
INFAMOUS, I SHOULD SAY, SYMBOL OF THE THIRD REICH. I SWEAR I DIDN'T KNOW.
YOUR DAD IS MEAN.
GODDAMN KIDS DON'T KNOW WHAT IT'S ALL ABOUT!!
W'LL HOW-R WE 'SPOSED TO KNOW IF YOU DON'T TELL US.
HA HA

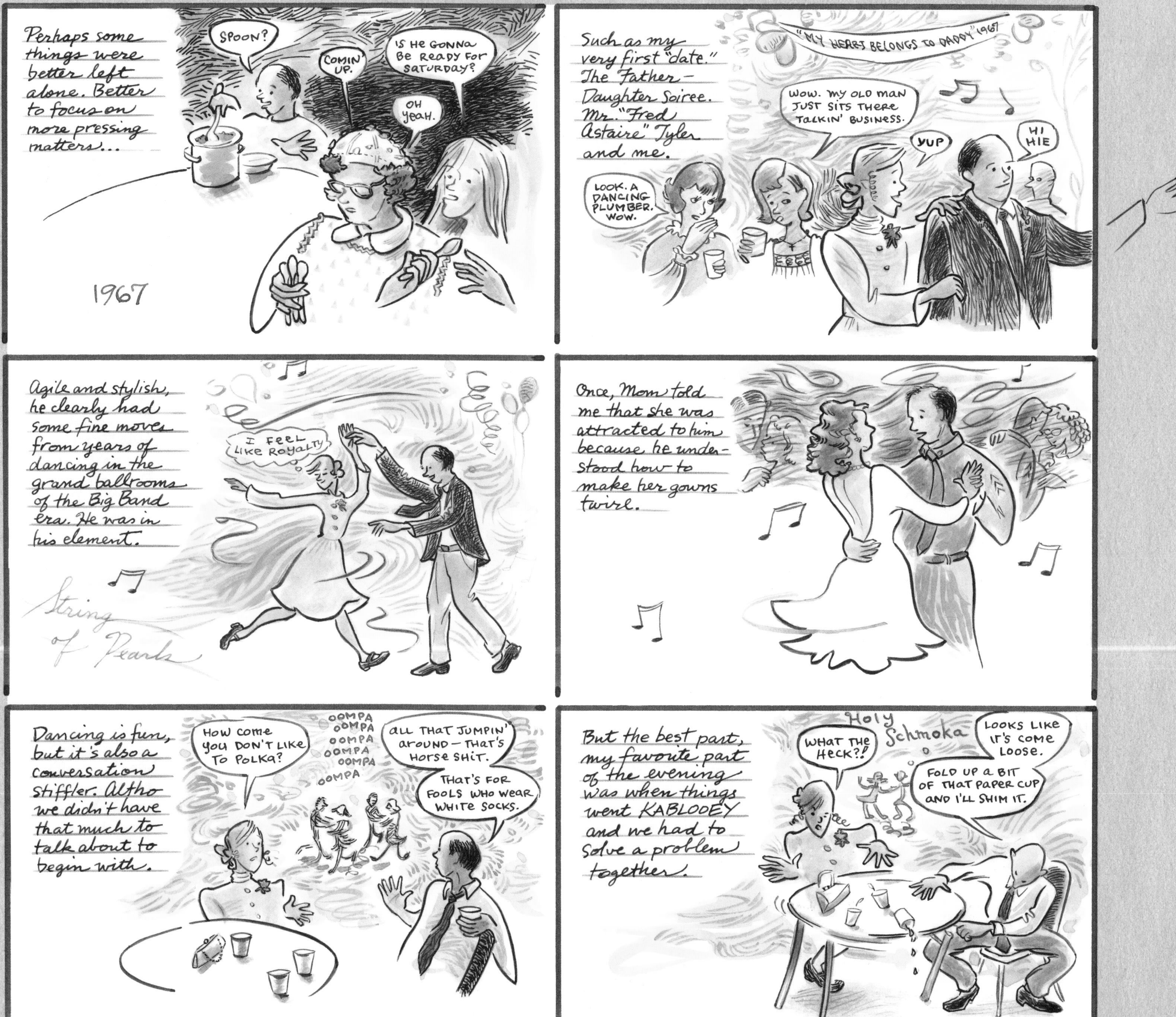
Perhaps some things were better left alone. Better to focus on more pressing matters...
SPOON?
COMIN' UP.
IS HE GONNA BE READY FOR SATURDAY?
OH YEAH.
1967
Such as my very first "date." The Father-Daughter Soiree. Mr. "Fred Astaire" Tyler and me.
"MY HEART BELONGS TO DADDY" 1967
WOW. MY OLD MAN JUST SITS THERE TALKIN' BUSINESS.
YUP
HI HIE
LOOK. A DANCING PLUMBER. WOW.
Agile and stylish, he clearly had some fine moves from years of dancing in the grand ballrooms of the Big Band era. He was in his element.
I FEEL LIKE ROYALTY
String of Pearls
Once, Mom told me that she was attracted to him because he understood how to make her gowns twirl.
Dancing is fun, but it's also a conversation stiffler. Altho we didn't have that much to talk about to begin with.
HOW COME YOU DON'T LIKE TO POLKA?
OOMPA OOMPA OOMPA OOMPA OOMPA OOMPA
ALL THAT JUMPIN' AROUND—THAT'S HORSE SHIT.
THAT'S FOR FOOLS WHO WEAR WHITE SOCKS.
But the best part, my favorite part of the evening was when things went KABLOOEY and we had to solve a problem together.
WHAT THE HECK?!
Holy Schmoka
LOOKS LIKE IT'S COME LOOSE.
FOLD UP A BIT OF THAT PAPER CUP AND I'LL SHIM IT.

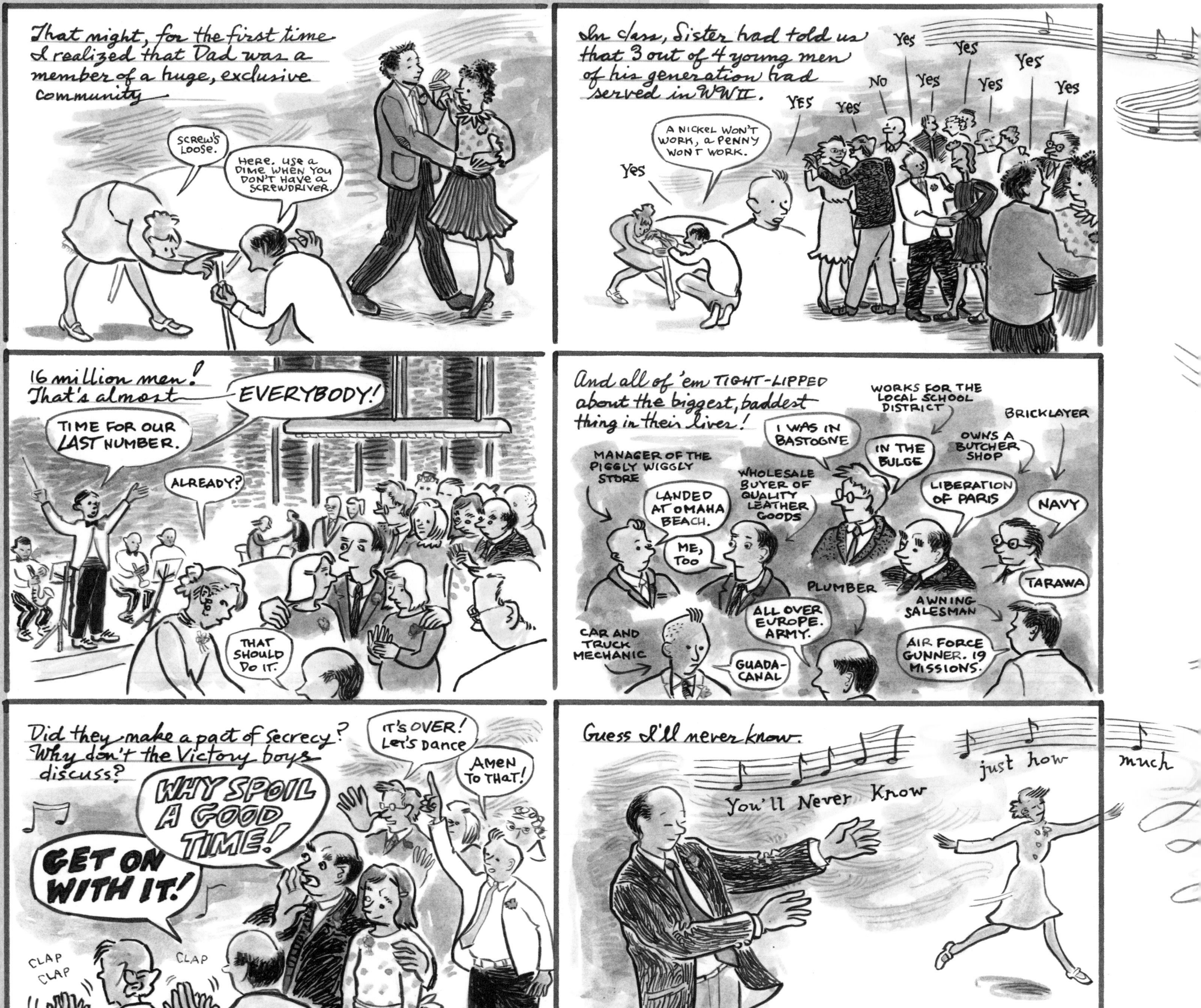

That night, for the first time I realized that Dad was a member of a huge, exclusive community
SCREW'S LOOSE.
HERE. USE A DIME WHEN YOU DON'T HAVE A SCREWDRIVER.
In class, Sister had told us that 3 out of 4 young men of his generation had served in WWII.
A NICKEL WON'T WORK, A PENNY WON'T WORK.
Yes
Yes
Yes
No
Yes
Yes
Yes
Yes
Yes
Yes
16 million men! That's almost
EVERYBODY!
TIME FOR OUR LAST NUMBER.
ALREADY?
THAT SHOULD DO IT.
And all of 'em TIGHT-LIPPED about the biggest, baddest thing in their lives!
MANAGER OF THE PIGGLY WIGGLY STORE
LANDED AT OMAHA BEACH.
ME, TOO
WHOLESALE BUYER OF QUALITY LEATHER GOODS
I WAS IN BASTOGNE
WORKS FOR THE LOCAL SCHOOL DISTRICT
IN THE BULGE
OWNS A BUTCHER SHOP
LIBERATION OF PARIS
BRICKLAYER
NAVY
TARAWA
PLUMBER
ALL OVER EUROPE. ARMY.
CAR AND TRUCK MECHANIC
GUADA-CANAL
AWNING SALESMAN
AIR FORCE GUNNER. 19 MISSIONS.
Did they make a pact of secrecy? Why don't the Victory boys discuss?
IT'S OVER! LET'S DANCE
AMEN TO THAT!
WHY SPOIL A GOOD TIME!
GET ON WITH IT!
CLAP
CLAP
CLAP
Guess I'll never know.
You'll Never Know
just how
much

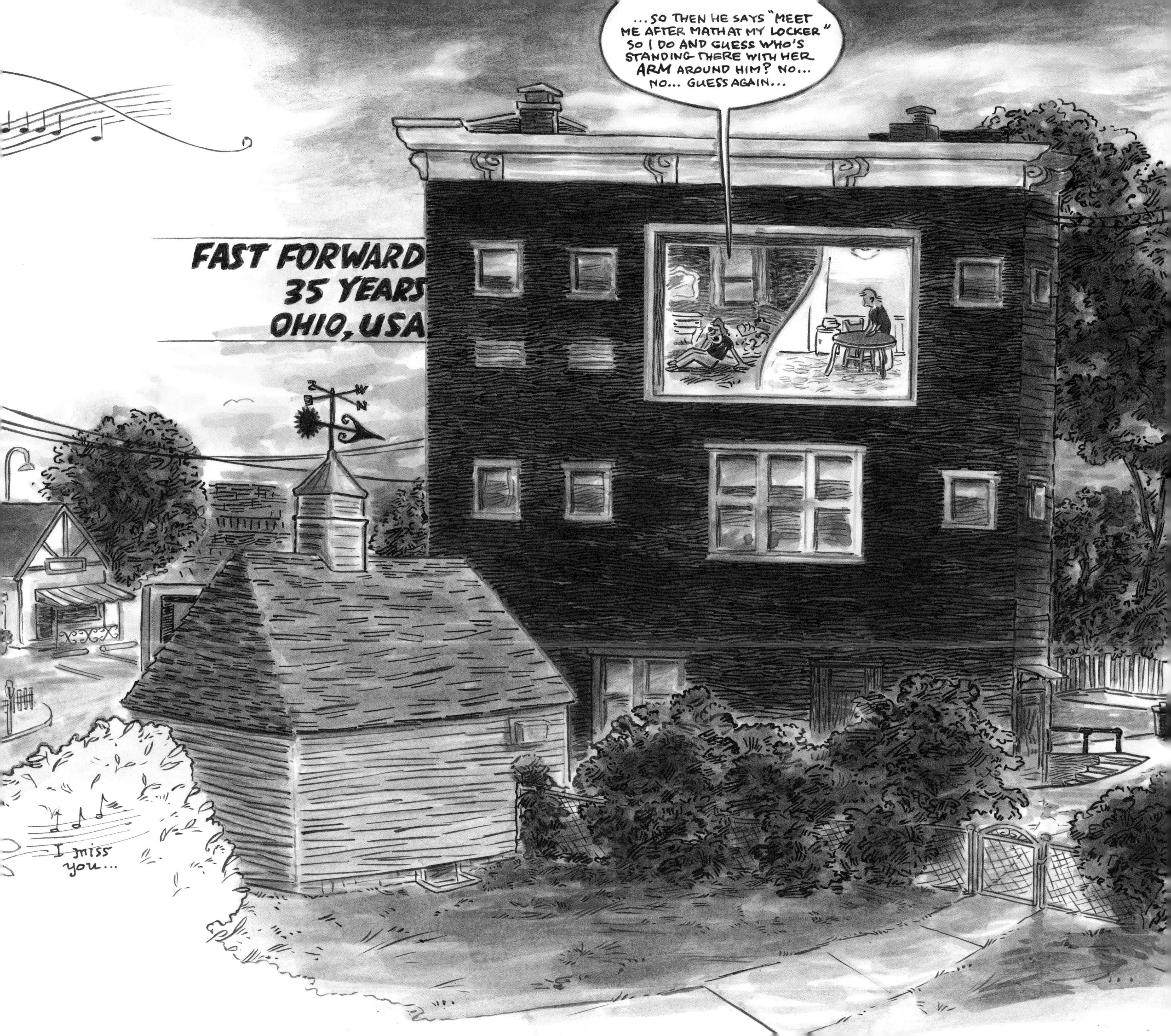
FAST FORWARD 35 YEARS OHIO, USA
...SO THEN HE SAYS "MEET ME AFTER MATH AT MY LOCKER" SO I DO AND GUESS WHO'S STANDING THERE WITH HER ARM AROUND HIM? NO... NO... GUESS AGAIN...
I miss you...

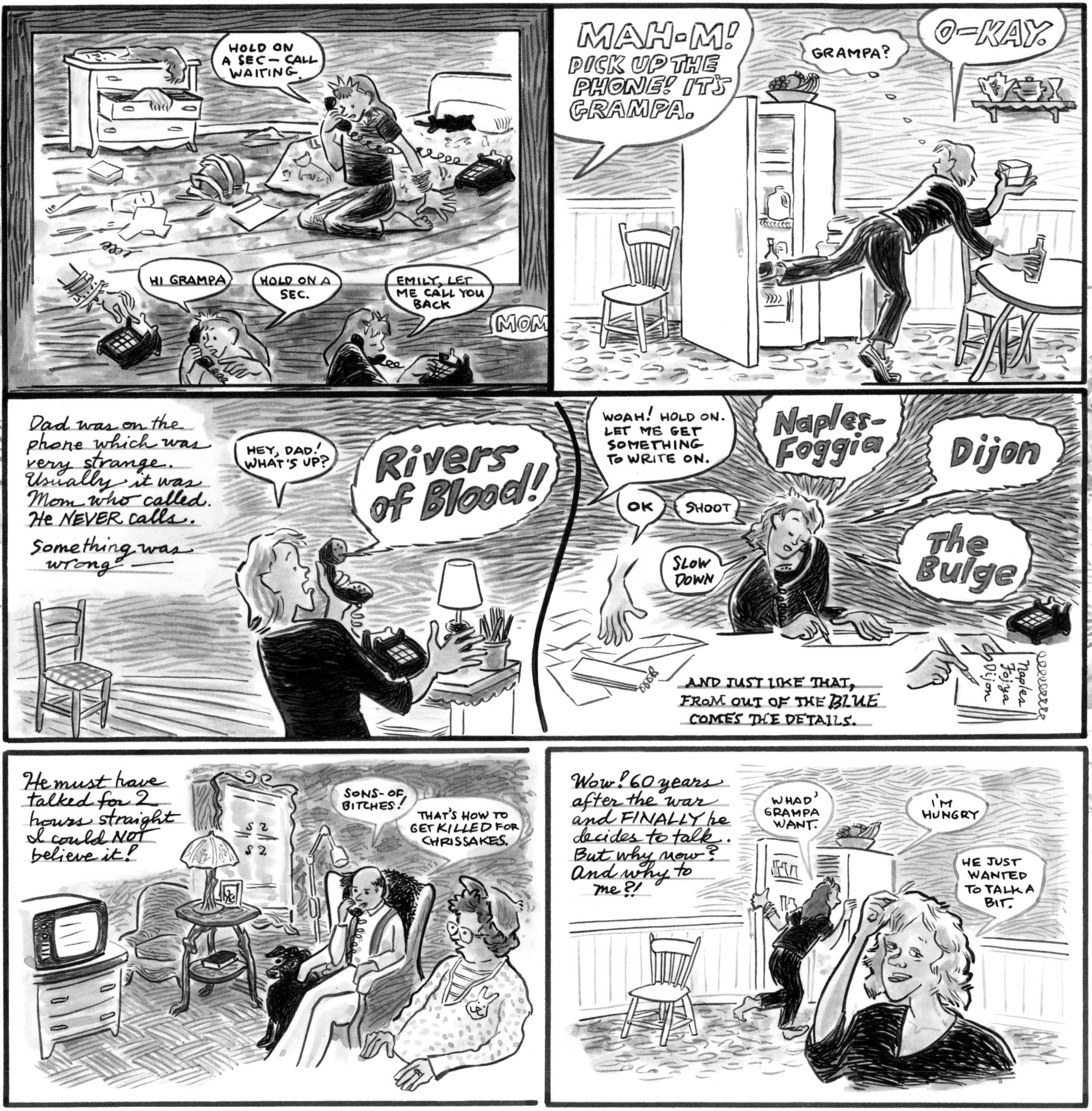
HOLD ON A SEC— CALL WAITING.
HI GRAMPA
HOLD ON A SEC.
EMILY, LET ME CALL YOU BACK
MOM
MAH-M! PICK UP THE PHONE! IT'S GRAMPA.
GRAMPA?
O-KAY.
Dad was on the phone which was very strange. Usually it was Mom who called. He NEVER calls.
Something was wrong—
HEY, DAD! WHAT'S UP?
Rivers of Blood!
WOAH! HOLD ON. LET ME GET SOMETHING TO WRITE ON.
OK
SHOOT
SLOW DOWN
Naples-Foggia
Dijon
The Bulge
AND JUST LIKE THAT, FROM OUT OF THE BLUE COMES THE DETAILS.
He must have talked for 2 hours straight I could NOT believe it!
SONS-OF-BITCHES!
THAT'S HOW TO GET KILLED FOR CHRISSAKES.
Wow! 60 years after the war and FINALLY he decides to talk. But why now? And why to me?!
WHAD' GRAMPA WANT.
I'M HUNGRY
HE JUST WANTED TO TALK A BIT.

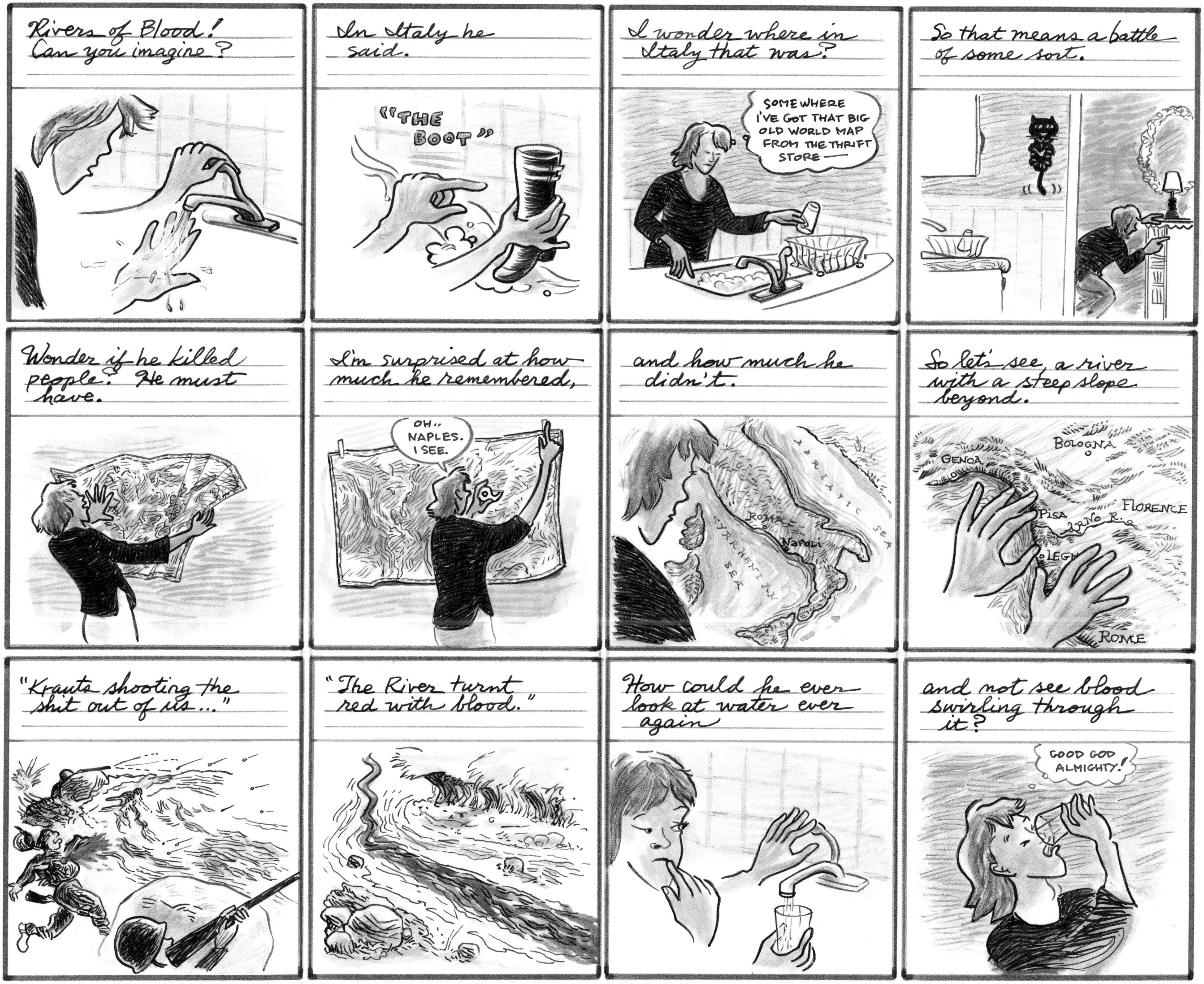

Rivers of Blood! Can you imagine?
In Italy he said.
"THE BOOT"
I wonder where in Italy that was?
SOMEWHERE I'VE GOT THAT BIG OLD WORLD MAP FROM THE THRIFT STORE —
So that means a battle of some sort.
Wonder if he killed people? He must have.
I'm surprised at how much he remembered,
OH.. NAPLES. I SEE.
and how much he didn't.
ADRIATIC SEA
ROMA
NAPOLI
TYRRHENIAN SEA
So let's see, a river with a steep slope beyond.
BOLOGNA
GENOA
PISA
FLORENCE
ARNO R.
ROME
"Krauts shooting the shit out of us..."
"The River turnt red with blood."
How could he ever look at water ever again
and not see blood swirling through it?
GOOD GOD ALMIGHTY!

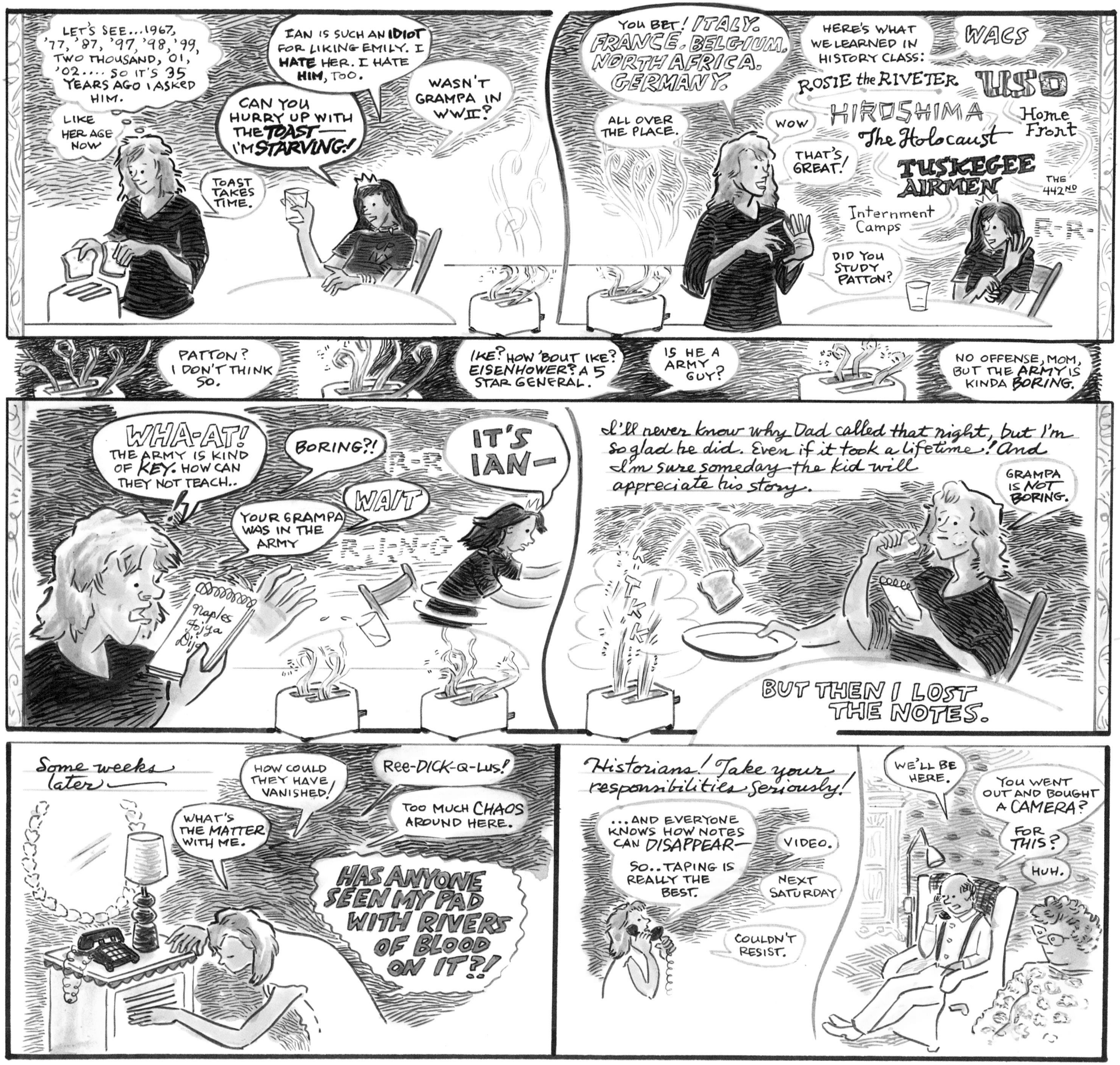
LET'S SEE...1967, '77, '87, '97, '98, '99, TWO THOUSAND, '01, '02.... SO IT'S 35 YEARS AGO I ASKED HIM.
LIKE HER AGE NOW
IAN IS SUCH AN IDIOT FOR LIKING EMILY. I HATE HER. I HATE HIM, TOO.
CAN YOU HURRY UP WITH THE TOAST— I'M STARVING!
WASN'T GRAMPA IN WWII?
TOAST TAKES TIME.
YOU BET! ITALY. FRANCE. BELGIUM. NORTH AFRICA. GERMANY.
ALL OVER THE PLACE.
WOW
THAT'S GREAT!
HERE'S WHAT WE LEARNED IN HISTORY CLASS:
WACS
ROSIE the RIVETER
USO
HIROSHIMA
Home Front
The Holocaust
TUSKEGEE AIRMEN
THE 442ND
Internment Camps
R-R-
DID YOU STUDY PATTON?
PATTON? I DON'T THINK SO.
IKE? HOW 'BOUT IKE? EISENHOWER? A 5 STAR GENERAL.
IS HE A ARMY GUY?
NO OFFENSE, MOM, BUT THE ARMY IS KINDA BORING.
WHA-AT! THE ARMY IS KIND OF KEY. HOW CAN THEY NOT TEACH..
BORING?!
R-R
IT'S IAN—
WAIT
YOUR GRAMPA WAS IN THE ARMY
R-I-N-G
Naples
I'll never know why Dad called that night, but I'm so glad he did. Even if it took a lifetime! And I'm sure someday the kid will appreciate his story.
GRAMPA IS NOT BORING.
BUT THEN I LOST THE NOTES.
Some weeks later
HOW COULD THEY HAVE VANISHED!
Ree-DICK-Q-Lus!
WHAT'S THE MATTER WITH ME.
TOO MUCH CHAOS AROUND HERE.
HAS ANYONE SEEN MY PAD WITH RIVERS OF BLOOD ON IT?!
Historians! Take your responsibilities Seriously!
...AND EVERYONE KNOWS HOW NOTES CAN DISAPPEAR—
SO.. TAPING IS REALLY THE BEST.
VIDEO.
NEXT SATURDAY
COULDN'T RESIST.
WE'LL BE HERE.
YOU WENT OUT AND BOUGHT A CAMERA?
FOR THIS?
HUH.

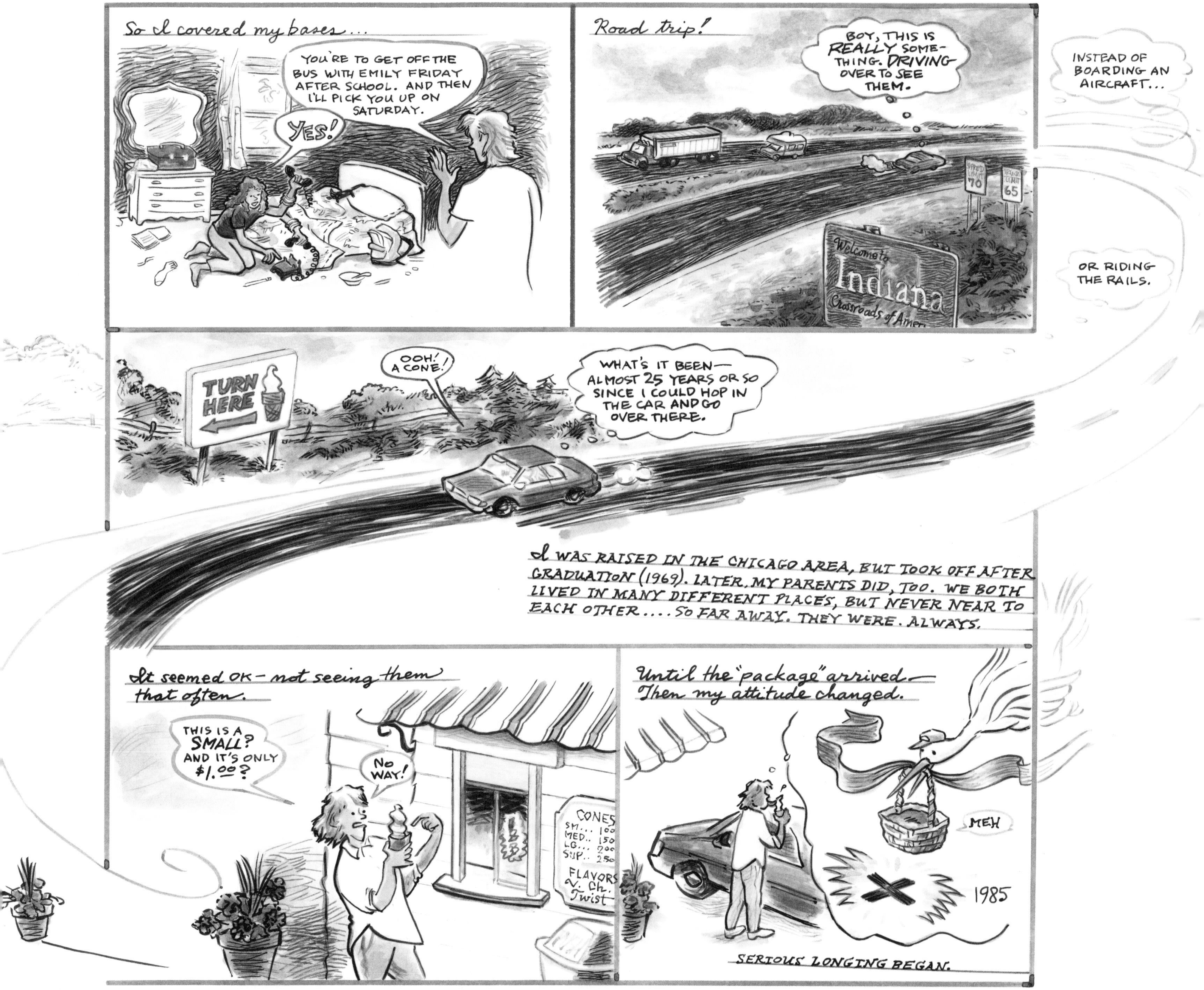
So I covered my bases...
YOU'RE TO GET OFF THE BUS WITH EMILY FRIDAY AFTER SCHOOL. AND THEN I'LL PICK YOU UP ON SATURDAY.
YES!
Road trip!
BOY, THIS IS REALLY SOMETHING. DRIVING OVER TO SEE THEM.
Welcome to Indiana Crossroads of Amer
INSTEAD OF BOARDING AN AIRCRAFT...
OR RIDING THE RAILS.
TURN HERE
OOH! A CONE!
WHAT'S IT BEEN— ALMOST 25 YEARS OR SO SINCE I COULD HOP IN THE CAR AND GO OVER THERE.
I WAS RAISED IN THE CHICAGO AREA, BUT TOOK OFF AFTER GRADUATION (1969). LATER, MY PARENTS DID, TOO. WE BOTH LIVED IN MANY DIFFERENT PLACES, BUT NEVER NEAR TO EACH OTHER.... SO FAR AWAY. THEY WERE. ALWAYS.
It seemed OK - not seeing them that often.
THIS IS A SMALL? AND IT'S ONLY $1.00?
NO WAY!
CONES
FLAVORS
Twist
Until the "package" arrived— Then my attitude changed.
MEH
1985
SERIOUS LONGING BEGAN.

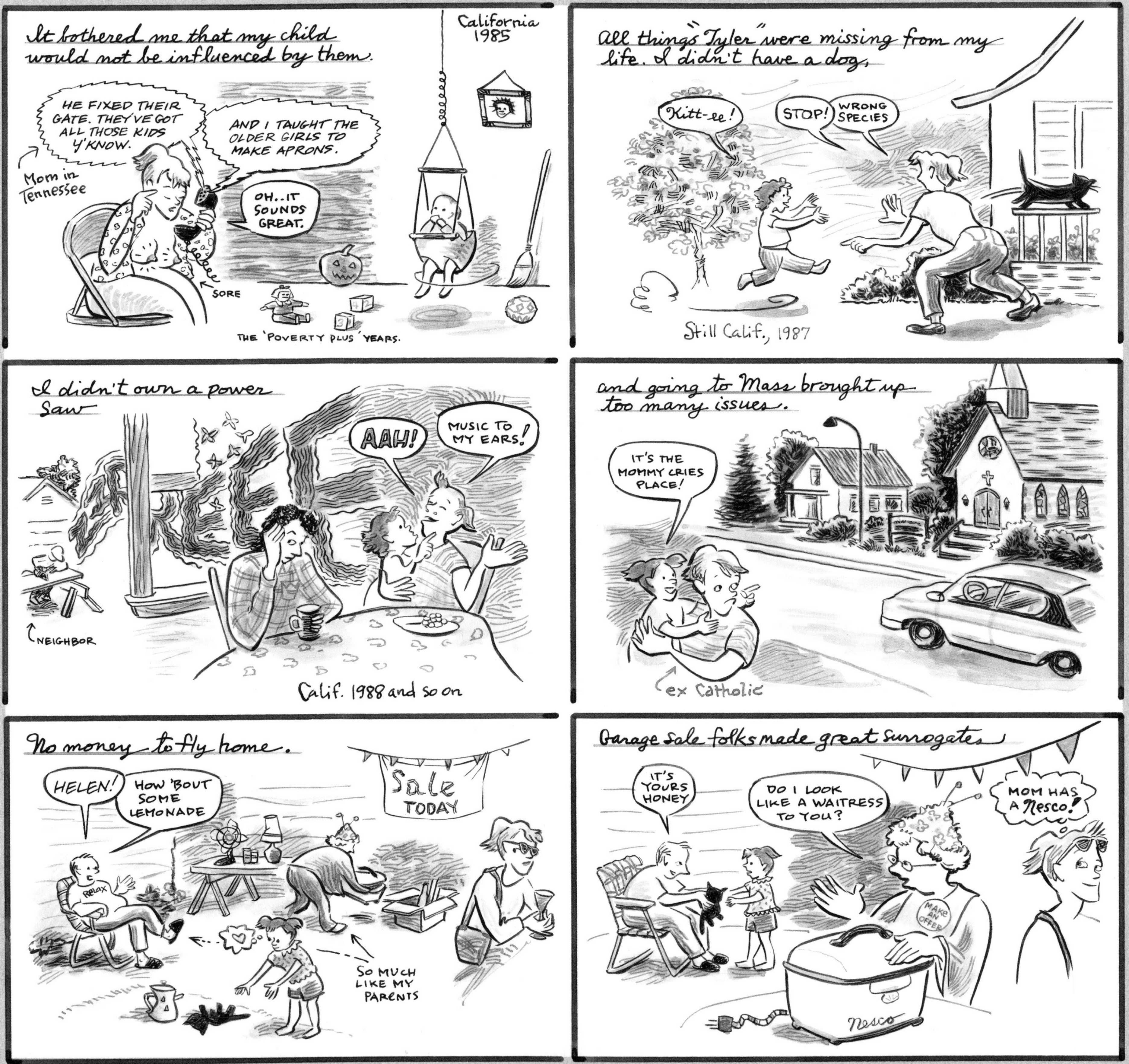
It bothered me that my child would not be influenced by them.
California 1985
HE FIXED THEIR GATE. THEY'VE GOT ALL THOSE KIDS Y'KNOW.
AND I TAUGHT THE OLDER GIRLS TO MAKE APRONS.
Mom in Tennessee
OH..IT SOUNDS GREAT.
SORE
THE 'POVERTY PLUS' YEARS.
All things "Tyler" were missing from my life. I didn't have a dog,
Kitt-ee!
STOP!
WRONG SPECIES
Still Calif., 1987
I didn't own a power saw
AAH!
MUSIC TO MY EARS!
NEIGHBOR
Calif. 1988 and so on
and going to Mass brought up too many issues.
IT'S THE MOMMY CRIES PLACE!
ex Catholic
No money to fly home.
HELEN!
How 'BOUT SOME LEMONADE
Sale TODAY
RELAX
SO MUCH LIKE MY PARENTS
Garage sale folks made great surrogates
IT'S YOURS HONEY
DO I LOOK LIKE A WAITRESS TO YOU?
MOM HAS A Nesco!
MAKE AN OFFER
Nesco

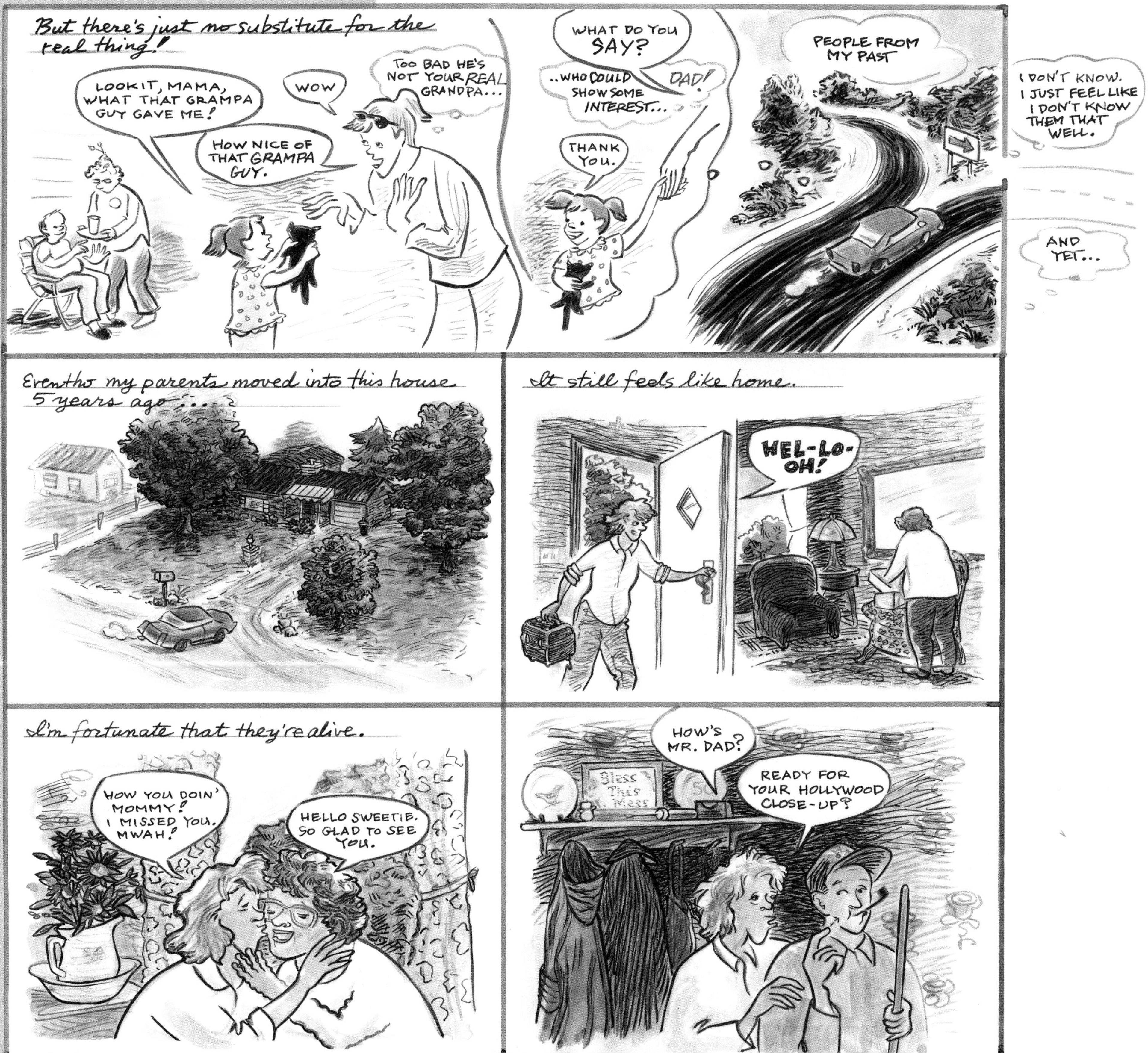
But there's just no substitute for the real thing!
LOOKIT, MAMA, WHAT THAT GRAMPA GUY GAVE ME!
WOW
HOW NICE OF THAT GRAMPA GUY.
TOO BAD HE'S NOT YOUR REAL GRANDPA...
WHAT DO YOU SAY?
..WHO COULD SHOW SOME INTEREST...
DAD!
THANK YOU.
PEOPLE FROM MY PAST
I DON'T KNOW. I JUST FEEL LIKE I DON'T KNOW THEM THAT WELL.
AND YET...
Even tho my parents moved into this house 5 years ago...
It still feels like home.
WEL-LO-OH!
I'm fortunate that they're alive.
HOW YOU DOIN' MOMMY! I MISSED YOU. MWAH!
HELLO SWEETIE. SO GLAD TO SEE YOU.
Bless This Mess
HOW'S MR. DAD?
READY FOR YOUR HOLLYWOOD CLOSE-UP?

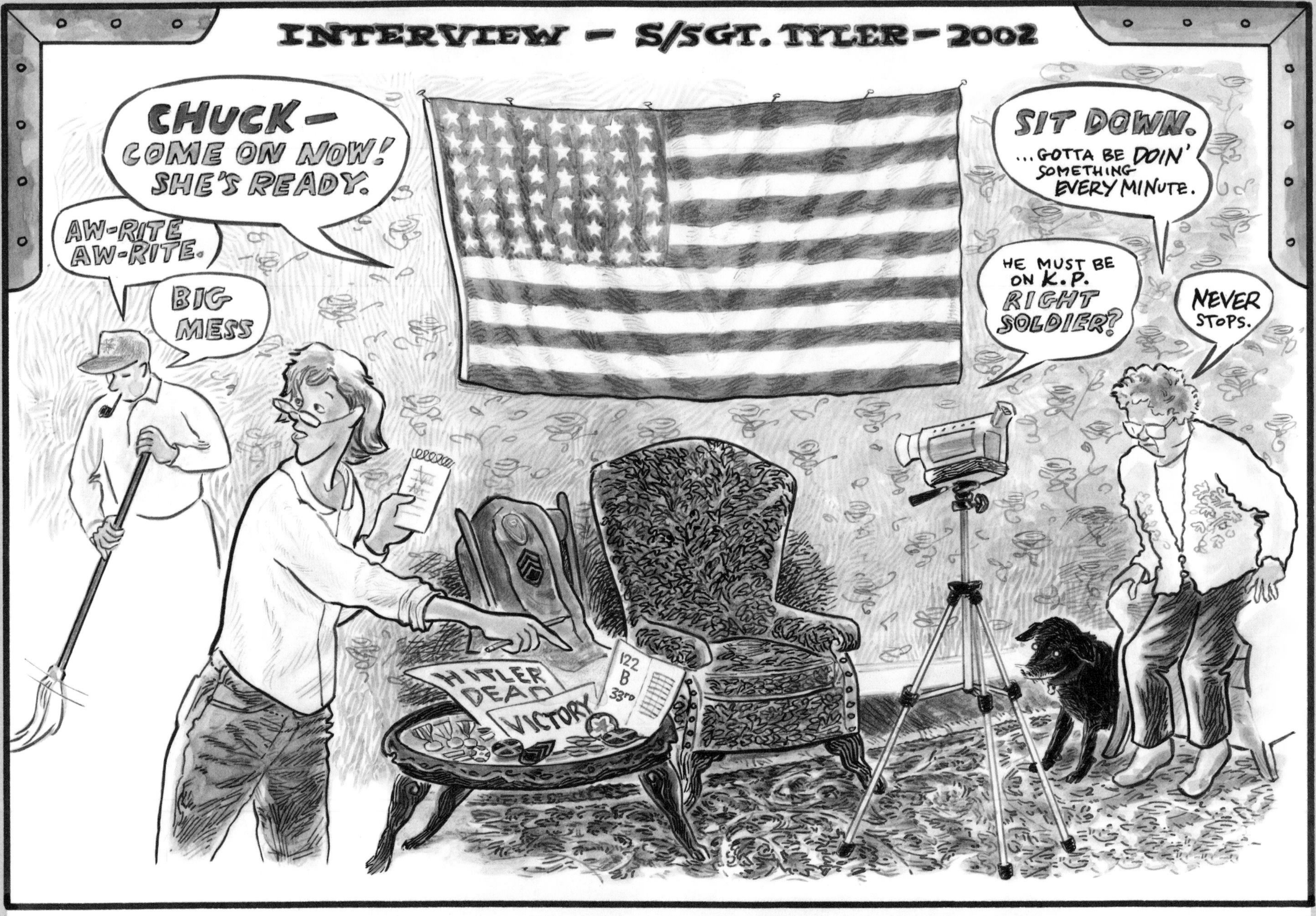
INTERVIEW – S/SGT. TYLER – 2002
CHUCK – COME ON NOW! SHE'S READY.
AW-RITE AW-RITE.
BIG MESS
SIT DOWN. ...GOTTA BE DOIN' SOMETHING EVERY MINUTE.
HE MUST BE ON K.P. RIGHT SOLDIER?
NEVER STOPS.
HITLER DEAD
VICTORY
122 B 33RD

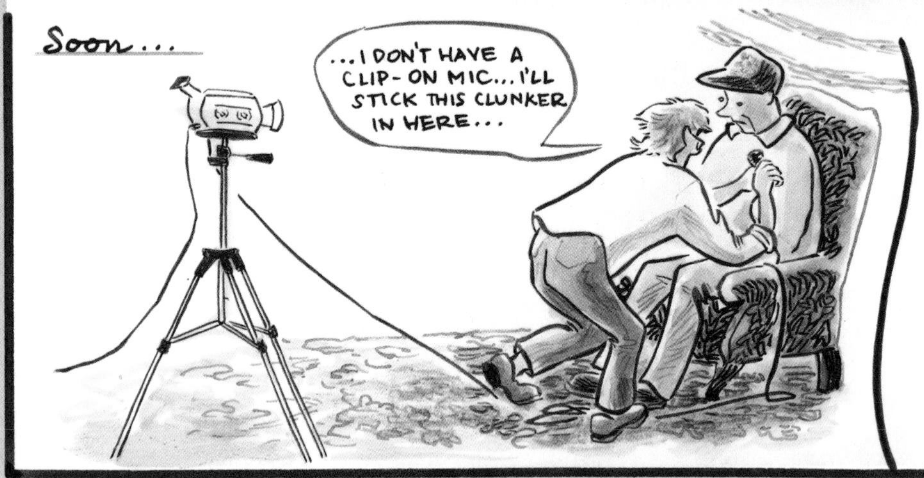
Soon...
...I DON'T HAVE A CLIP-ON MIC...I'LL STICK THIS CLUNKER IN HERE...

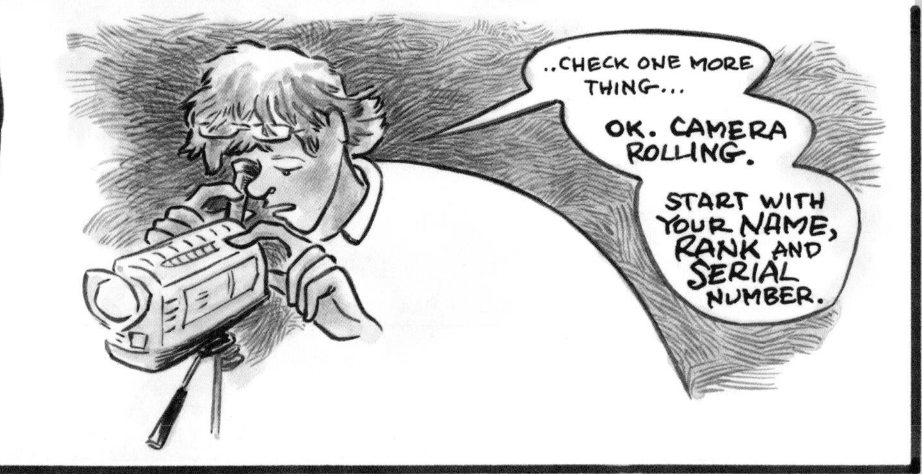
..CHECK ONE MORE THING...
OK. CAMERA ROLLING.
START WITH YOUR NAME, RANK AND SERIAL NUMBER.

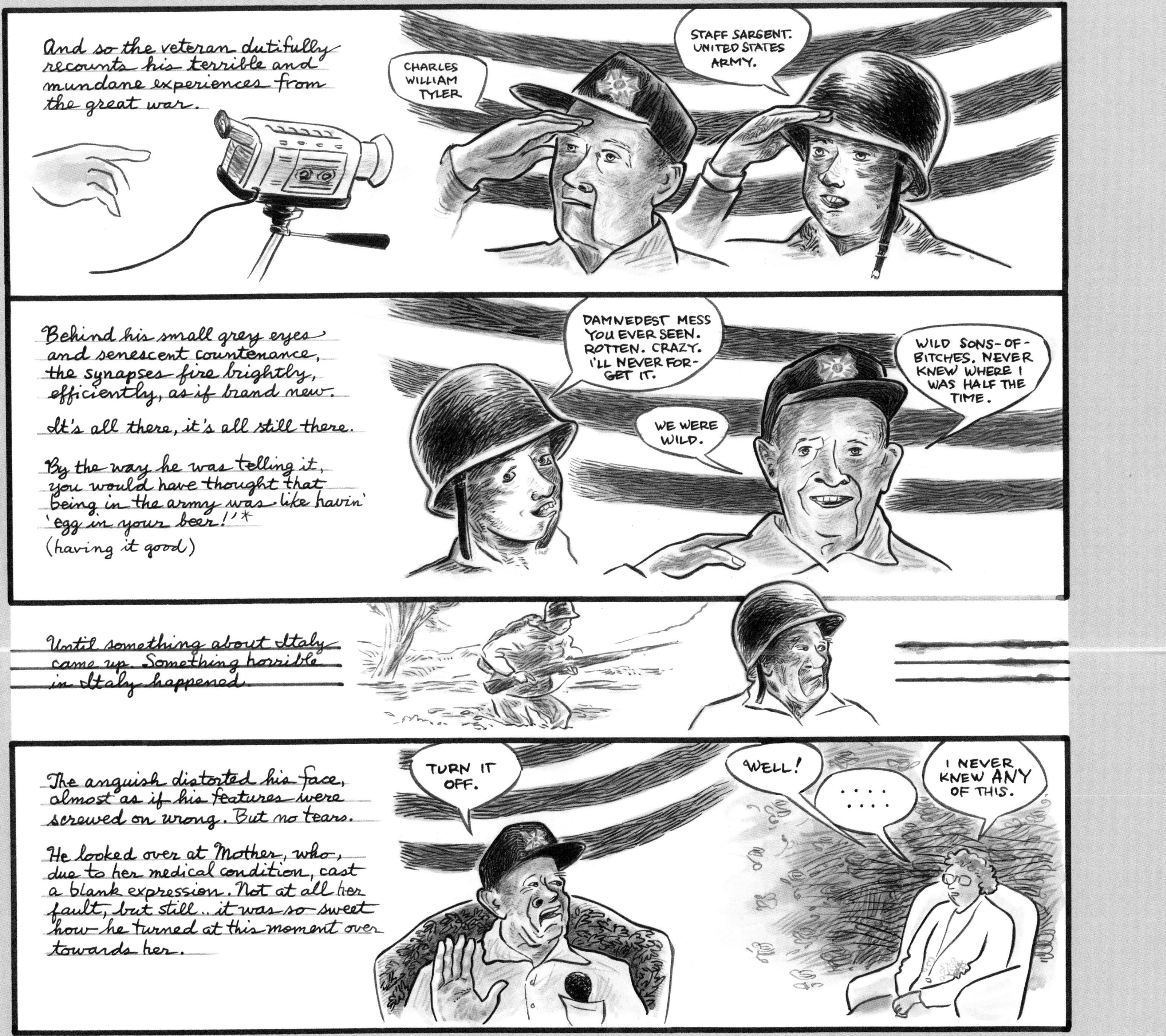
And so the veteran dutifully recounts his terrible and mundane experiences from the great war.
CHARLES WILLIAM TYLER
STAFF SARGENT. UNITED STATES ARMY.
Behind his small grey eyes and senescent countenance, the synapses fire brightly, efficiently, as if brand new.
It's all there, it's all still there.
By the way he was telling it, you would have thought that being in the army was like havin' 'egg in your beer!'*
(having it good)
DAMNEDEST MESS YOU EVER SEEN. ROTTEN. CRAZY. I'LL NEVER FORGET IT.
WE WERE WILD.
WILD SONS-OF-BITCHES. NEVER KNEW WHERE I WAS HALF THE TIME.
Until something about Italy came up. Something horrible in Italy happened.
The anguish distorted his face, almost as if his features were screwed on wrong. But no tears.
He looked over at Mother, who, due to her medical condition, cast a blank expression. Not at all her fault, but still.. it was so sweet how he turned at this moment over towards her.
TURN IT OFF.
WELL!
. . . .
. . . .
I NEVER KNEW ANY OF THIS.

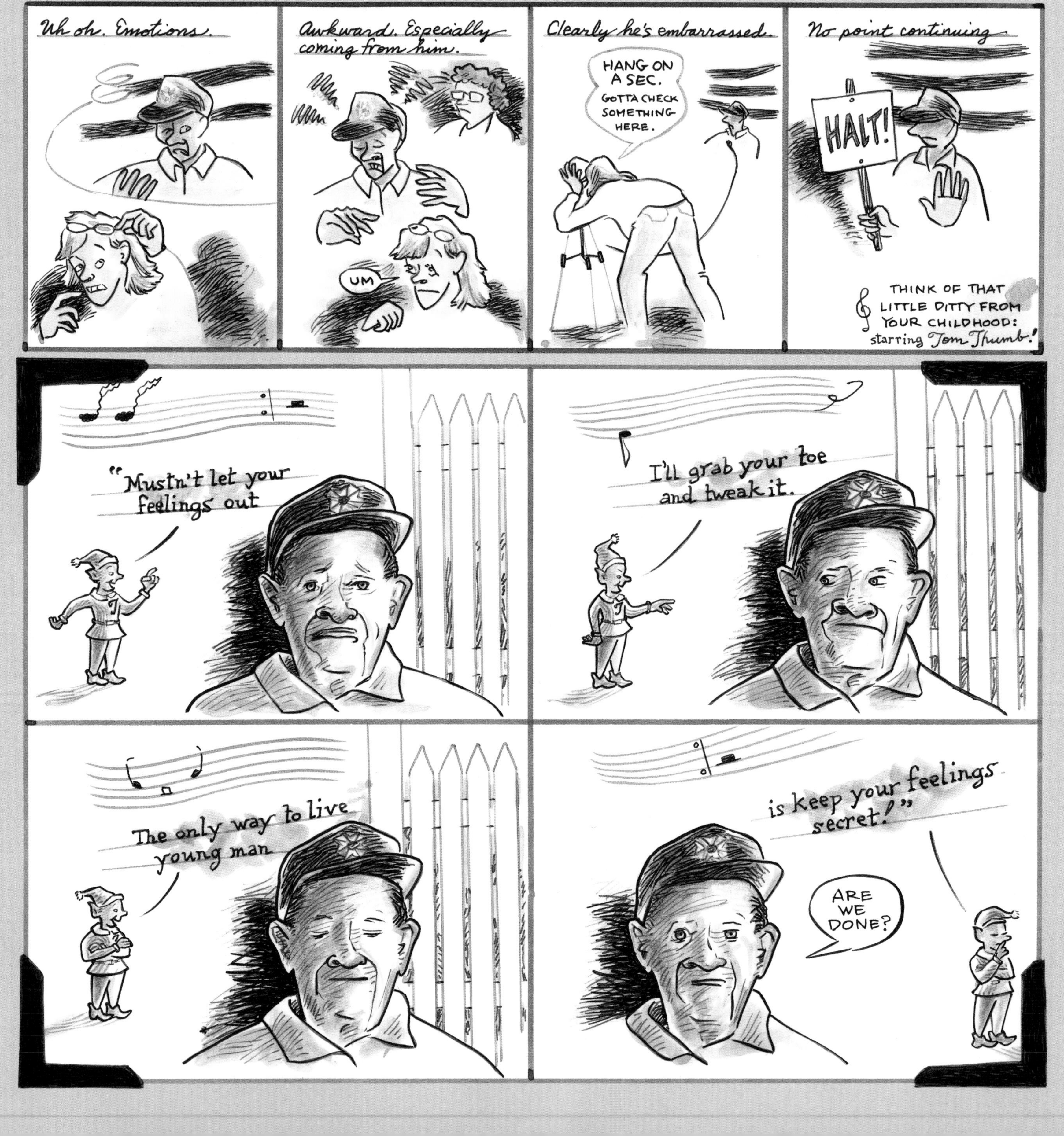

Uh oh. Emotions.
Awkward. Especially coming from him.
UM
Clearly he's embarrassed.
HANG ON A SEC. GOTTA CHECK SOMETHING HERE.
No point continuing
HALT!
THINK OF THAT LITTLE DITTY FROM YOUR CHILDHOOD: starring Tom Thumb!
"Mustn't let your feelings out
I'll grab your toe and tweak it.
The only way to live young man
is keep your feelings secret!"
ARE WE DONE?

Now I was even MORE curious.
ARE WE DONE? 'CAUSE I'M DONE.
WE'RE DONE.
HITLER DEAD
VICTORY
Sure, he had gone over all the facts and details—
HOW COME YOU NEVER TOLD ME ANY OF THIS?
YOU NEVER ASKED, DOLL.
STILL LOVE ME EVEN THOUGH I STOLE A JEEP?
but Italy, you bad boy, what did you do to my Dad.
YES I DID ASK— YEARS AGO.
YOU MIGHT HAVE.
I DON'T KNOW
Vague Discharge Papers
I HAD to know what happened!
PERHAPS THAT STUFF ON THE TABLE WILL PROVIDE A CLUE—
HITLER DEAD
VICTORY
VICTORY
WORLD WAR II
U.S.
5 FRANCS 5
AMERICAN DEFENSE
Charles W. Tyler T42
Chicago, Ill.
60331
HITLER DEAD!

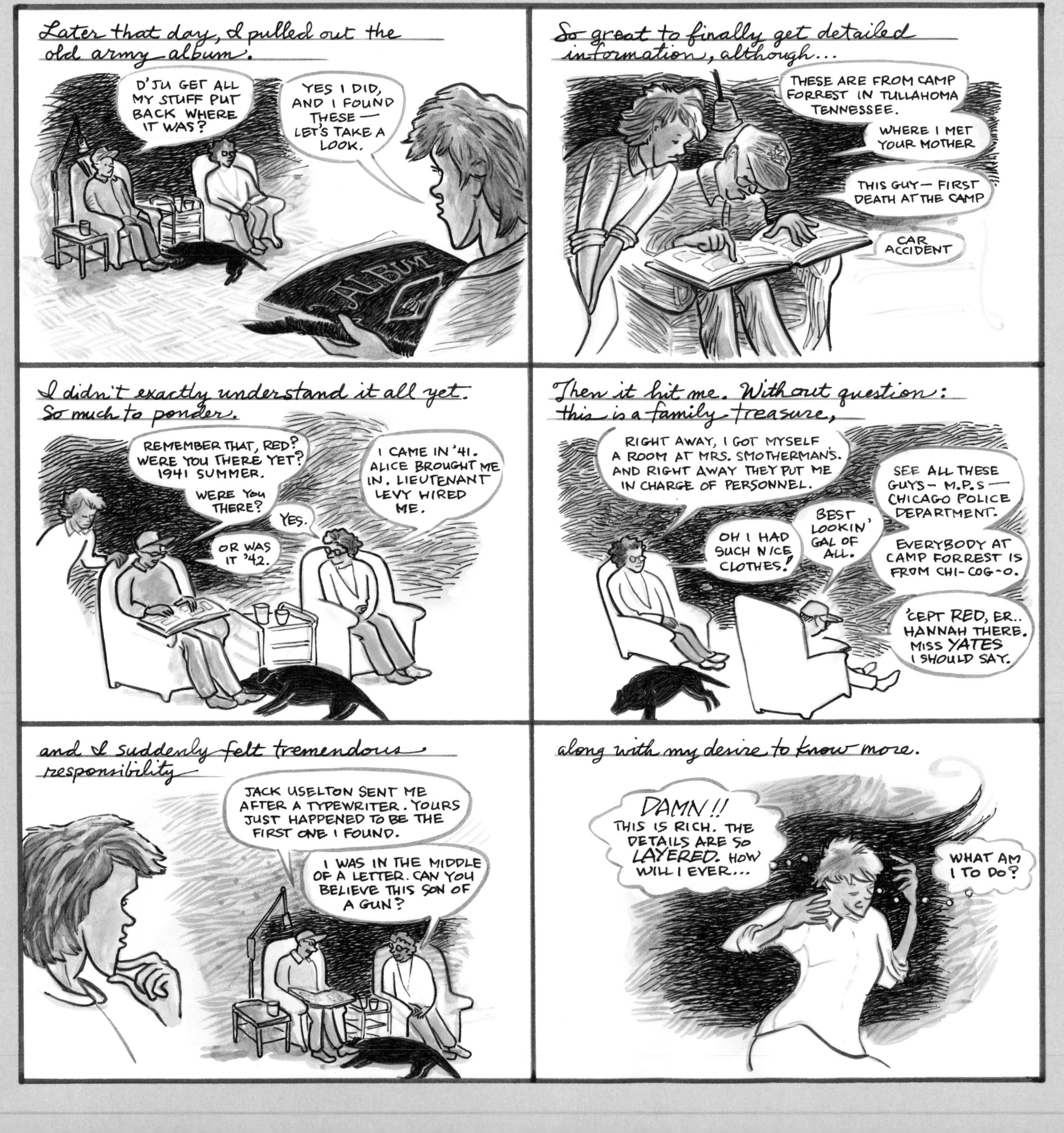
Later that day, I pulled out the old army album.
D'JU GET ALL MY STUFF PUT BACK WHERE IT WAS?
YES I DID, AND I FOUND THESE— LET'S TAKE A LOOK.
ALBUM
So great to finally get detailed information, although...
THESE ARE FROM CAMP FORREST IN TULLAHOMA TENNESSEE.
WHERE I MET YOUR MOTHER
THIS GUY— FIRST DEATH AT THE CAMP
CAR ACCIDENT
I didn't exactly understand it all yet. So much to ponder.
REMEMBER THAT, RED? WERE YOU THERE YET? 1941 SUMMER.
WERE YOU THERE?
OR WAS IT '42.
YES.
I CAME IN '41. ALICE BROUGHT ME IN. LIEUTENANT LEVY HIRED ME.
Then it hit me. Without question: this is a family treasure,
RIGHT AWAY, I GOT MYSELF A ROOM AT MRS. SMOTHERMAN'S. AND RIGHT AWAY THEY PUT ME IN CHARGE OF PERSONNEL.
OH I HAD SUCH NICE CLOTHES!
BEST LOOKIN' GAL OF ALL.
SEE ALL THESE GUYS— M.P.S— CHICAGO POLICE DEPARTMENT.
EVERYBODY AT CAMP FORREST IS FROM CHI-COG-O.
'CEPT RED, ER.. HANNAH THERE. MISS YATES I SHOULD SAY.
and I suddenly felt tremendous responsibility
JACK USELTON SENT ME AFTER A TYPEWRITER. YOURS JUST HAPPENED TO BE THE FIRST ONE I FOUND.
I WAS IN THE MIDDLE OF A LETTER. CAN YOU BELIEVE THIS SON OF A GUN?
along with my desire to know more.
DAMN!! THIS IS RICH. THE DETAILS ARE SO LAYERED. HOW WILL I EVER...
WHAT AM I TO DO?

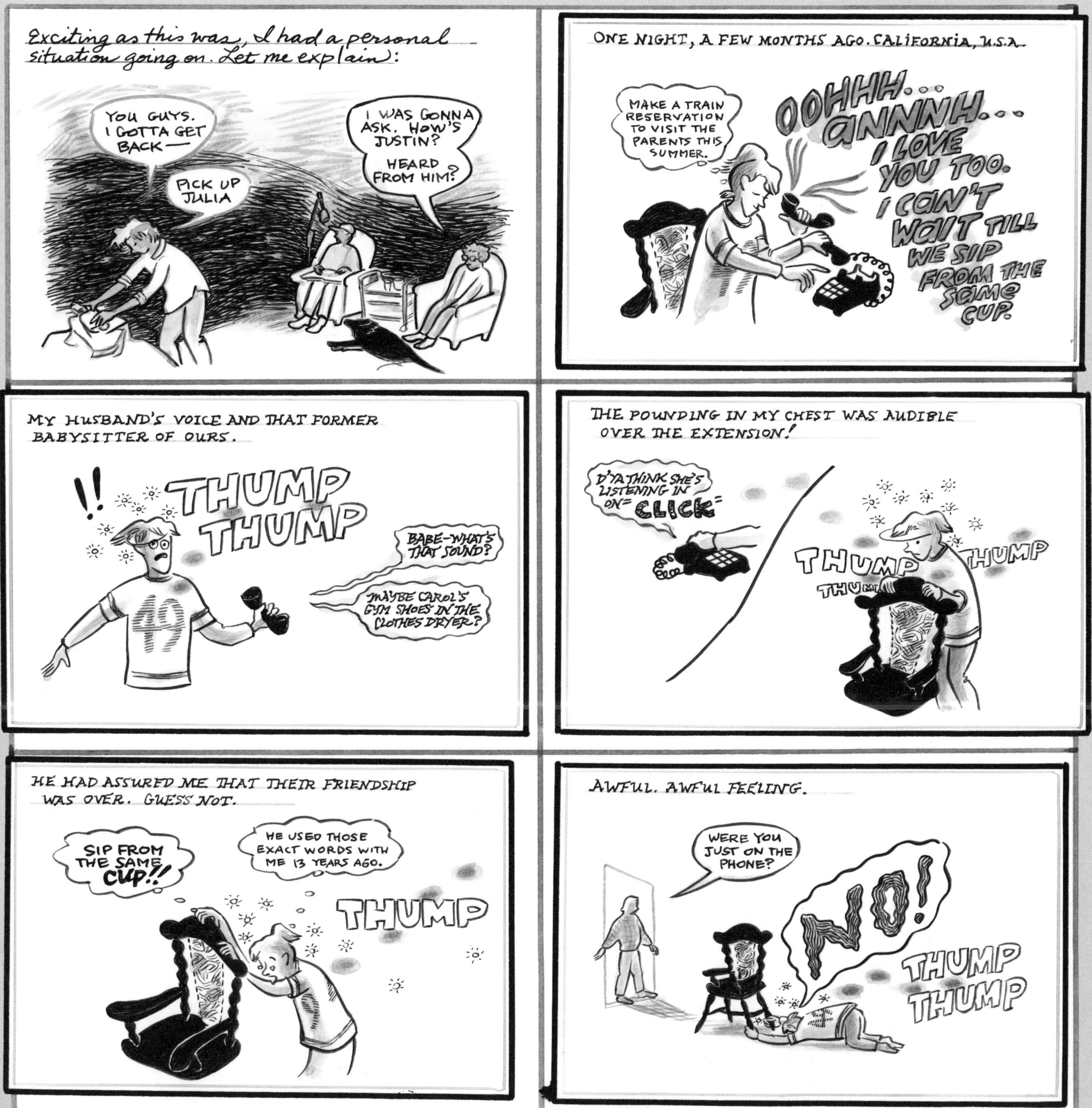
Exciting as this was, I had a personal situation going on. Let me explain:
YOU GUYS. I GOTTA GET BACK—
PICK UP JULIA
I WAS GONNA ASK. HOW'S JUSTIN?
HEARD FROM HIM?
ONE NIGHT, A FEW MONTHS AGO. CALIFORNIA, U.S.A.
MAKE A TRAIN RESERVATION TO VISIT THE PARENTS THIS SUMMER.
OOHHH... AHNNH... I LOVE YOU TOO. I CAN'T WAIT TILL WE SIP FROM THE SAME CUP.
MY HUSBAND'S VOICE AND THAT FORMER BABYSITTER OF OURS.
!!
THUMP THUMP
BABE-WHAT'S THAT SOUND?
MAYBE CAROL'S GYM SHOES IN THE CLOTHES DRYER?
THE POUNDING IN MY CHEST WAS AUDIBLE OVER THE EXTENSION!
D'YA THINK SHE'S LISTENING IN ON= CLICK=
THUMP THUMP THUMP
HE HAD ASSURED ME THAT THEIR FRIENDSHIP WAS OVER. GUESS NOT.
SIP FROM THE SAME CUP!!
HE USED THOSE EXACT WORDS WITH ME 13 YEARS AGO.
THUMP
AWFUL. AWFUL FEELING.
WERE YOU JUST ON THE PHONE?
NO!
THUMP THUMP

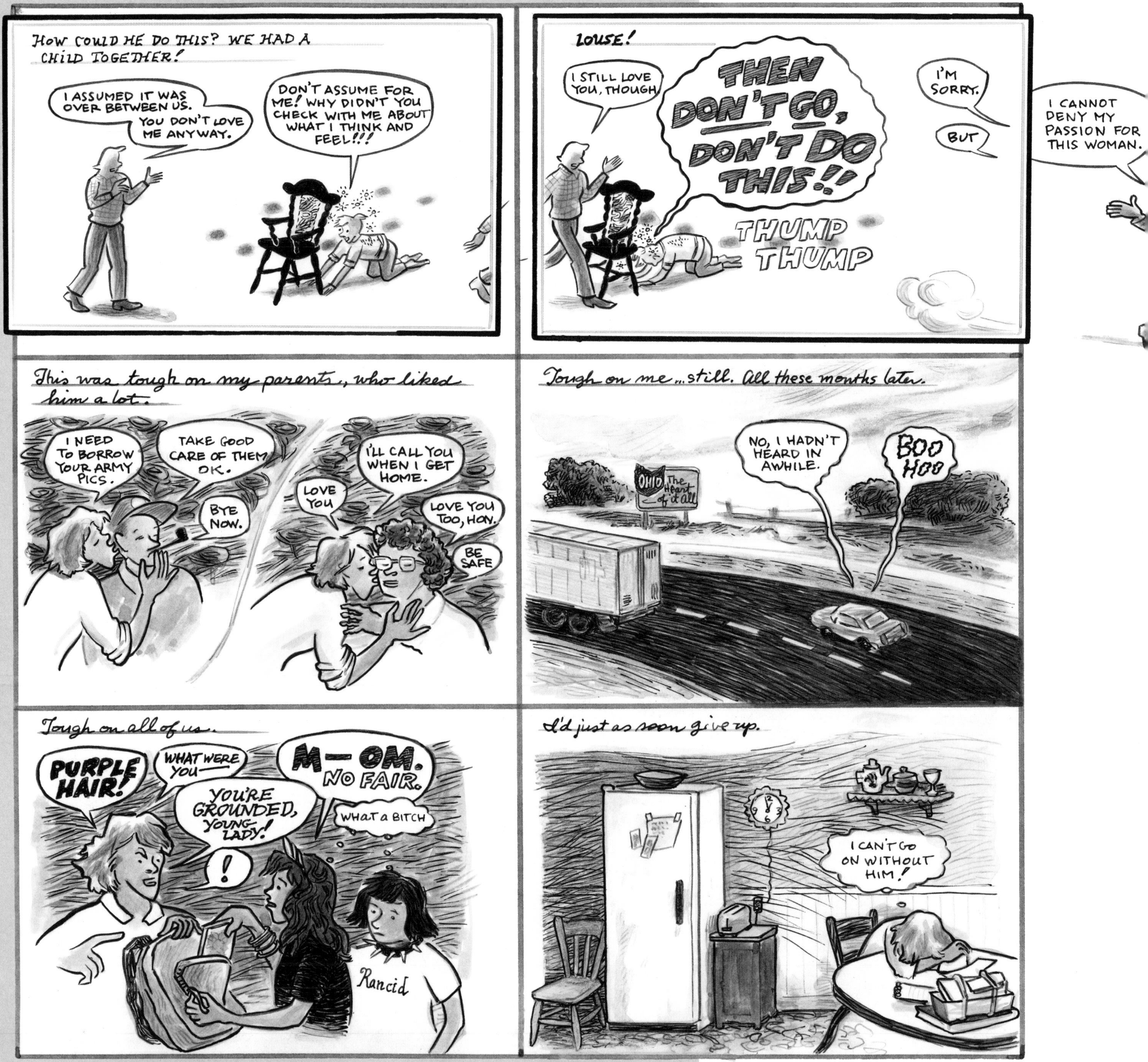
HOW COULD HE DO THIS? WE HAD A CHILD TOGETHER!
I ASSUMED IT WAS OVER BETWEEN US. YOU DON'T LOVE ME ANYWAY.
DON'T ASSUME FOR ME! WHY DIDN'T YOU CHECK WITH ME ABOUT WHAT I THINK AND FEEL!!!
LOUSE!
I STILL LOVE YOU, THOUGH
THEN DON'T GO, DON'T DO THIS!!
I'M SORRY.
BUT
I CANNOT DENY MY PASSION FOR THIS WOMAN.
THUMP THUMP
This was tough on my parents, who liked him a lot.
I NEED TO BORROW YOUR ARMY PICS.
TAKE GOOD CARE OF THEM OK.
BYE NOW.
LOVE YOU
I'LL CALL YOU WHEN I GET HOME.
LOVE YOU TOO, HON.
BE SAFE
Tough on me... still. All these months later.
OHIO The Heart of it all
NO, I HADN'T HEARD IN AWHILE.
BOO HOO
Tough on all of us.
PURPLE HAIR!
WHAT WERE YOU—
YOU'RE GROUNDED, YOUNG LADY!
M—OM. NO FAIR.
WHAT A BITCH
!
Rancid
I'd just as soon give up.
I CAN'T GO ON WITHOUT HIM!

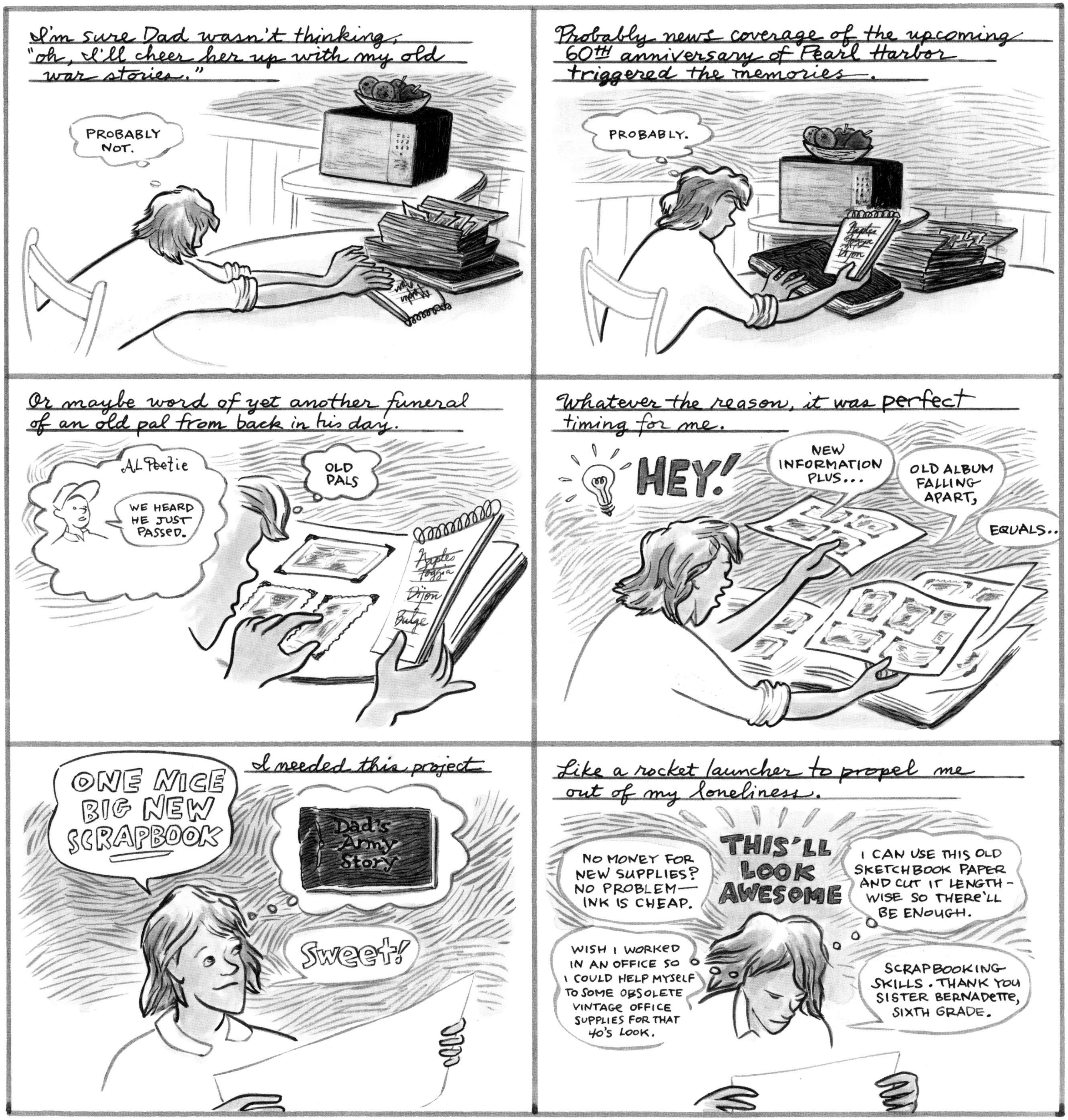

I'm sure Dad wasn't thinking, "oh, I'll cheer her up with my old war stories."
PROBABLY NOT.
Probably news coverage of the upcoming 60TH anniversary of Pearl Harbor triggered the memories.
PROBABLY.
Or maybe word of yet another funeral of an old pal from back in his day.
AL Peetie
WE HEARD HE JUST PASSED.
OLD PALS
Whatever the reason, it was perfect timing for me.
HEY!
NEW INFORMATION PLUS...
OLD ALBUM FALLING APART,
EQUALS..
I needed this project
ONE NICE BIG NEW SCRAPBOOK
Dad's Army Story
Sweet!
Like a rocket launcher to propel me out of my loneliness.
NO MONEY FOR NEW SUPPLIES? NO PROBLEM— INK IS CHEAP.
THIS'LL LOOK AWESOME
I CAN USE THIS OLD SKETCHBOOK PAPER AND CUT IT LENGTH-WISE SO THERE'LL BE ENOUGH.
WISH I WORKED IN AN OFFICE SO I COULD HELP MYSELF TO SOME OBSOLETE VINTAGE OFFICE SUPPLIES FOR THAT 40'S LOOK.
SCRAPBOOKING SKILLS. THANK YOU SISTER BERNADETTE, SIXTH GRADE.

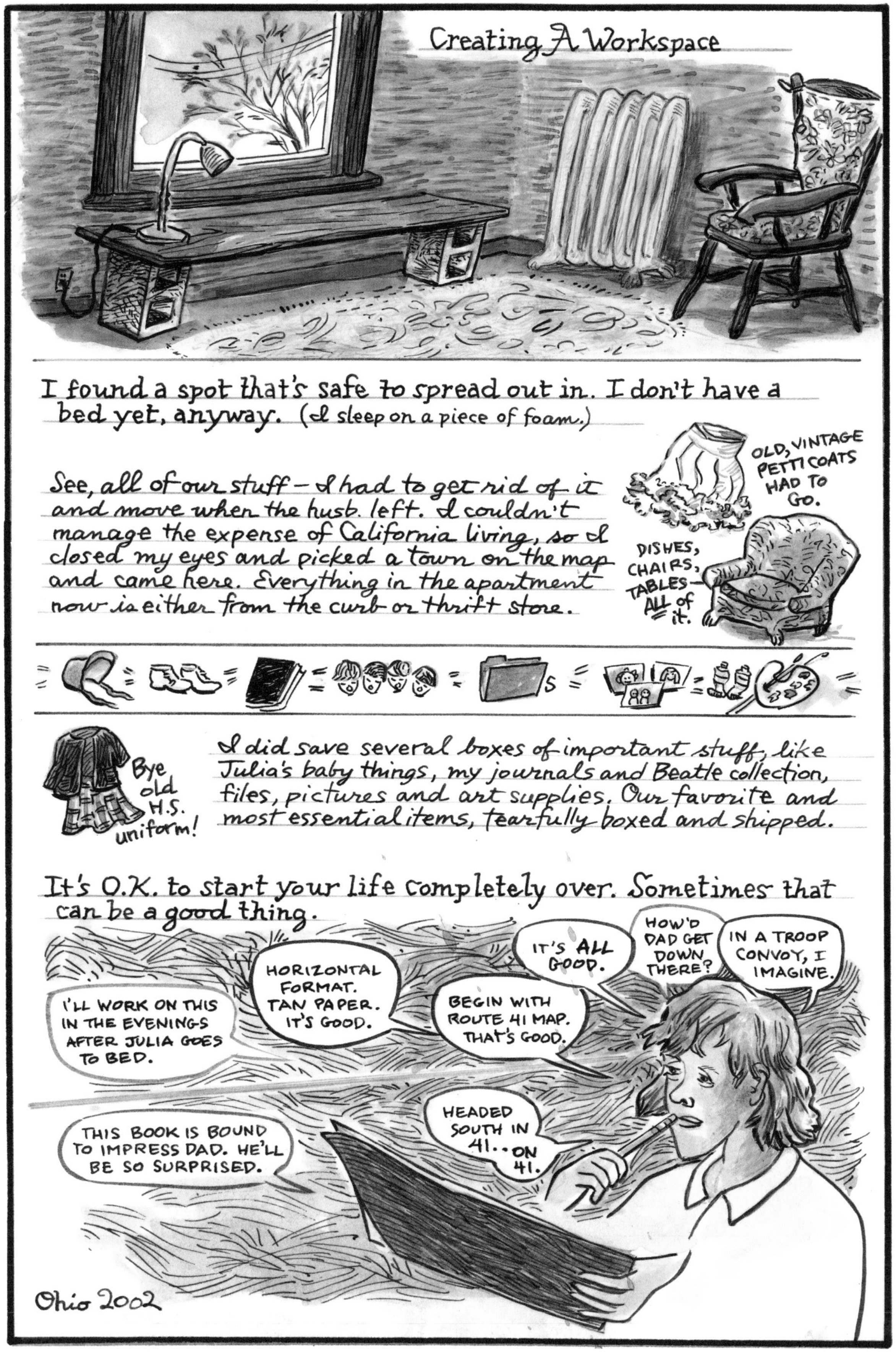
Creating A Workspace
I found a spot that's safe to spread out in. I don't have a bed yet, anyway. (I sleep on a piece of foam.)
See, all of our stuff - I had to get rid of it and move when the husb. left. I couldn't manage the expense of California living, so I closed my eyes and picked a town on the map and came here. Everything in the apartment now is either from the curb or thrift store.
OLD, VINTAGE PETTICOATS HAD TO GO.
DISHES, CHAIRS, TABLES - ALL of it.
I did save several boxes of important stuff, like Julia's baby things, my journals and Beatle collection, files, pictures and art supplies. Our favorite and most essential items, tearfully boxed and shipped.
Bye old H.S. uniform!
It's O.K. to start your life completely over. Sometimes that can be a good thing.
I'LL WORK ON THIS IN THE EVENINGS AFTER JULIA GOES TO BED.
HORIZONTAL FORMAT. TAN PAPER. IT'S GOOD.
BEGIN WITH ROUTE 41 MAP. THAT'S GOOD.
IT'S ALL GOOD.
HOW'D DAD GET DOWN THERE?
IN A TROOP CONVOY, I IMAGINE.
THIS BOOK IS BOUND TO IMPRESS DAD. HE'LL BE SO SURPRISED.
HEADED SOUTH IN 41.. ON 41.
Ohio 2002

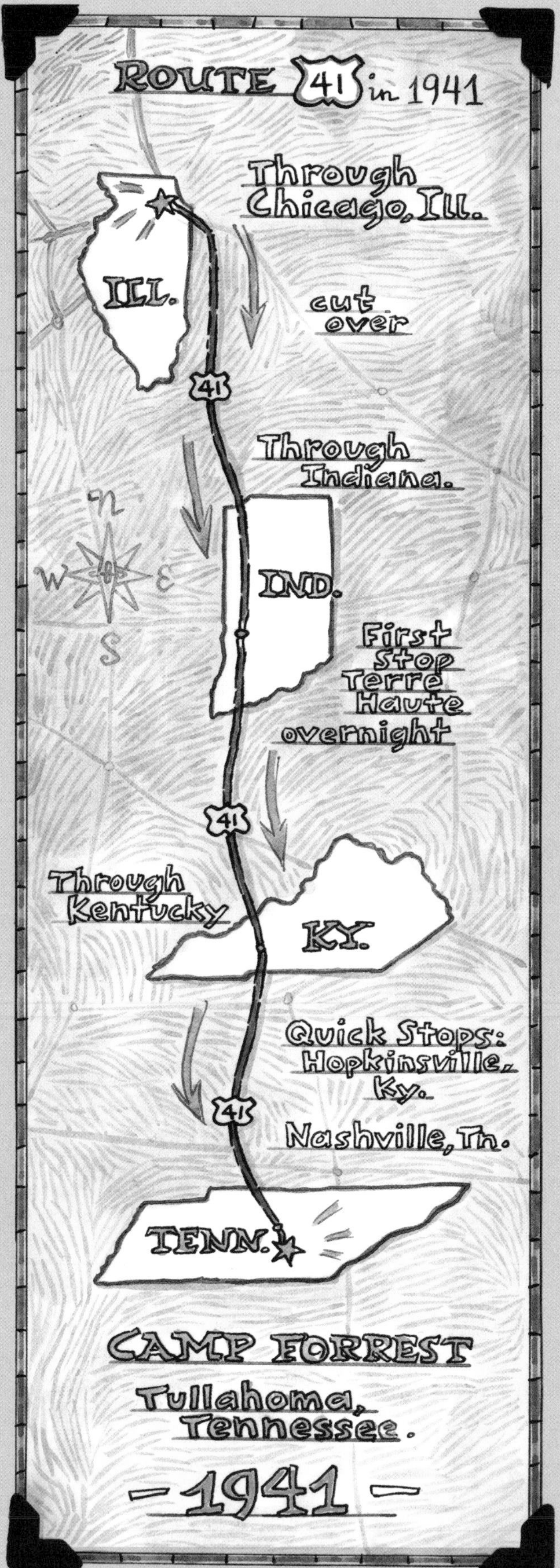
ROUTE 41 in 1941
Through Chicago, Ill.
ILL.
cut over
41
Through Indiana.
N
W
E
S
IND.
First Stop Terre Haute overnight
41
Through Kentucky
KY.
Quick Stops: Hopkinsville, Ky.
41
Nashville, Tn.
TENN.
CAMP FORREST
Tullahoma, Tennessee.
- 1941 -

DAD'S ARMY SCRAPBOOK
AND
TOUR OF DUTY HIGHLIGHTS

PART I

CAMP FORREST
&
POST ENGINEER SERVICE

MARCH 1941 — JUNE 1944

★

Dumb Luck!

In February 1941, Chuck decided to join the Illinois National Guard "because all my buddies from the neighborhood joined." Battery B, First Battalion, 122 Field Artillery, 33RD Division. A Chicago unit with the motto: Ready and Prepared. About a month later, the Division was put on ACTIVE status.

You're in the Army *now*, pal!

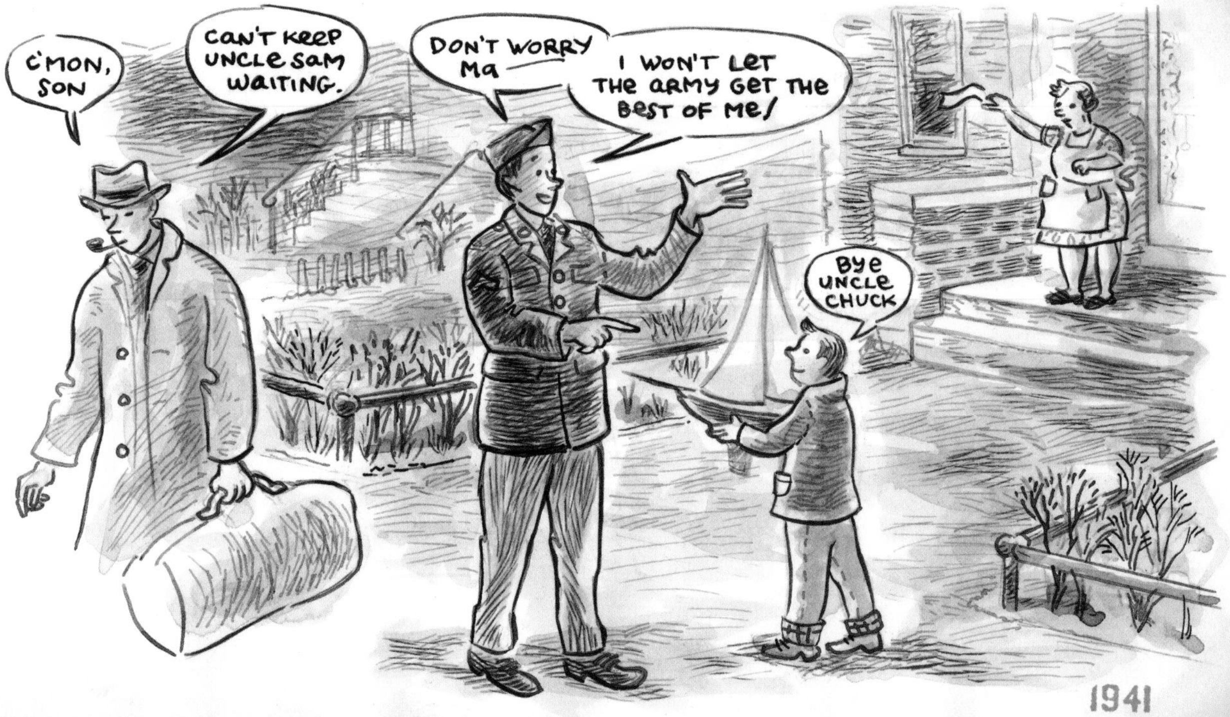
C'MON, SON
CAN'T KEEP UNCLE SAM WAITING.
DON'T WORRY MA—
I WON'T LET THE ARMY GET THE BEST OF ME!
BYE UNCLE CHUCK
1941

2

So the Division, along with many other units, descended upon quaint Tullahoma, Tennessee for training at the newly being built Camp Forrest. Overnight, the little town is overrun by thousands and thousands of young men, arriving in big truck convoys, coming in by train.

Lots of opportunity for civilians, too. Especially attractive redheads with excellent secretarial skills.

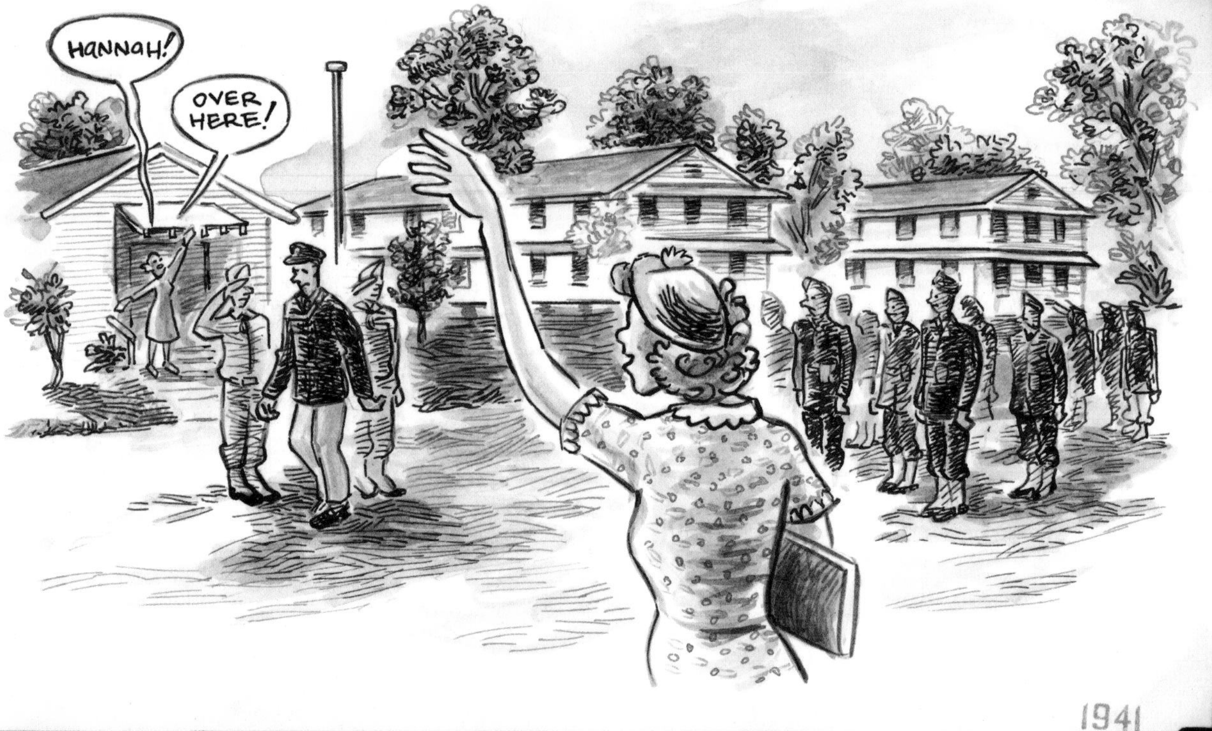
HANNAH!
OVER HERE!
1941

3

Camp Forrest was bursting at the seams! They couldn't build facilities fast enough, let alone maintain them. One night, so many pipes froze and then burst, the whole camp flooded. Chuck spoke up. He had worked as a plumber before enlisting, with his dad who was also a plumber. He knew what had to be done. Soon the Colonel had papers drawn up for his transfer out of artillery into the Post Engineers.

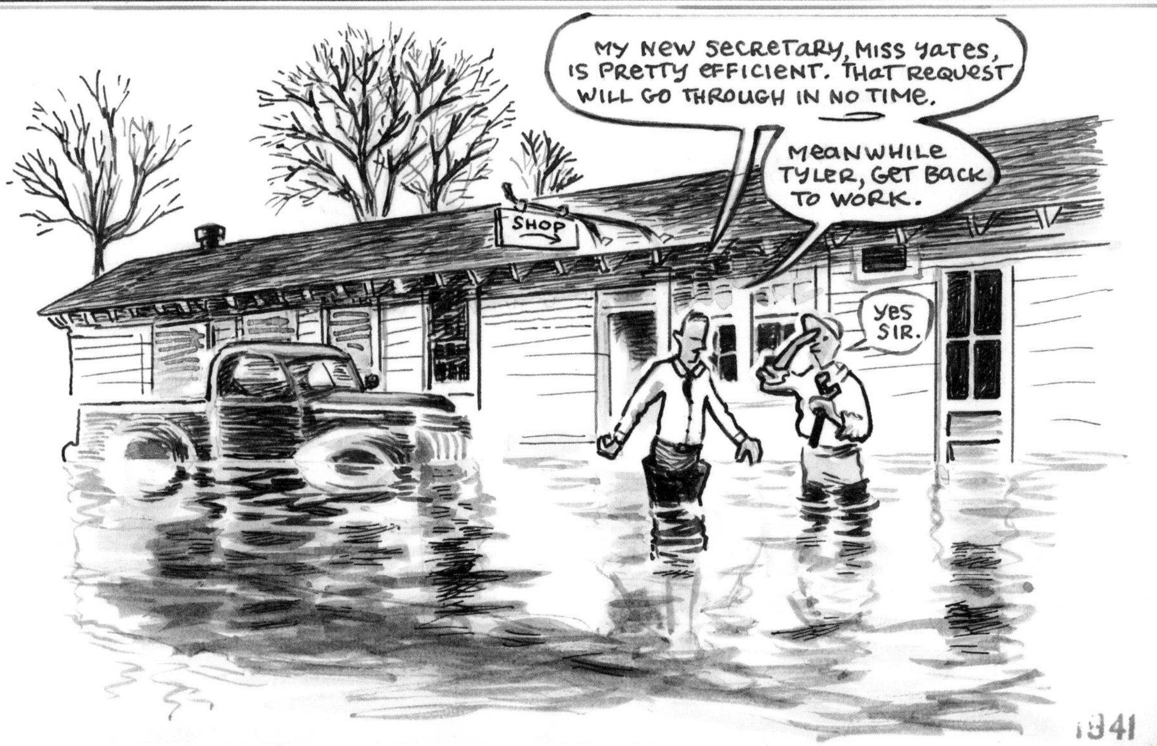
MY NEW SECRETARY, MISS YATES, IS PRETTY EFFICIENT. THAT REQUEST WILL GO THROUGH IN NO TIME.
MEANWHILE TYLER, GET BACK TO WORK.
YES SIR.
SHOP
1941

4

A critical component of military training is this male bonding thing, the 'band of brothers' and all that. Strong group identity insures better outcomes on the battlefield.

'Horseshit' thought Chuck. He was so glad when that transfer went through. It meant no more reveille, nicer sleeping quarters, a civilian boss. He could have his car. He had autonomy, like back at home.

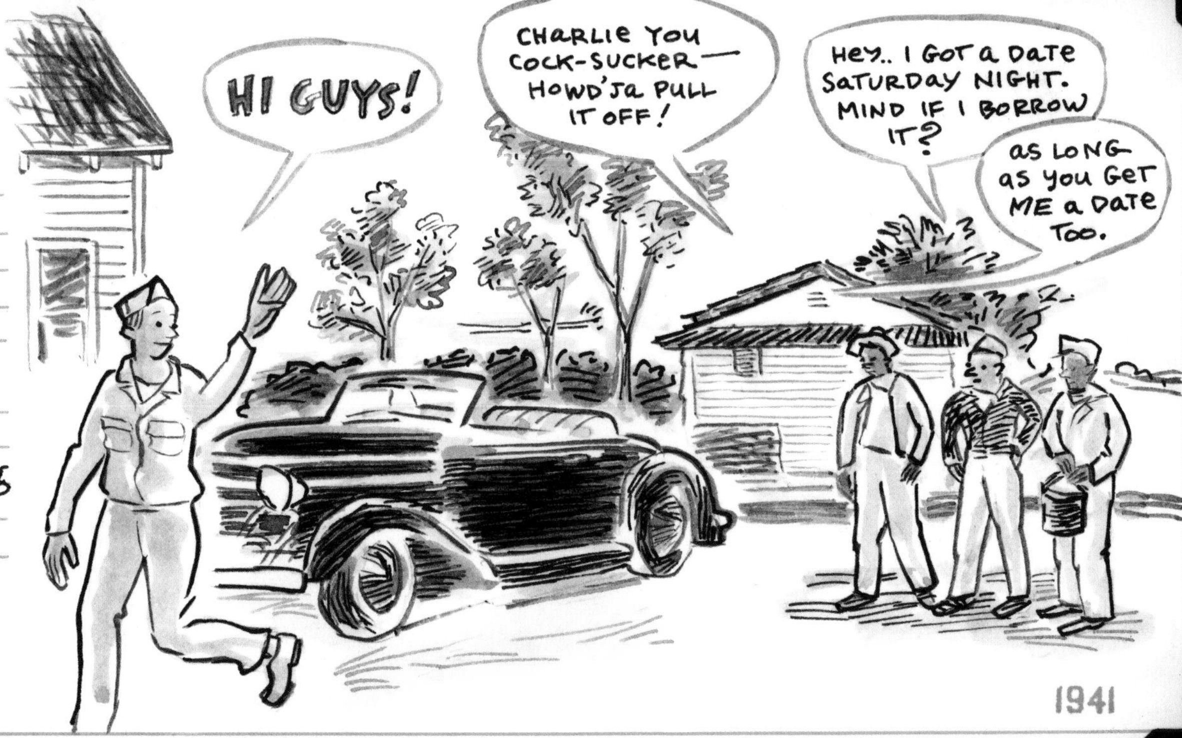
HI GUYS!
CHARLIE YOU COCK-SUCKER— HOWD'JA PULL IT OFF!
HEY.. I GOT A DATE SATURDAY NIGHT. MIND IF I BORROW IT?
AS LONG AS YOU GET ME A DATE TOO.
1941

5

But not before basic training and a trip with the 2ND Army down to Louisiana for maneuvers - aka dress rehearsal for war. The guys had to lug around Howitzers and learn how to shoot them, too, while living in bivouac conditions.

One guy, a coral snake bit him on the ankle and SNAP, just like that he was dead. That's why I never slept in a tent while I was in the Army. I slept on the gun turret.

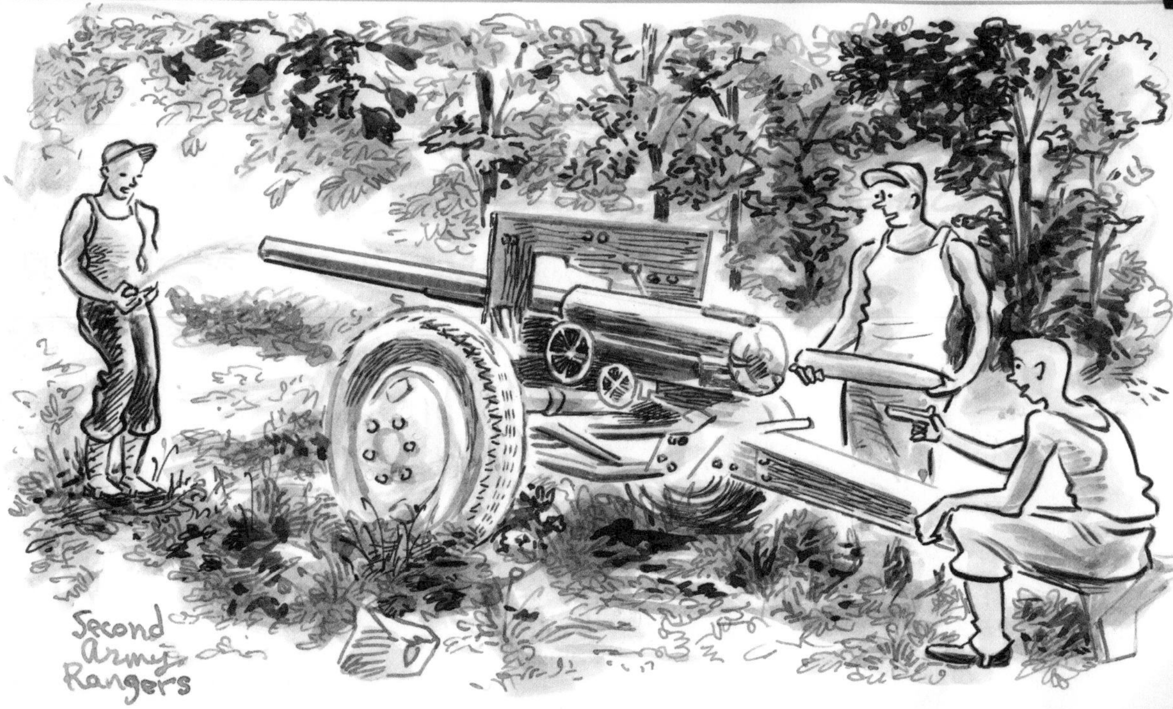
Second Army Rangers

6

"On the way back from maneuvers, while crossing the Mississippi, I tried to take a picture of a paddle wheeler. My foot got hung up, and I was hanging out of the truck, just missing the girders and cross pieces by inches. Turned my ankle pretty bad. They took me to the Marine Hospital in Memphis. Nice nurse from Alton, Ill. Not enough eats there, so she brought me rationed fruit in her blouse each day.

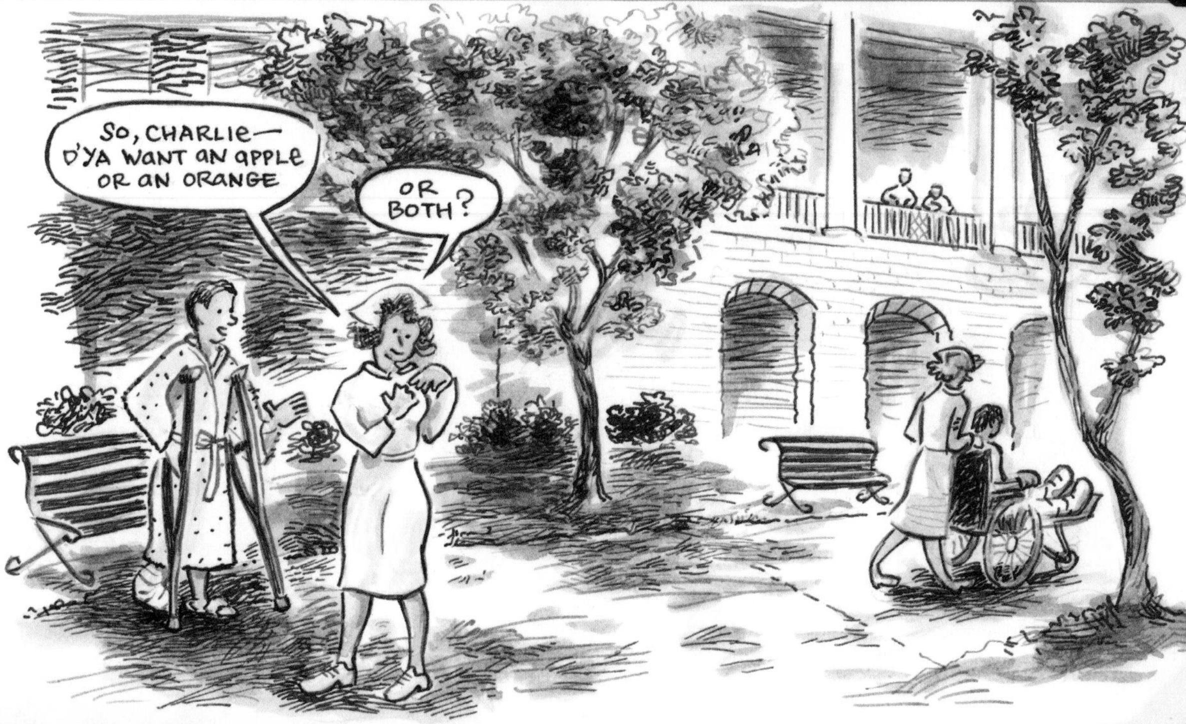
SO, CHARLIE— D'YA WANT AN APPLE OR AN ORANGE
OR BOTH?

7

"I don't even care that much about paddlewheelers but I hated being on crutches, so as soon as I could, I climbed up a smokestack, cast and all, so I could see better to snap a picture. Next thing I know, there's a bunch of nurses hollerin' up at me 'Dont jump! There's too much to live for!' Ha ha, those crazy broads thought I was tryin' to commit suicide.

"Wasn't long till they got rid of me.

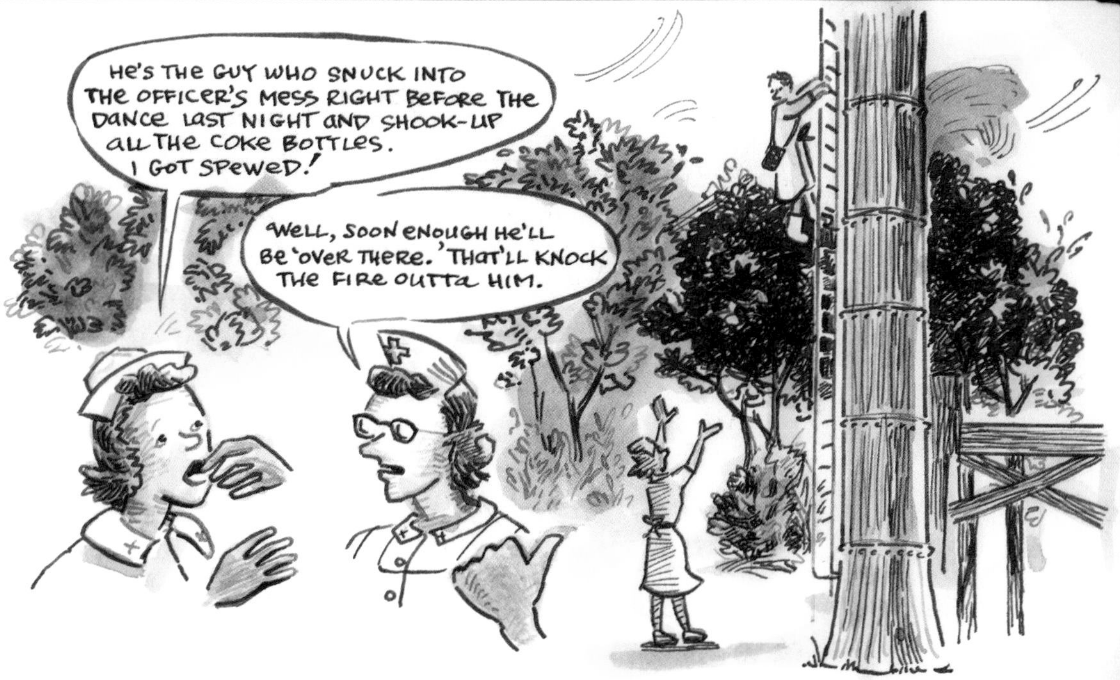
HE'S THE GUY WHO SNUCK INTO THE OFFICER'S MESS RIGHT BEFORE THE DANCE LAST NIGHT AND SHOOK-UP ALL THE COKE BOTTLES. I GOT SPEWED!
WELL, SOON ENOUGH HE'LL BE 'OVER THERE.' THAT'LL KNOCK THE FIRE OUTTA HIM.

8

Every now and then, we'd go to Chattanooga dancin.' A rough bunch of characters we were. We decided to beat up the dress blues with the gold buttons because the girls went for them. (Marines).

Same thing when we saw all those paratroopers with their nice boots. We had a little confrontation. At reveille, we had those boots on. Boy we got hell for that!

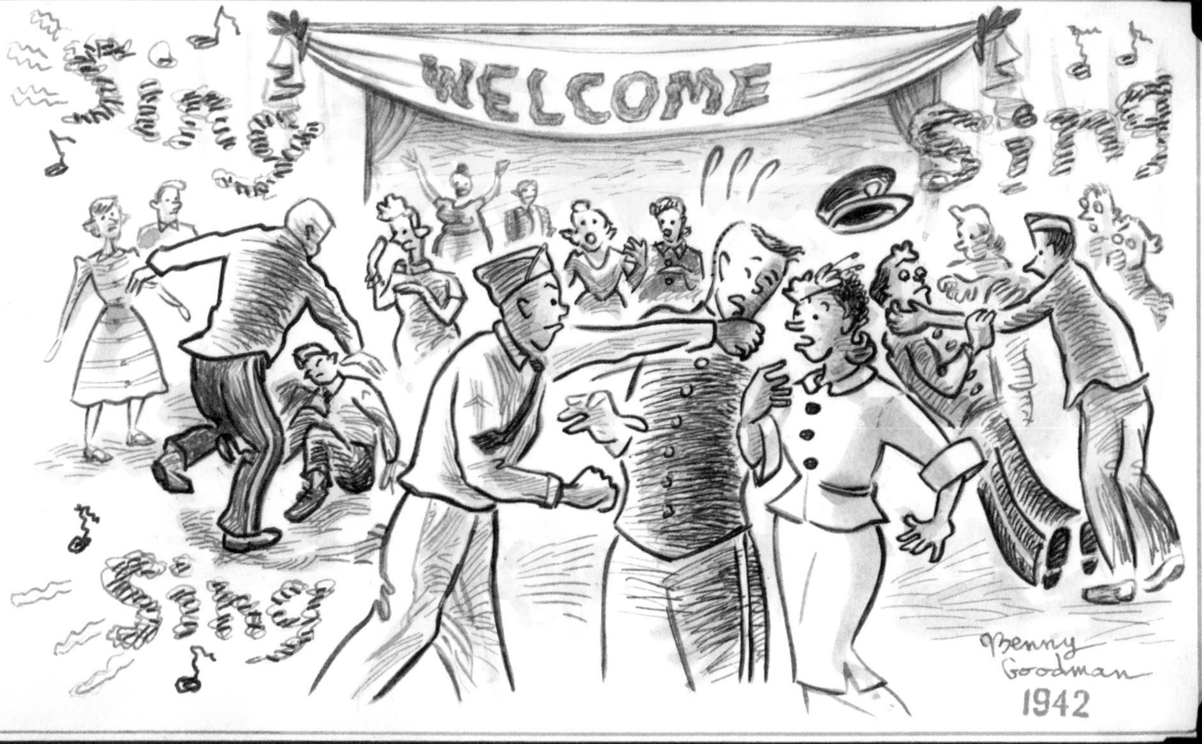
WELCOME
Benny Goodman
1942

9

"Yeah, I banged myself up pretty good in the Army. I skidded bare chested down a tree while trimming wires. My spurs gummed up and I had nothing to grip with. Then that steam burn on my hand from the Chapel boiler. Some son-of-a bitch didn't read the sign I posted and made a fire anyway.

"I waded knee-deep through gas to shut off a leaky valve and got skin burns. Also, I twisted my knee. Lucky, or I would have been hangin' from a tree in Normandy."

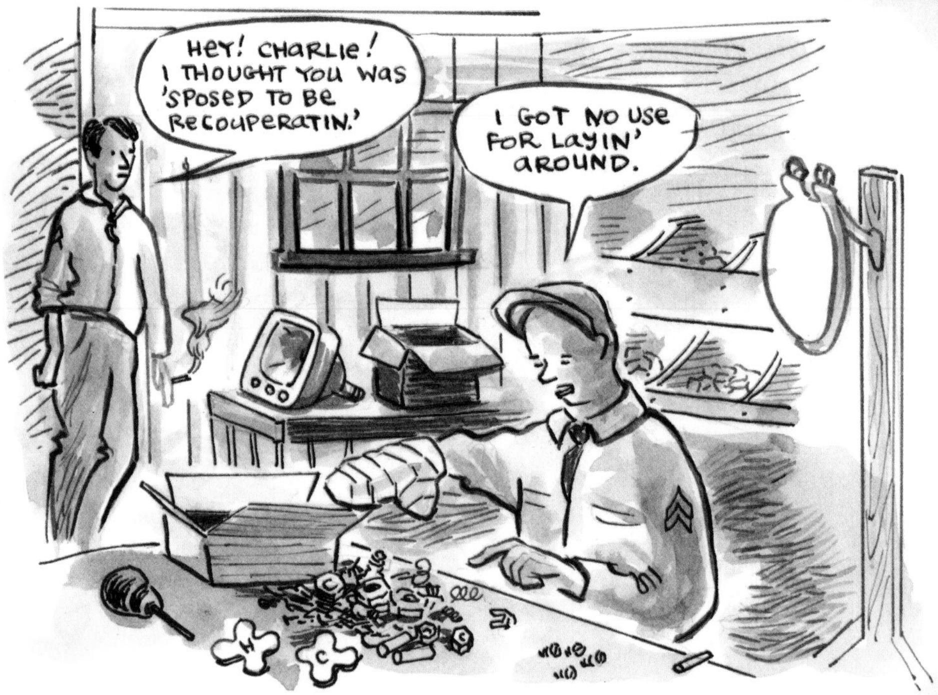

HEY! CHARLIE! I THOUGHT YOU WAS 'SPOSED TO BE RECOUPERATIN.'
I GOT NO USE FOR LAYIN' AROUND.

10

Hannah, in the meantime moved in with an established family in town. Rented a room there with her saucy friend Alice, who was also her boss. With such a desperate need for clerical personnel, Alice had Hannah call in all of her old pals from the McKenzie Business School in Chattanooga.

Hannah became the top dog when Alice resigned to get married. Such a dreadful outcome. The guy was killed at Anzio. She cried and cried. It broke her spirit.

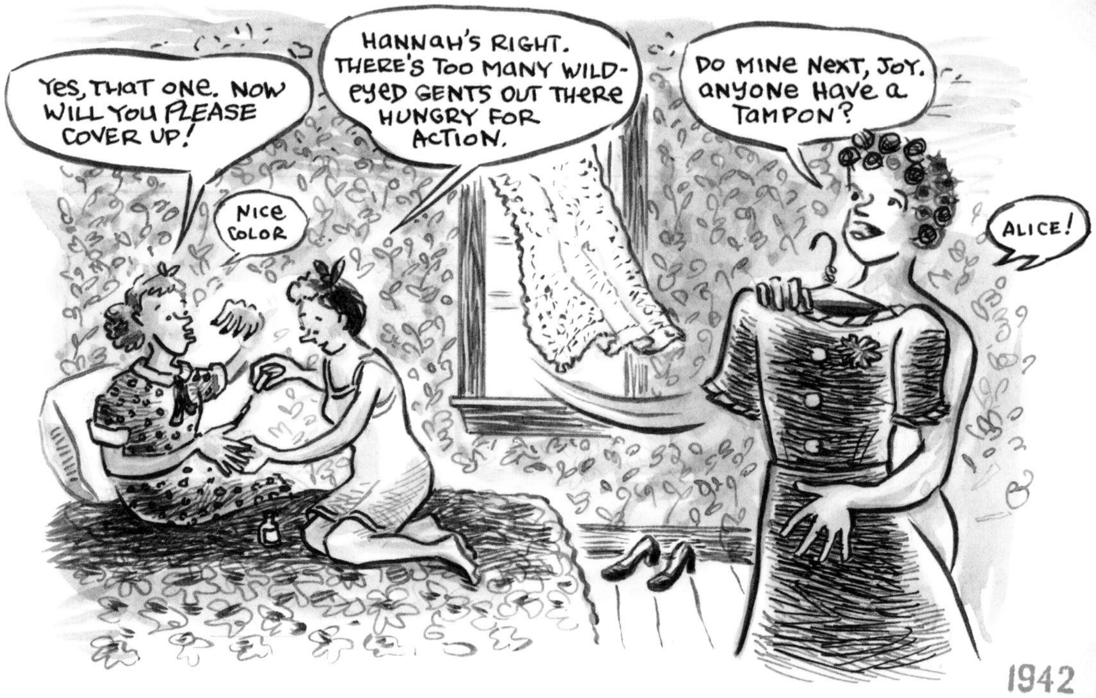

YES, THAT ONE. NOW WILL YOU PLEASE COVER UP!
NICE COLOR
HANNAH'S RIGHT. THERE'S TOO MANY WILD-EYED GENTS OUT THERE HUNGRY FOR ACTION.
DO MINE NEXT, JOY. ANYONE HAVE A TAMPON?
ALICE!

1942

11

Come and go, life in wartime. People come into your life and can be there maybe only for a minute and then be gone in an instant. It can have a wildly big impact. With so much at stake and everything so tenuous, relationships intensified. Everything: urgent.

There's a grand scale operation, and then there's this tenderness target for that expert marksman, Cupid.

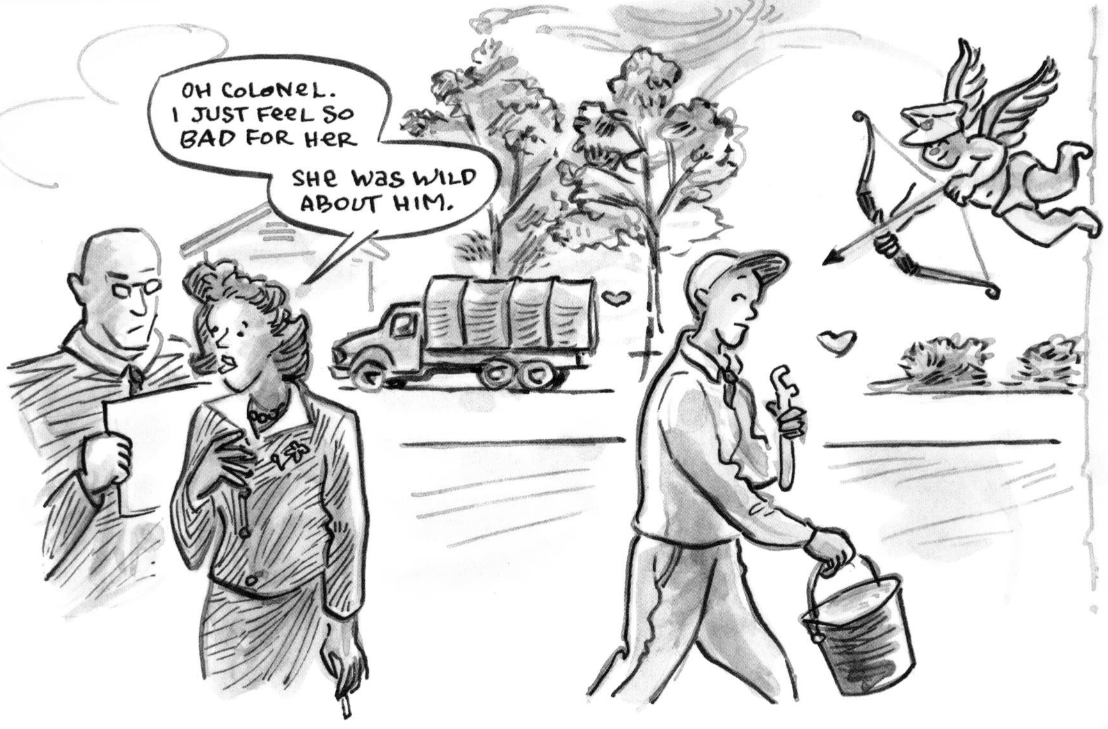
OH COLONEL. I JUST FEEL SO BAD FOR HER
SHE WAS WILD ABOUT HIM.

12

Chuck Tyler, dude, sharp dresser, clown.
Hannah Yates, clothes horse, wit, knockout.

She, using her paychecks to buy the latest in everything, suits, purses, shoes, ball gowns, furs... Putting the feed-sack calicos of childhood poverty behind her.

He, beneficiary of a comfortable middle class life, earned by the tradesmen before him. Great role models—clean, snappy, nothing but the humble best.

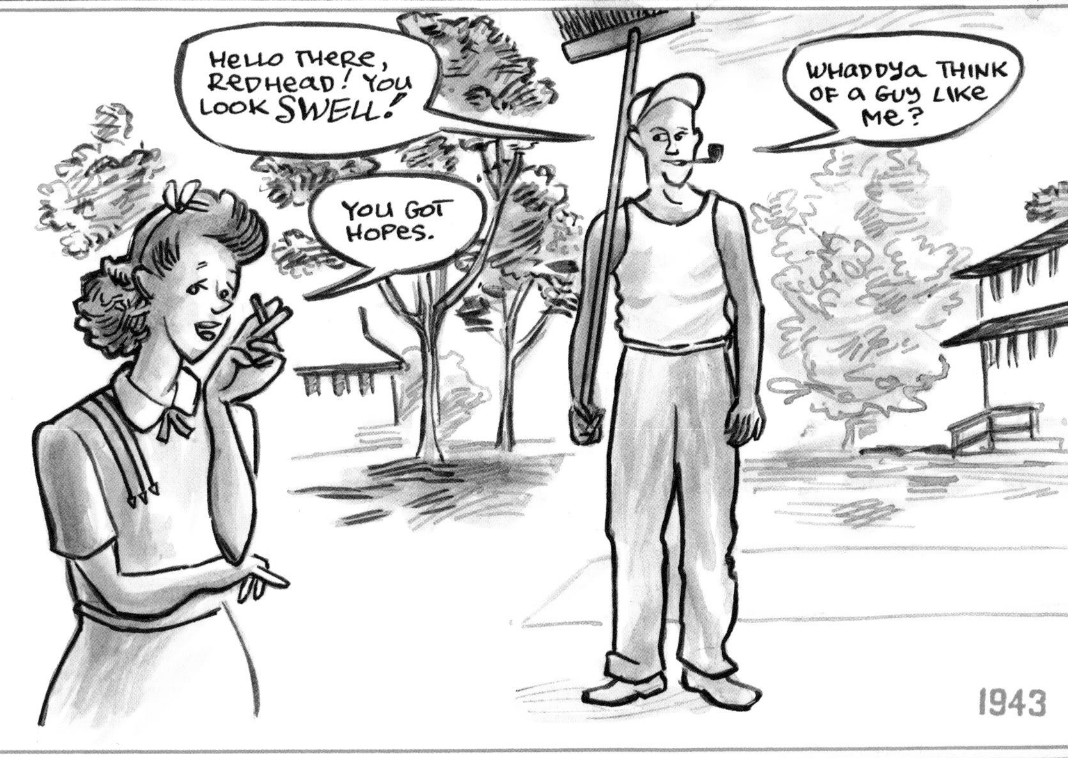
HELLO THERE, REDHEAD! YOU LOOK SWELL!
WHADDYA THINK OF A GUY LIKE ME?
YOU GOT HOPES.
1943

13

"One day my boss Jack said, 'Go get me a typewriter.' I guess he knew I had my eye on a certain redhead from over in personnel. I'd seen her around and at U.S.O. dances. The best lookin' one of the bunch. So, I walked in and took the typewriter while she was typing a letter! She was not too happy with me."

Flying fingers, flawless, furious... Miss Yates was the next target.

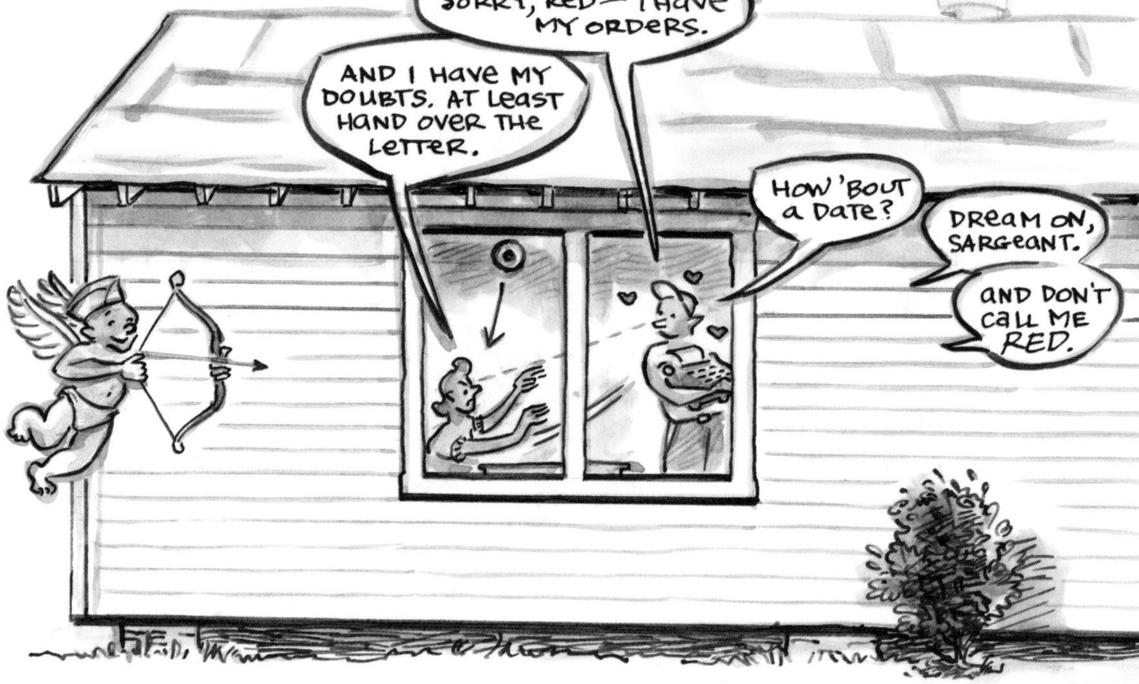
SORRY, RED— I HAVE MY ORDERS.
AND I HAVE MY DOUBTS. AT LEAST HAND OVER THE LETTER.
HOW 'BOUT A DATE?
DREAM ON, SARGEANT.
AND DON'T CALL ME RED.

14

Nonpariel, ditto.
Back in Chicago, he dated a different girl every night of the week. "..but this Red, she... wow. She..." (starts tearing up.)

She had been dating this lieutenant. Maybe things were getting serious. Walking away to his car one night, she noticed something about him that just seemed wrong— unlike that Chuck, who really had something to him. Eyes ready to see.

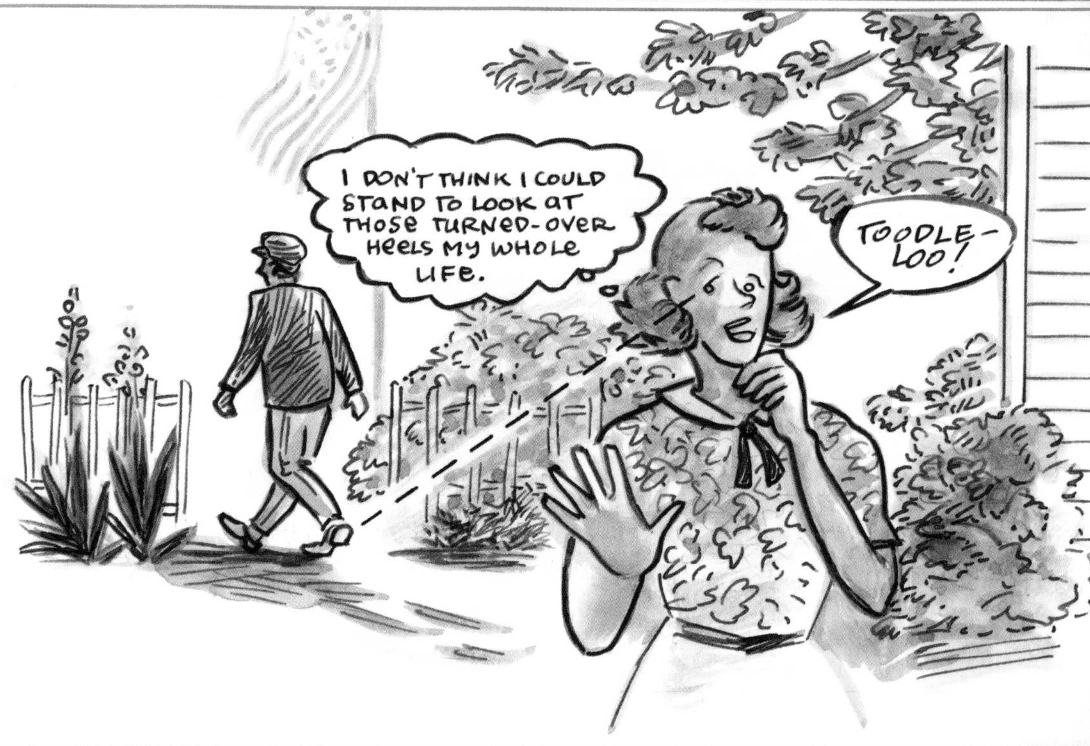
I DON'T THINK I COULD STAND TO LOOK AT THOSE TURNED-OVER HEELS MY WHOLE LIFE.
TOODLE-LOO!

15

"I knew the guys from the motor pool. They worked on the car and kept it in tip-top shape so we could all use it. M.P.'s and all that gang. We were an elite class of hell-raisers. We'd siphon off gas from the tank units, claiming it was for maintenance, but it was for the car. Quart here, gallon there. But I would need a whole lot more to get home to Chicago. Wouldn't you know who was in charge of ration tickets? This Miss Yates."

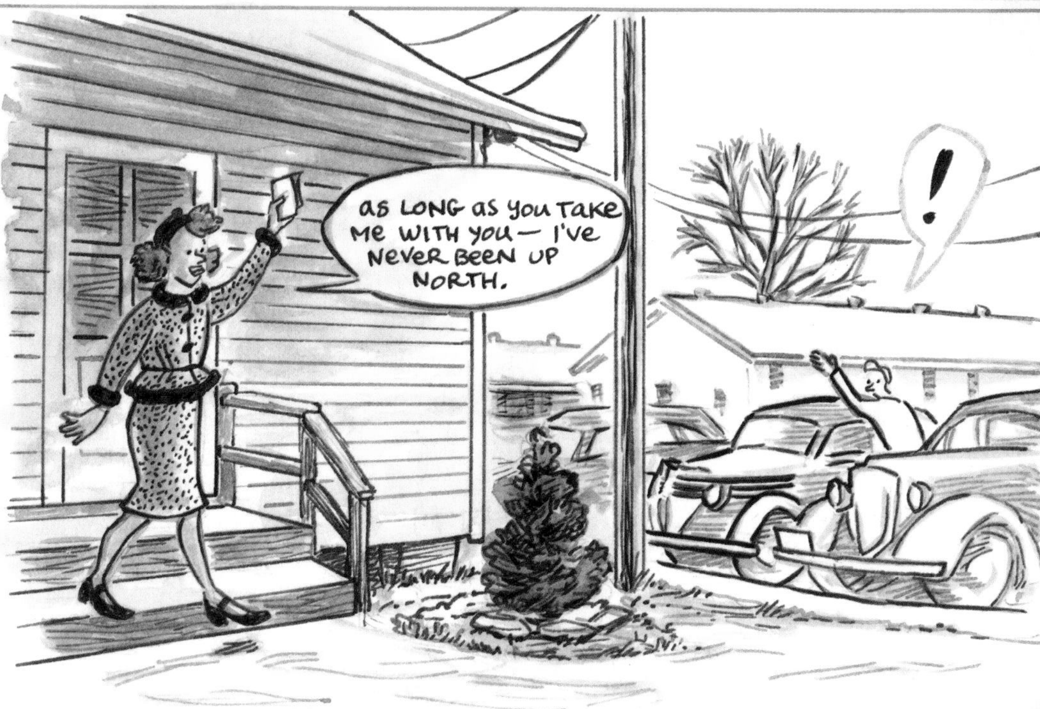
AS LONG AS YOU TAKE ME WITH YOU — I'VE NEVER BEEN UP NORTH.
!

16

"We took off up Highway 41 with all these jerry cans in the back. Every so often, I'd pull onto a farm road to fuel-up. I'd say to Red, 'keep a lookout.' 'For what?!' she'd say, 'farmers? Rabbits?' 'You never know,' I said.

Before even going to the house, it was an evening of enchantment at Chicago's Aragon Ballroom (known for elegance and its springs, cork and felt-backed dance floor.) 'Magic' struck while the orchestra played their favorite song.

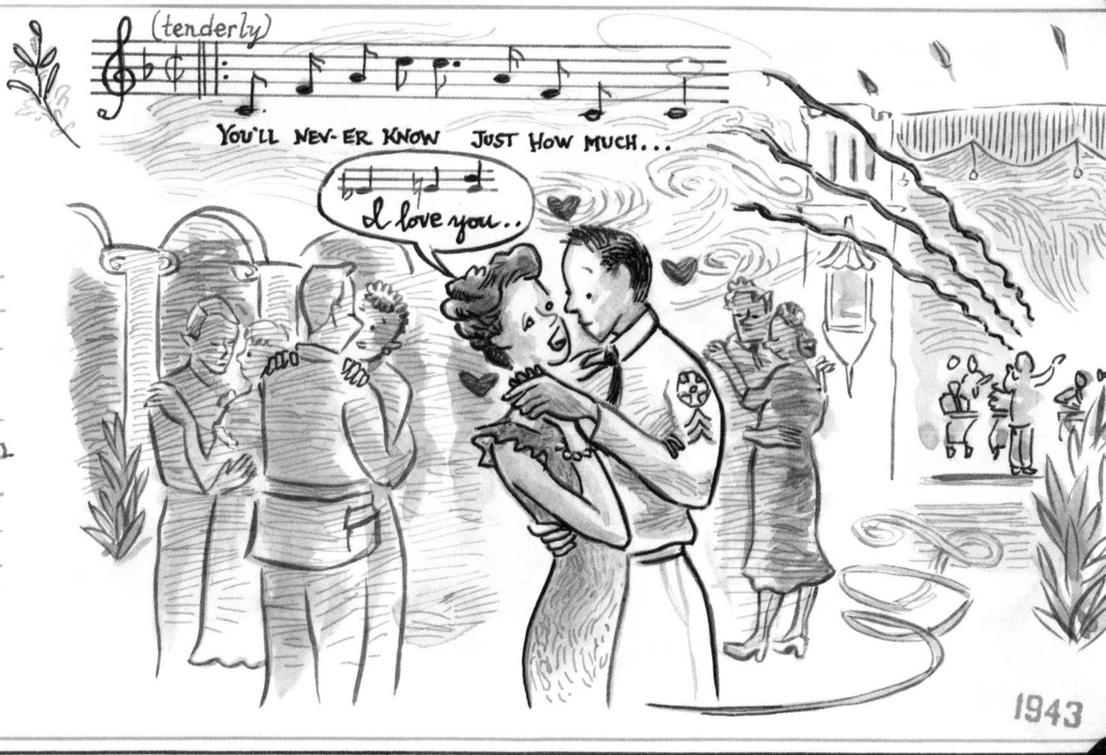
(tenderly)
YOU'LL NEV-ER KNOW JUST HOW MUCH...
I love you...
1943

17

"We got in late and the folks had already gone to bed. Ma had fixed up the guest room for Red and I went up to my old room.

"Red froze up in Chicago — not used to it. Even in her fur coat, the one she bought from Burshays in Chattanooga. So she figured 'I'll just sit on the sofa here until I warm up a bit.' Well, lo and behold, she fell asleep. Ma found her there the next morning and had a fit. First impressions, you know, they last.

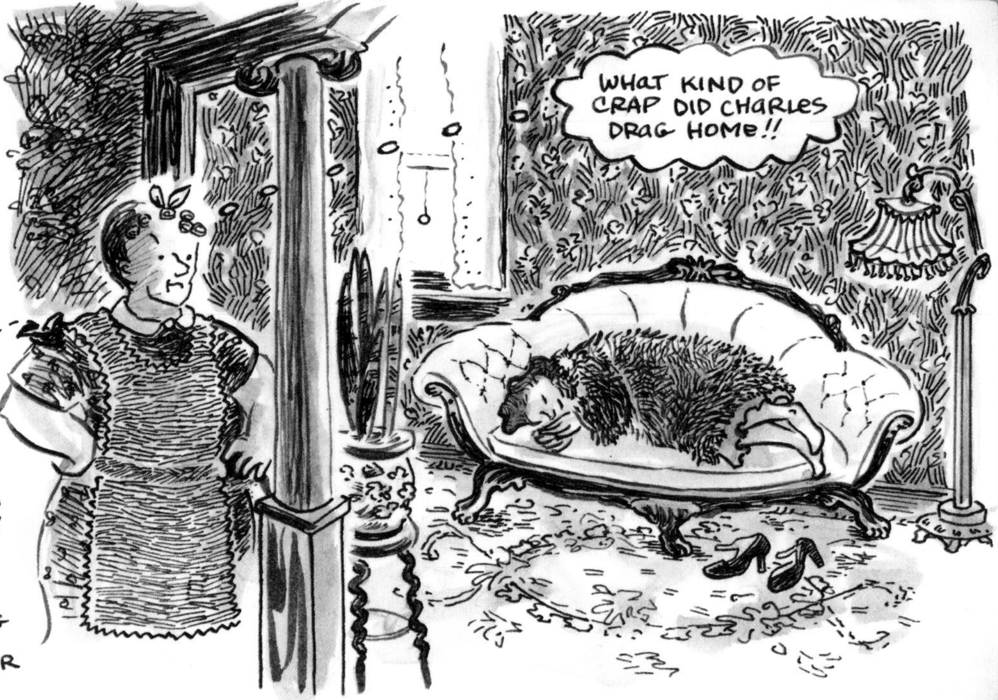
WHAT KIND OF CRAP DID CHARLES DRAG HOME!!
LIFELONG CHIP ON SHOULDER

18

"When we got back to Tennessee, I knew it was time to propose. So I went to see a jeweler in Nashville. He handed me the ring and a box of matches. 'What's this for,' I says. 'She'll want to see it in the dark.'

"Since it looked like I'd be headed overseas, Ma insisted we marry up there at St. Andrews on Thanksgiving. No such thing as going away on a honeymoon during a war, so we 'maneuvered' over to the Edgewater Beach Hotel on Lake Michigan for a few days."

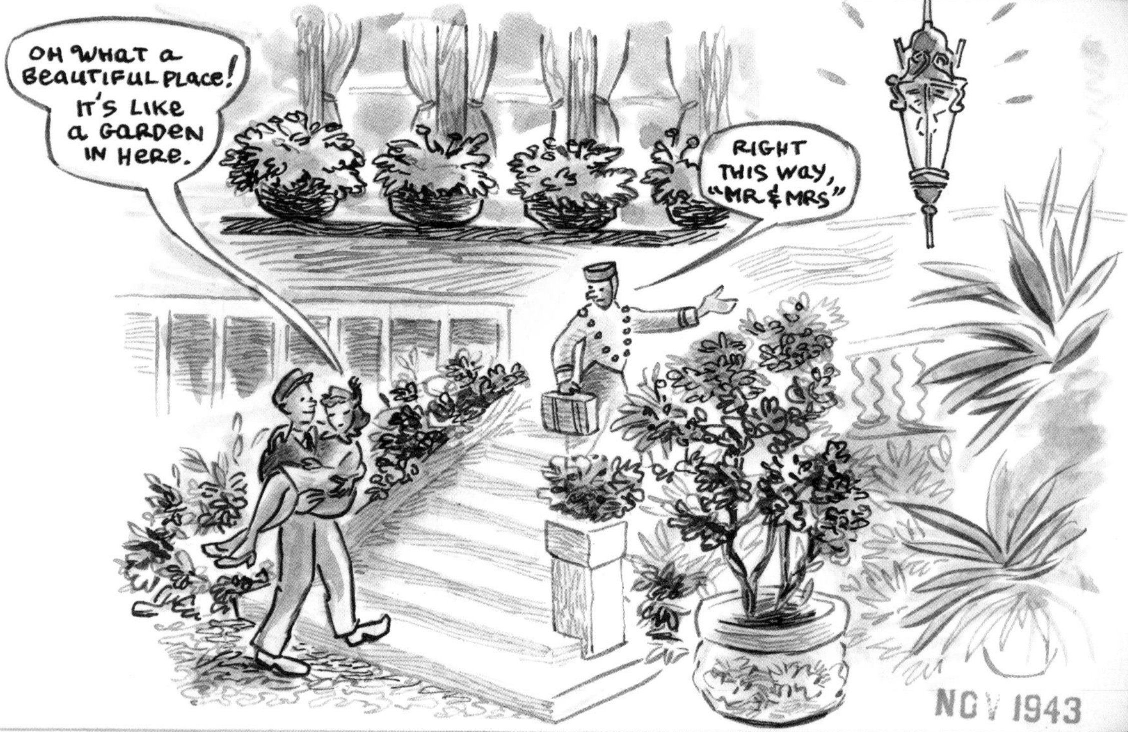
OH WHAT A BEAUTIFUL PLACE! IT'S LIKE A GARDEN IN HERE.
RIGHT THIS WAY, "MR & MRS"
NOV 1943

19

First meal: The bride decides on a romantic chicken-n-rice dinner – with no cooking experience. Bride dumps an entire bag of rice into a pot with a little water, and then sets the chicken into a 550° oven. Before long, the rice is boiling over, so she gets another pot, and another, and a big bowl and so on. Meanwhile, the groom decides to "toast-up" the place by firing-up the old stove there in the front, not knowing it has flue problems. Soon, their cute little cottage is full of smoke with pots and bowls of rice everywhere.

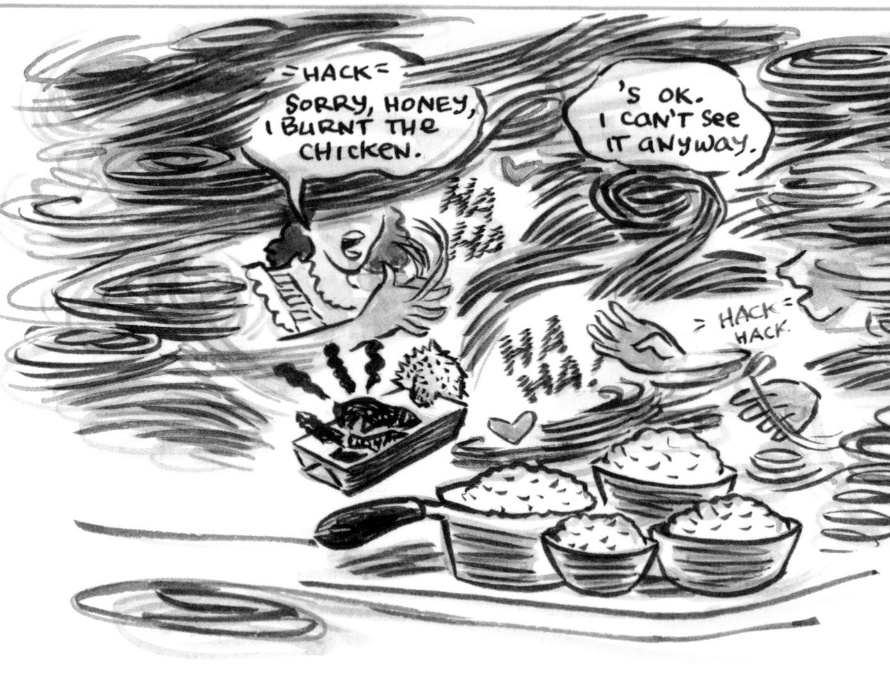
=HACK=
SORRY, HONEY, I BURNT THE CHICKEN.
'S OK. I CAN'T SEE IT ANYWAY.
HA HA
HA HA!
=HACK= HACK

20

"On to Ft. Bragg. They had me sorting scrap at a dump, I don't know why... I loved when Dad would come visit and we'd go fishin'. I guess what was to come was hard on my mind. And I hated to say bye to Red, but it was time to go.

"If I had stayed with the 122ND, I would have ended up in the Pacific. So many of those Chicago boys lost. If it wasn't for that transfer... Dumb luck, huh? I join the Army to be with my buddies, but instead I find the girl of my dreams."

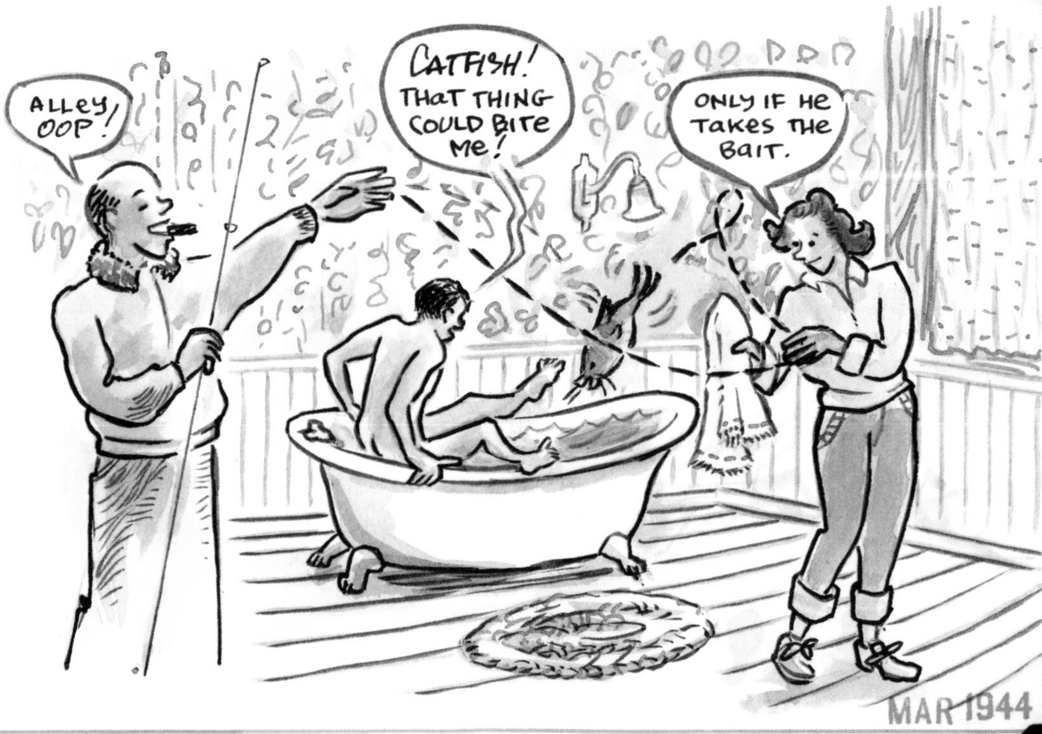
ALLEY OOP!
CATFISH! THAT THING COULD BITE ME!
ONLY IF HE TAKES THE BAIT.
MAR 1944

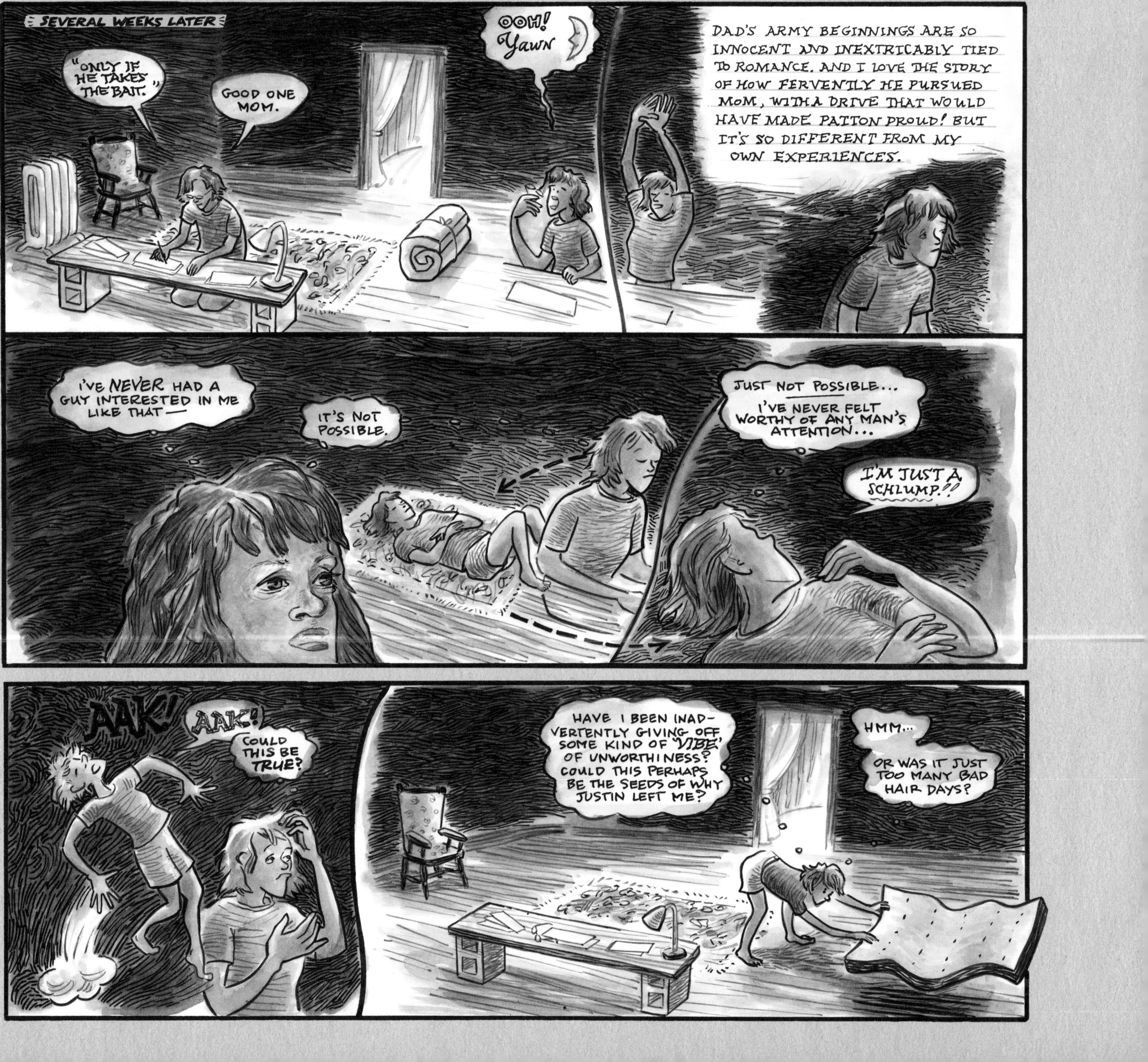
SEVERAL WEEKS LATER
"ONLY IF HE TAKES THE BAIT."
GOOD ONE MOM.
OOH! Yawn
DAD'S ARMY BEGINNINGS ARE SO INNOCENT AND INEXTRICABLY TIED TO ROMANCE. AND I LOVE THE STORY OF HOW FERVENTLY HE PURSUED MOM, WITH A DRIVE THAT WOULD HAVE MADE PATTON PROUD! BUT IT'S SO DIFFERENT FROM MY OWN EXPERIENCES.
I'VE NEVER HAD A GUY INTERESTED IN ME LIKE THAT—
IT'S NOT POSSIBLE.
JUST NOT POSSIBLE...
I'VE NEVER FELT WORTHY OF ANY MAN'S ATTENTION...
I'M JUST A SCHLUMP.
AAK!
AAK!
COULD THIS BE TRUE?
HAVE I BEEN INADVERTENTLY GIVING OFF SOME KIND OF 'VIBE' OF UNWORTHINESS? COULD THIS PERHAPS BE THE SEEDS OF WHY JUSTIN LEFT ME?
HMM...
OR WAS IT JUST TOO MANY BAD HAIR DAYS?

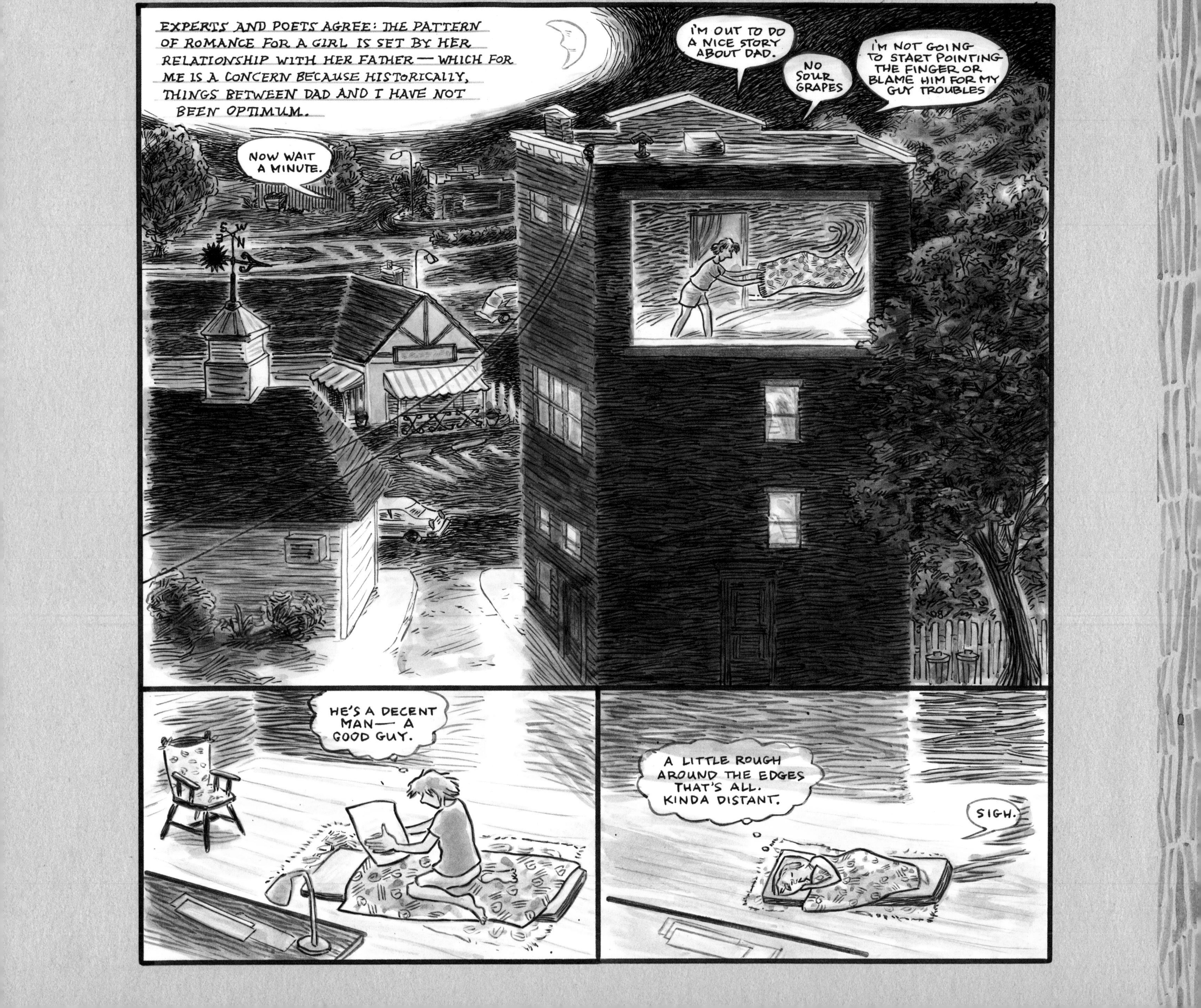
EXPERTS AND POETS AGREE: THE PATTERN OF ROMANCE FOR A GIRL IS SET BY HER RELATIONSHIP WITH HER FATHER — WHICH FOR ME IS A CONCERN BECAUSE HISTORICALLY, THINGS BETWEEN DAD AND I HAVE NOT BEEN OPTIMUM.
I'M OUT TO DO A NICE STORY ABOUT DAD.
NO SOUR GRAPES
I'M NOT GOING TO START POINTING THE FINGER OR BLAME HIM FOR MY GUY TROUBLES
NOW WAIT A MINUTE.
HE'S A DECENT MAN— A GOOD GUY.
A LITTLE ROUGH AROUND THE EDGES THAT'S ALL. KINDA DISTANT.
SIGH.

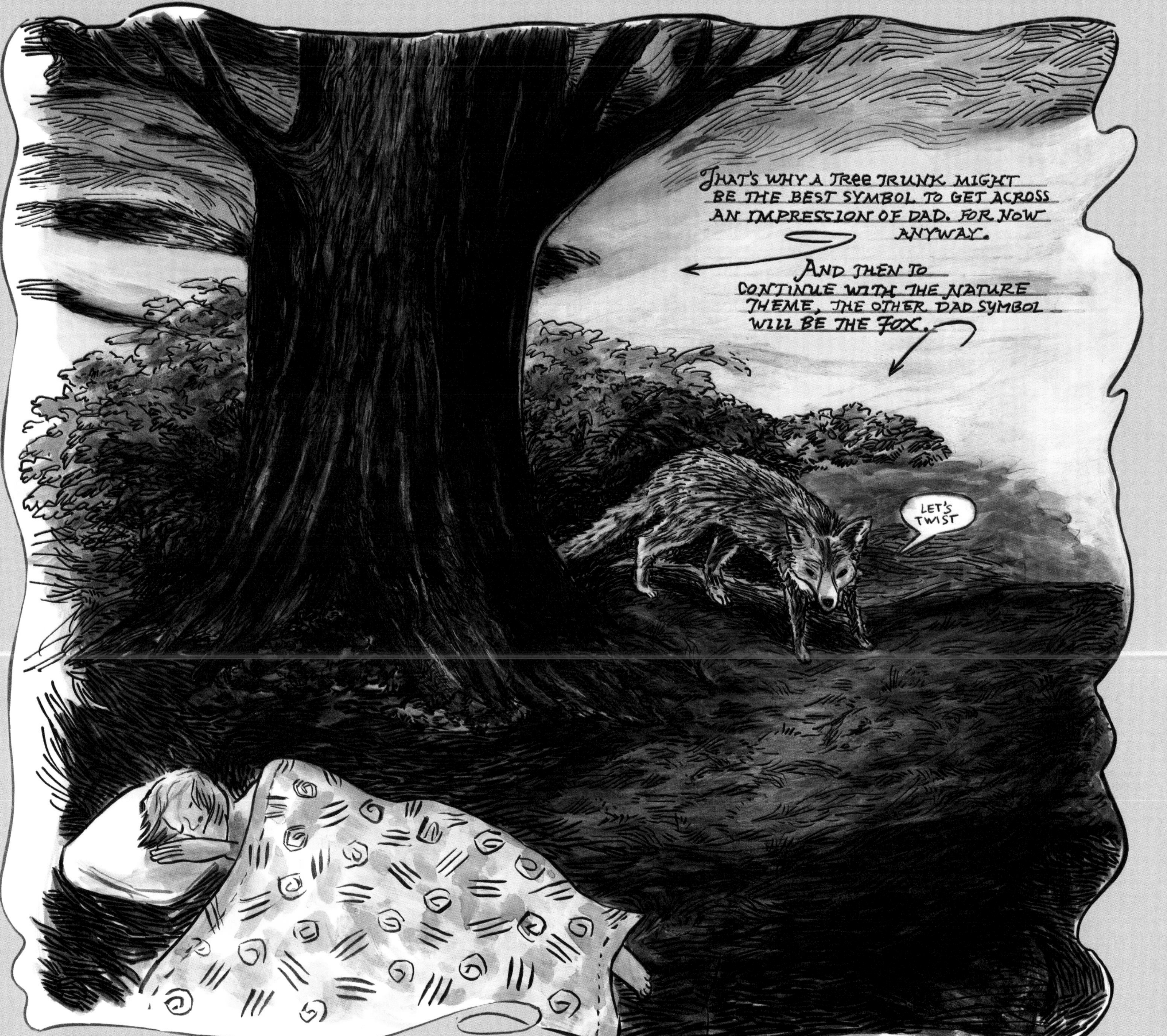
THAT'S WHY A TREE TRUNK MIGHT BE THE BEST SYMBOL TO GET ACROSS AN IMPRESSION OF DAD. FOR NOW ANYWAY.
AND THEN TO CONTINUE WITH THE NATURE THEME, THE OTHER DAD SYMBOL WILL BE THE FOX.
LET'S TWIST

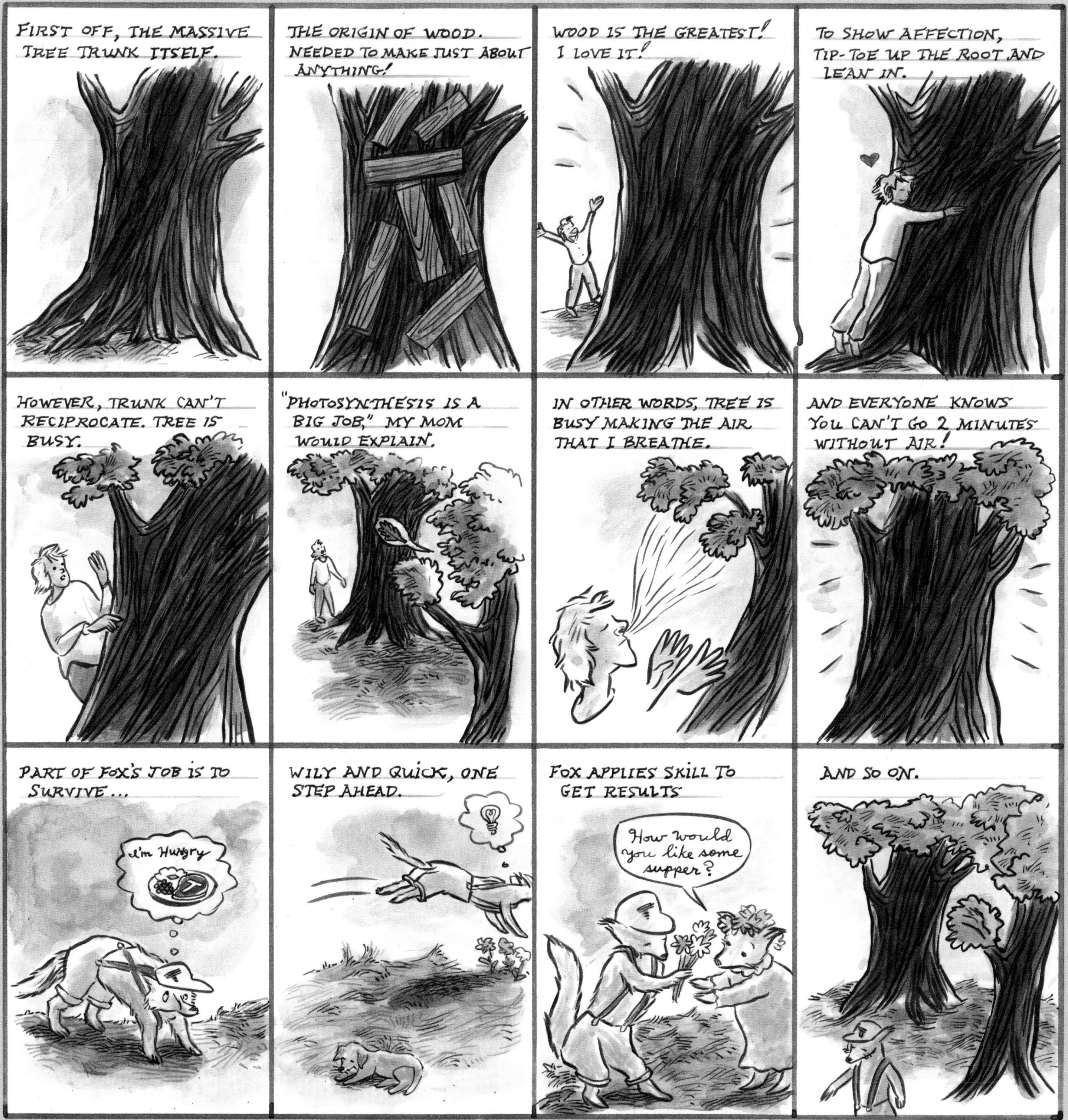
FIRST OFF, THE MASSIVE TREE TRUNK ITSELF.
THE ORIGIN OF WOOD. NEEDED TO MAKE JUST ABOUT ANYTHING!
WOOD IS THE GREATEST! I LOVE IT!
TO SHOW AFFECTION, TIP-TOE UP THE ROOT AND LEAN IN.
HOWEVER, TRUNK CAN'T RECIPROCATE. TREE IS BUSY.
"PHOTOSYNTHESIS IS A BIG JOB," MY MOM WOULD EXPLAIN.
IN OTHER WORDS, TREE IS BUSY MAKING THE AIR THAT I BREATHE.
AND EVERYONE KNOWS YOU CAN'T GO 2 MINUTES WITHOUT AIR!
PART OF FOX'S JOB IS TO SURVIVE...
I'm Hungry
WILY AND QUICK, ONE STEP AHEAD.
FOX APPLIES SKILL TO GET RESULTS
How would you like some supper?
AND SO ON.

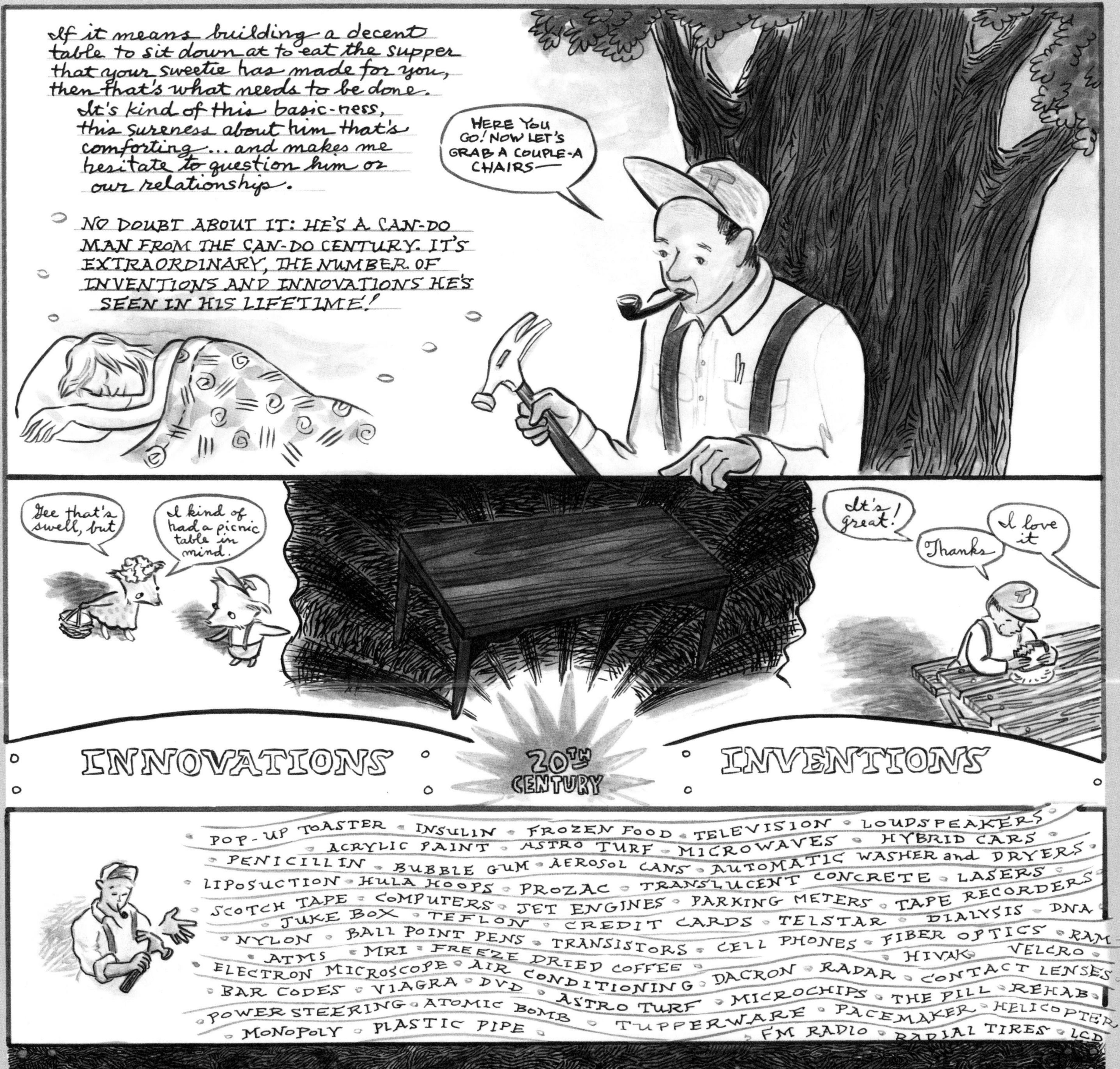
If it means building a decent table to sit down at to eat the supper that your sweetie has made for you, then that's what needs to be done.
It's kind of this basic-ness, this sureness about him that's comforting... and makes me hesitate to question him or our relationship.
HERE YOU GO! NOW LET'S GRAB A COUPLE-A CHAIRS—
NO DOUBT ABOUT IT: HE'S A CAN-DO MAN FROM THE CAN-DO CENTURY. IT'S EXTRAORDINARY, THE NUMBER OF INVENTIONS AND INNOVATIONS HE'S SEEN IN HIS LIFETIME!
Gee that's swell, but
I kind of had a picnic table in mind.
It's great!
Thanks
I love it
INNOVATIONS
20TH CENTURY
INVENTIONS
POP-UP TOASTER • INSULIN • FROZEN FOOD • TELEVISION • LOUDSPEAKERS
ACRYLIC PAINT • ASTRO TURF • MICROWAVES • HYBRID CARS
PENICILLIN • BUBBLE GUM • AEROSOL CANS • AUTOMATIC WASHER and DRYERS
LIPOSUCTION • HULA HOOPS • PROZAC • TRANSLUCENT CONCRETE • LASERS
SCOTCH TAPE • COMPUTERS • JET ENGINES • PARKING METERS • TAPE RECORDERS
JUKE BOX • TEFLON • CREDIT CARDS • TELSTAR • DIALYSIS • DNA
NYLON • BALL POINT PENS • TRANSISTORS • CELL PHONES • FIBER OPTICS • RAM
ATMS • MRI • FREEZE DRIED COFFEE • HIVAK • VELCRO
ELECTRON MICROSCOPE • AIR CONDITIONING • DACRON • RADAR • CONTACT LENSES
BAR CODES • VIAGRA • DVD • ASTRO TURF • MICROCHIPS • THE PILL • REHAB
POWER STEERING • ATOMIC BOMB • TUPPERWARE • PACEMAKER • HELICOPTER
MONOPOLY • PLASTIC PIPE • FM RADIO • RADIAL TIRES • LCD

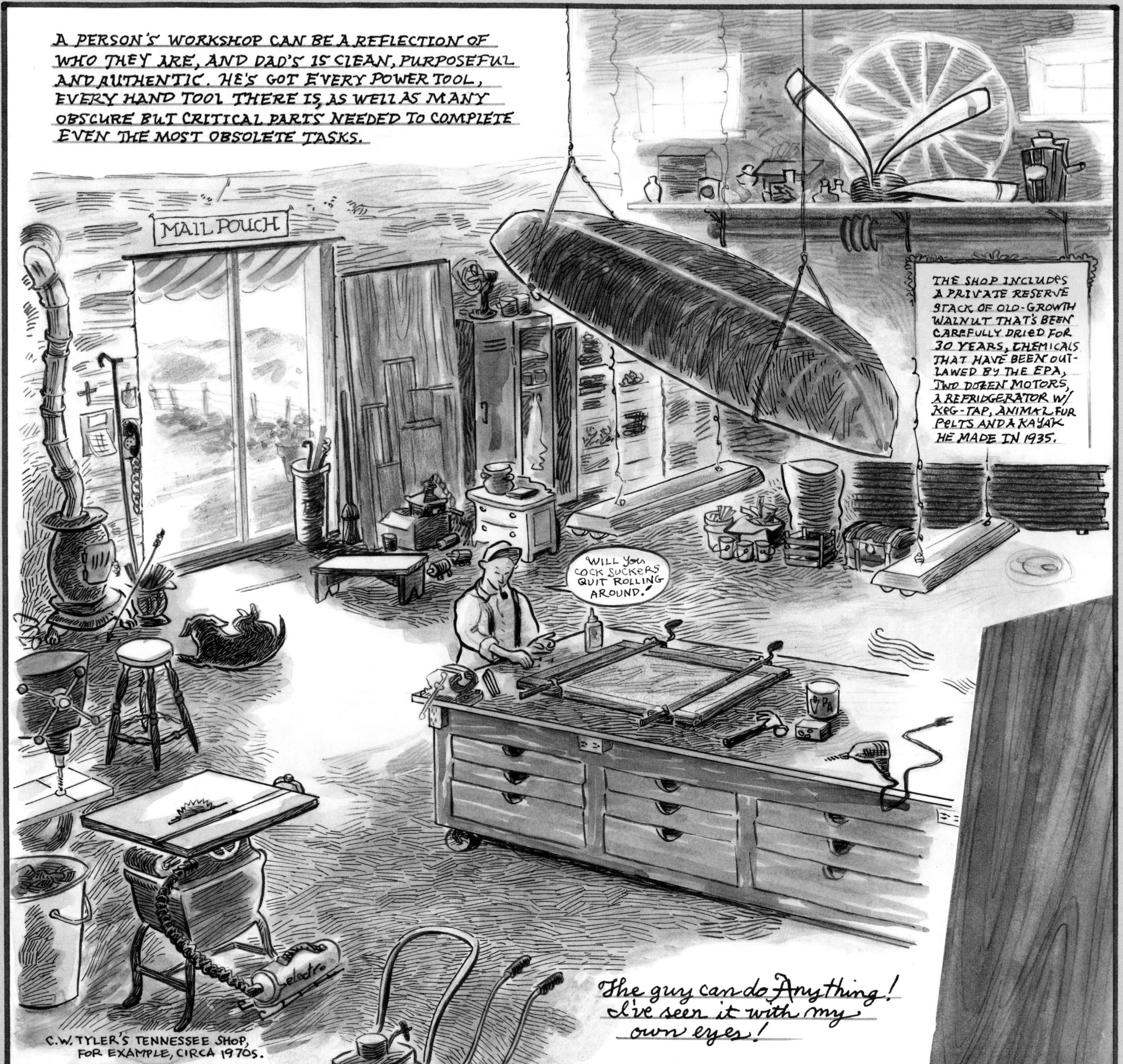
A PERSON'S WORKSHOP CAN BE A REFLECTION OF WHO THEY ARE, AND DAD'S IS CLEAN, PURPOSEFUL AND AUTHENTIC. HE'S GOT EVERY POWER TOOL, EVERY HAND TOOL THERE IS, AS WELL AS MANY OBSCURE BUT CRITICAL PARTS NEEDED TO COMPLETE EVEN THE MOST OBSOLETE TASKS.
MAIL POUCH
THE SHOP INCLUDES A PRIVATE RESERVE STACK OF OLD-GROWTH WALNUT THAT'S BEEN CAREFULLY DRIED FOR 30 YEARS, CHEMICALS THAT HAVE BEEN OUTLAWED BY THE EPA, TWO DOZEN MOTORS, A REFRIDGERATOR W/ KEG-TAP, ANIMAL FUR PELTS AND A KAYAK HE MADE IN 1935.
WILL YOU COCK SUCKERS QUIT ROLLING AROUND!
EPA
electro
C.W. TYLER'S TENNESSEE SHOP, FOR EXAMPLE, CIRCA 1970S.
The guy can do Anything! I've seen it with my own eyes!

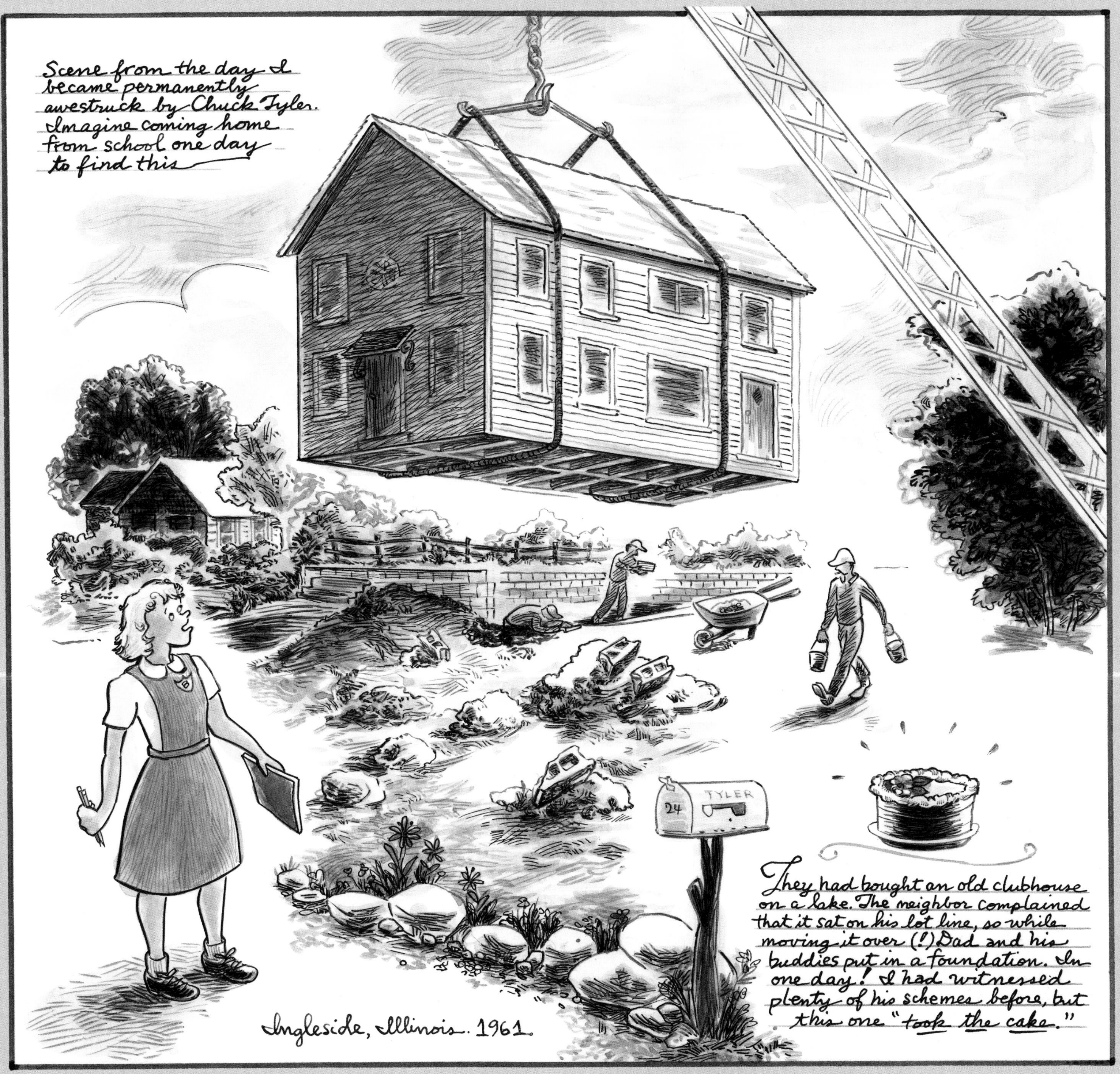
Scene from the day I became permanently awestruck by Chuck Tyler. Imagine coming home from school one day to find this
TYLER
24
They had bought an old clubhouse on a lake. The neighbor complained that it sat on his lot line, so while moving it over (!) Dad and his buddies put in a foundation. In one day! I had witnessed plenty of his schemes before, but this one "took the cake."
Ingleside, Illinois. 1961.

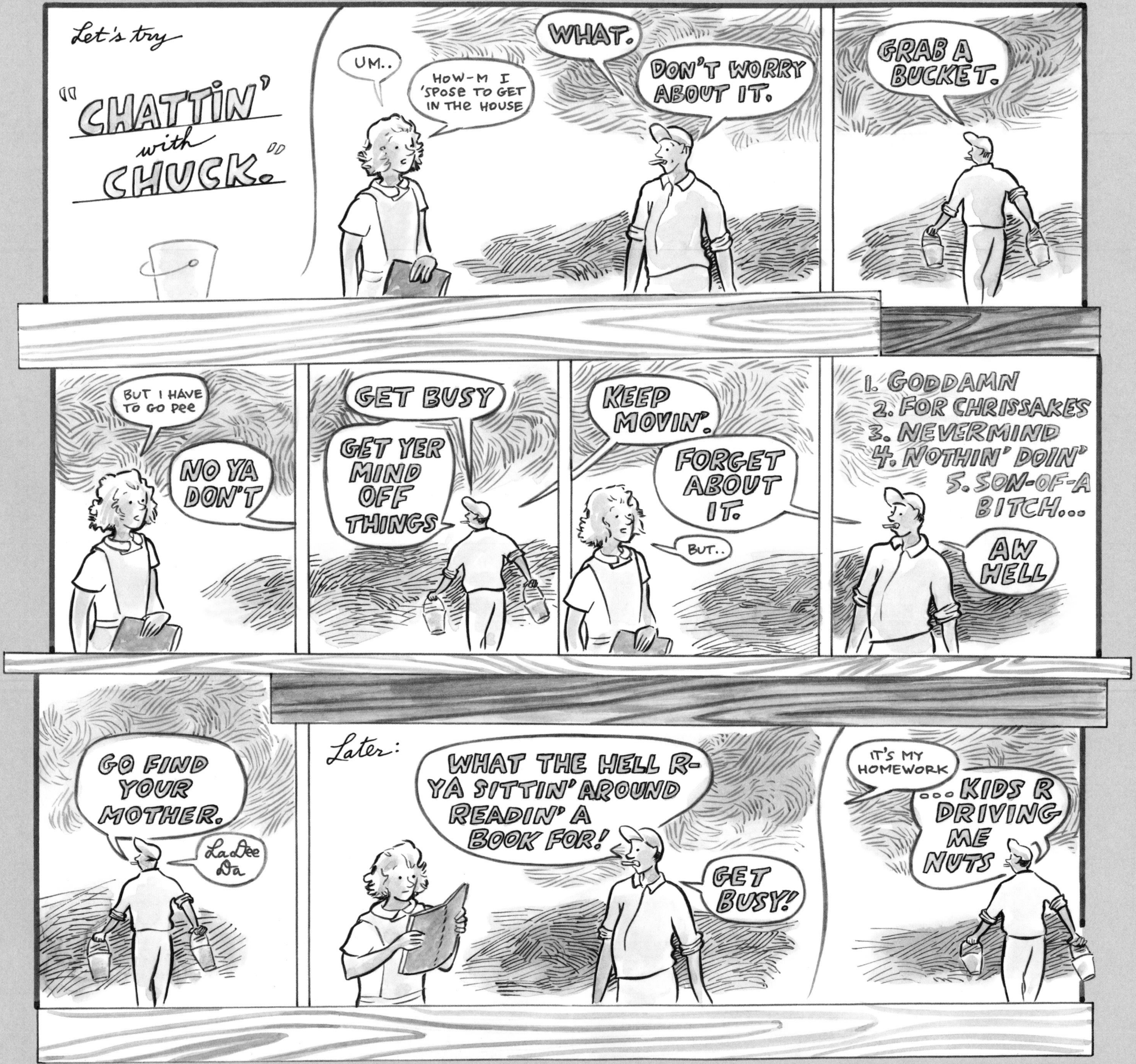
Let's try
"CHATTIN' with CHUCK."
UM..
HOW-M I 'SPOSE TO GET IN THE HOUSE
WHAT.
DON'T WORRY ABOUT IT.
GRAB A BUCKET.
BUT I HAVE TO GO PEE
NO YA DON'T
GET BUSY
GET YER MIND OFF THINGS
KEEP MOVIN'.
FORGET ABOUT IT.
BUT..
1. GODDAMN
2. FOR CHRISSAKES
3. NEVERMIND
4. NOTHIN' DOIN'
5. SON-OF-A BITCH...
AW HELL
GO FIND YOUR MOTHER.
La Dee Da
Later:
WHAT THE HELL R-YA SITTIN' AROUND READIN' A BOOK FOR!
GET BUSY!
IT'S MY HOMEWORK
...KIDS R DRIVING ME NUTS

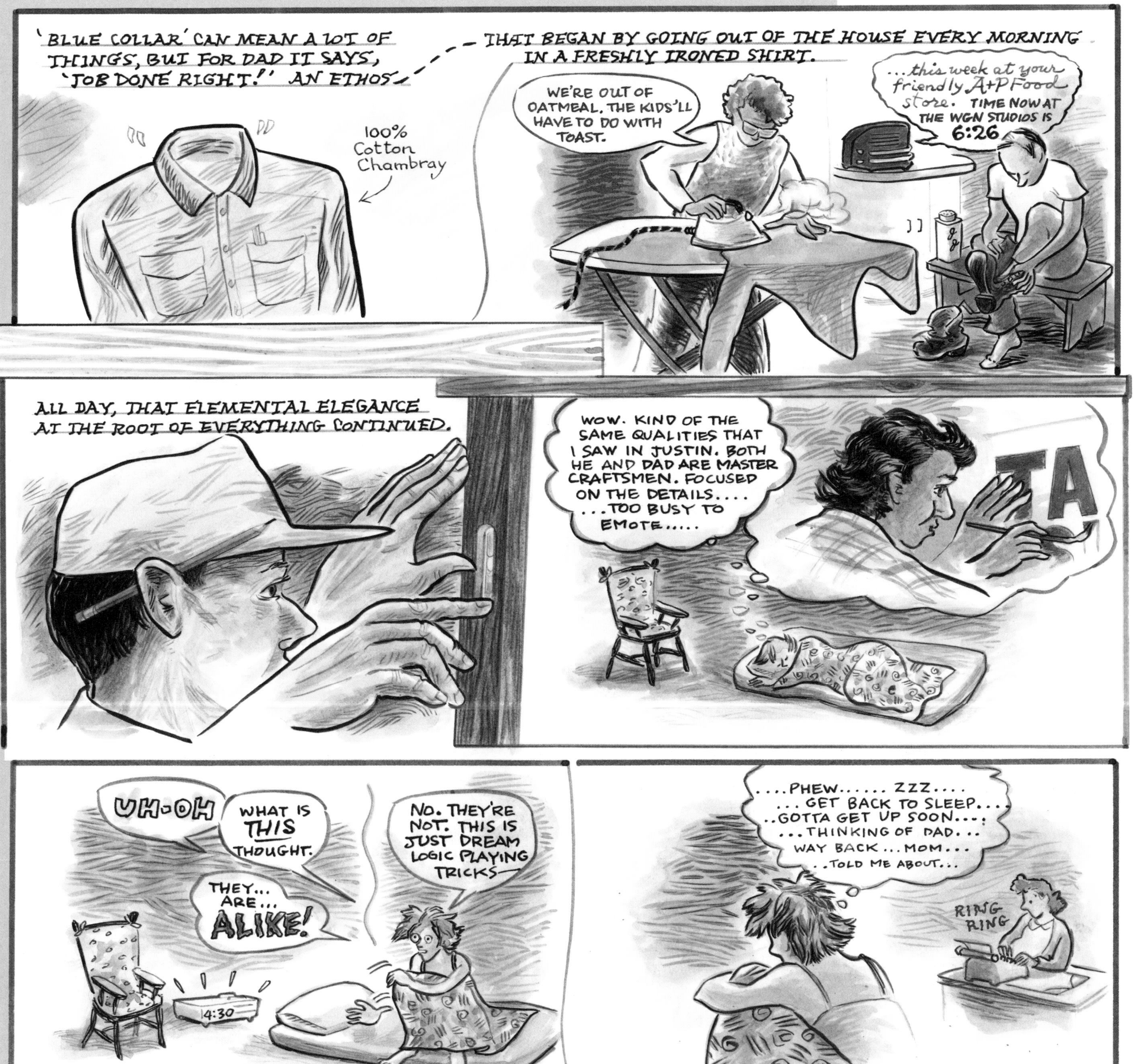
'BLUE COLLAR' CAN MEAN A LOT OF THINGS, BUT FOR DAD IT SAYS, 'JOB DONE RIGHT!' AN ETHOS
100% Cotton Chambray
THAT BEGAN BY GOING OUT OF THE HOUSE EVERY MORNING IN A FRESHLY IRONED SHIRT.
WE'RE OUT OF OATMEAL. THE KIDS'LL HAVE TO DO WITH TOAST.
...this week at your friendly A+P Food store. TIME NOW AT THE WGN STUDIOS IS 6:26
ALL DAY, THAT ELEMENTAL ELEGANCE AT THE ROOT OF EVERYTHING CONTINUED.
WOW. KIND OF THE SAME QUALITIES THAT I SAW IN JUSTIN. BOTH HE AND DAD ARE MASTER CRAFTSMEN. FOCUSED ON THE DETAILS.... ...TOO BUSY TO EMOTE.....
TA
UH-OH
WHAT IS THIS THOUGHT.
THEY... ARE... ALIKE!
NO. THEY'RE NOT. THIS IS JUST DREAM LOGIC PLAYING TRICKS—
4:30
....PHEW...... ZZZ.... ...GET BACK TO SLEEP... ..GOTTA GET UP SOON.... ...THINKING OF DAD... WAY BACK...MOM... ..TOLD ME ABOUT...
RING RING

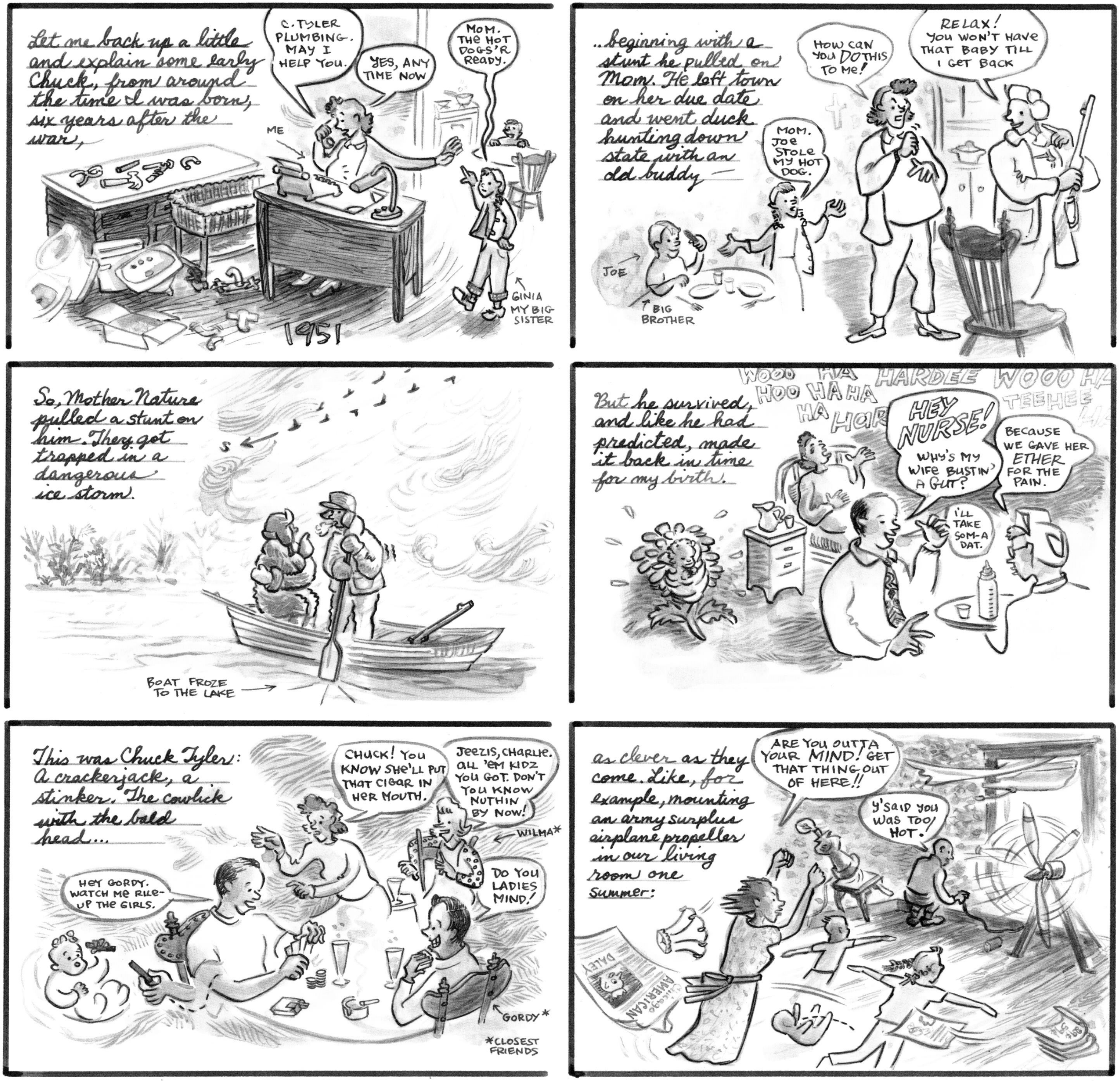
Let me back up a little and explain some early Chuck, from around the time I was born, six years after the war,
C. TYLER PLUMBING. MAY I HELP YOU.
YES, ANY TIME NOW
MOM. THE HOT DOGS'R READY.
ME
GINIA MY BIG SISTER
1951
..beginning with a stunt he pulled on Mom. He left town on her due date and went duck hunting down state with an old buddy
HOW CAN YOU DO THIS TO ME!
RELAX! YOU WON'T HAVE THAT BABY TILL I GET BACK
MOM. JOE STOLE MY HOT DOG.
JOE
BIG BROTHER
So, Mother Nature pulled a stunt on him. They got trapped in a dangerous ice storm.
BOAT FROZE TO THE LAKE
But he survived, and like he had predicted, made it back in time for my birth.
WOOO HA HARDEE WOOO HA
HOO HAHA TEEHEE
HA HAR
HEY NURSE! WHY'S MY WIFE BUSTIN' A GUT?
BECAUSE WE GAVE HER ETHER FOR THE PAIN.
I'LL TAKE SOM-A DAT.
This was Chuck Tyler: A crackerjack, a stinker. The cowlick with the bald head...
CHUCK! YOU KNOW SHE'LL PUT THAT CIGAR IN HER MOUTH.
JEEZIS, CHARLIE. ALL 'EM KIDZ YOU GOT. DON'T YOU KNOW NUTHIN BY NOW!
WILMA*
HEY GORDY. WATCH ME RILE-UP THE GIRLS.
DO YOU LADIES MIND!
GORDY*
*CLOSEST FRIENDS
as clever as they come. Like, for example, mounting an army surplus airplane propeller in our living room one summer:
ARE YOU OUTTA YOUR MIND! GET THAT THING OUT OF HERE!!
Y'SAID YOU WAS TOO HOT.
DALEY
Chicago AMERICAN

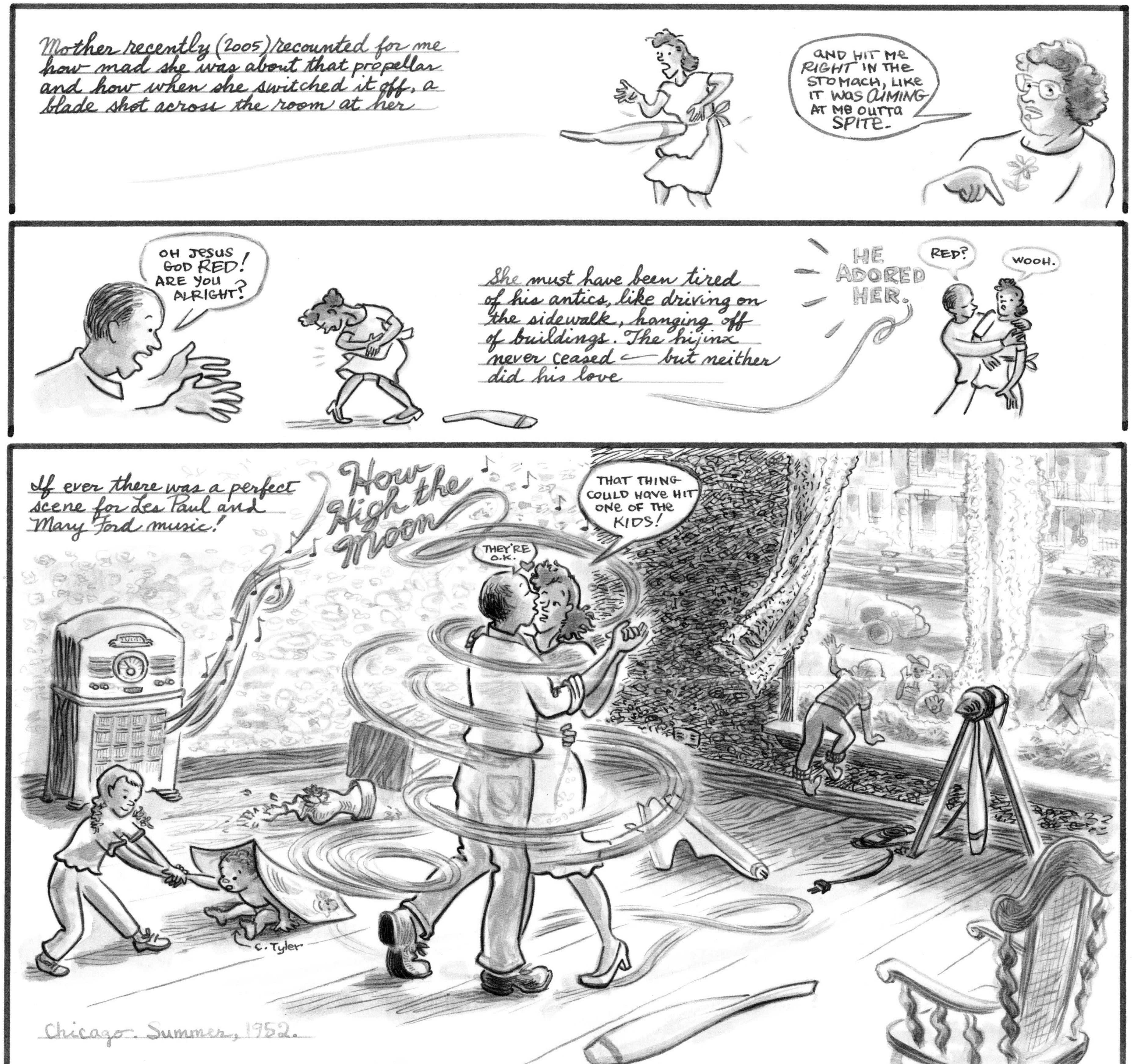
Mother recently (2005) recounted for me how mad she was about that propellar and how when she switched it off, a blade shot across the room at her
AND HIT ME RIGHT IN THE STOMACH, LIKE IT WAS AIMING AT ME OUTTA SPITE.
OH JESUS GOD RED! ARE YOU ALRIGHT?
She must have been tired of his antics, like driving on the sidewalk, hanging off of buildings. The hijinx never ceased — but neither did his love
HE ADORED HER.
RED?
WOOH.
If ever there was a perfect scene for Les Paul and Mary Ford music!
How High the Moon
THAT THING COULD HAVE HIT ONE OF THE KIDS!
THEY'RE O.K.
C. Tyler
Chicago. Summer, 1952.

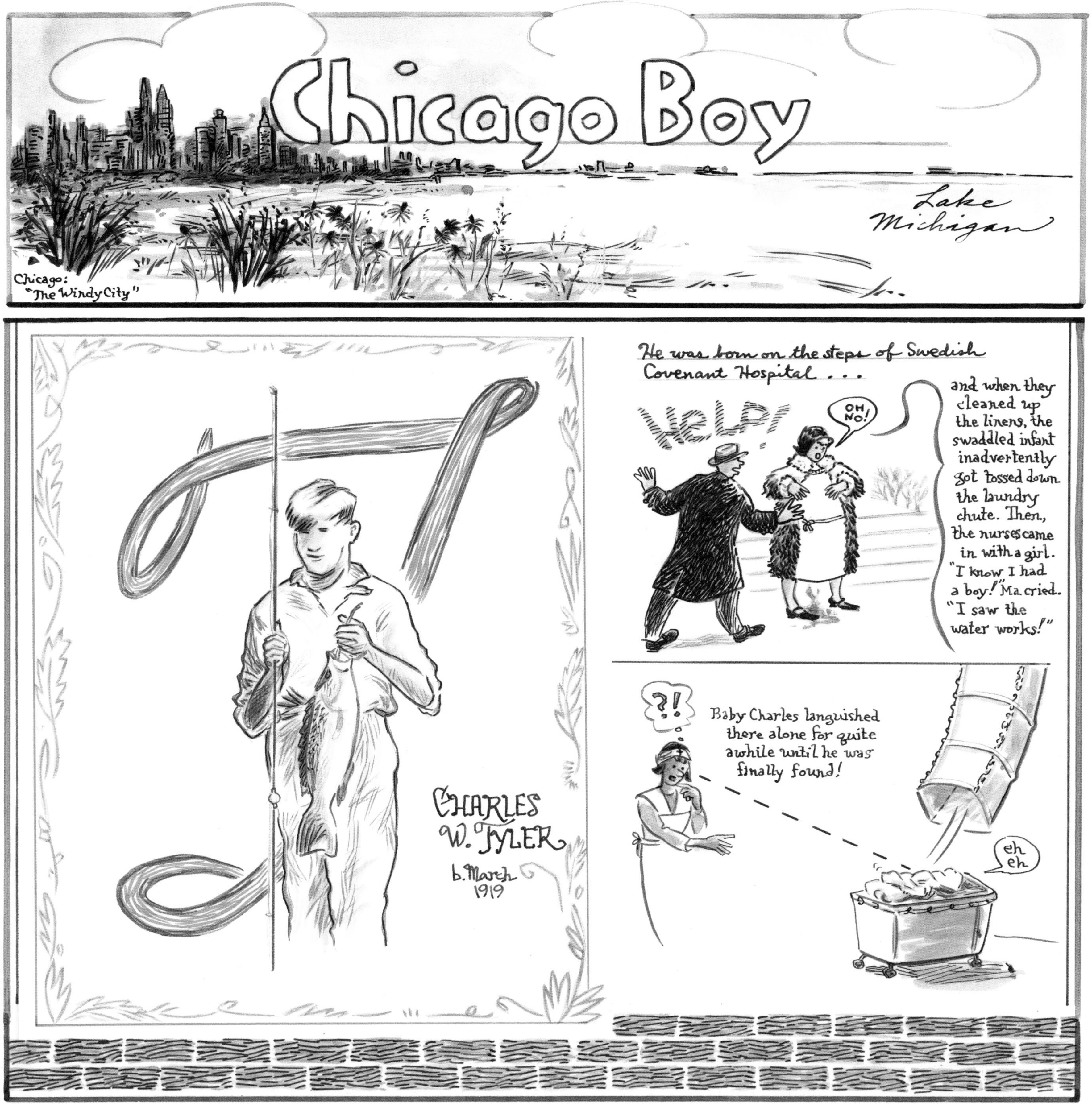
Chicago Boy
Lake Michigan
Chicago: "The Windy City"
CHARLES W. TYLER
b. March 1919
He was born on the steps of Swedish Covenant Hospital . . .
HELP!
OH NO!
and when they cleaned up the linens, the swaddled infant inadvertently got tossed down the laundry chute. Then, the nurses came in with a girl. "I know I had a boy!" Ma cried. "I saw the water works!"
?!
Baby Charles languished there alone for quite awhile until he was finally found!
eh eh

His parents were good people, a pipe-fitter and a cook.
TIME FOR MOTHER'S BEST PANCAKES. CLEAN UP, NOW.
USE THE TURPENTINE.
It was understood that little Charles would follow his dad into the plumbing trade.
NOW WHAT!
Theirs was a typical Catholic family, doing their Saturday Nights....
STRAIGHT BEATS A PAIR
A PAIR OF FEET! FATHER....
HEH HEH
I SEE 'EM. YOU KIDS GET TO BED!
AWW UH
...and Sunday Mornings.
Agnus Dei
Qui tollis peccata mundi
*a bit devil-ish
His dad taught him all things boy: hunting, fishing,
SOMEDAY I'LL HAVE A GIRL TO TAKE OUT FOR A RIDE.
And shooting. Once he stumbled upon a gangland hit—
HOLY KEE-RI-IST.
DAD
COME QUICK!
CHICAGO - 1920S.

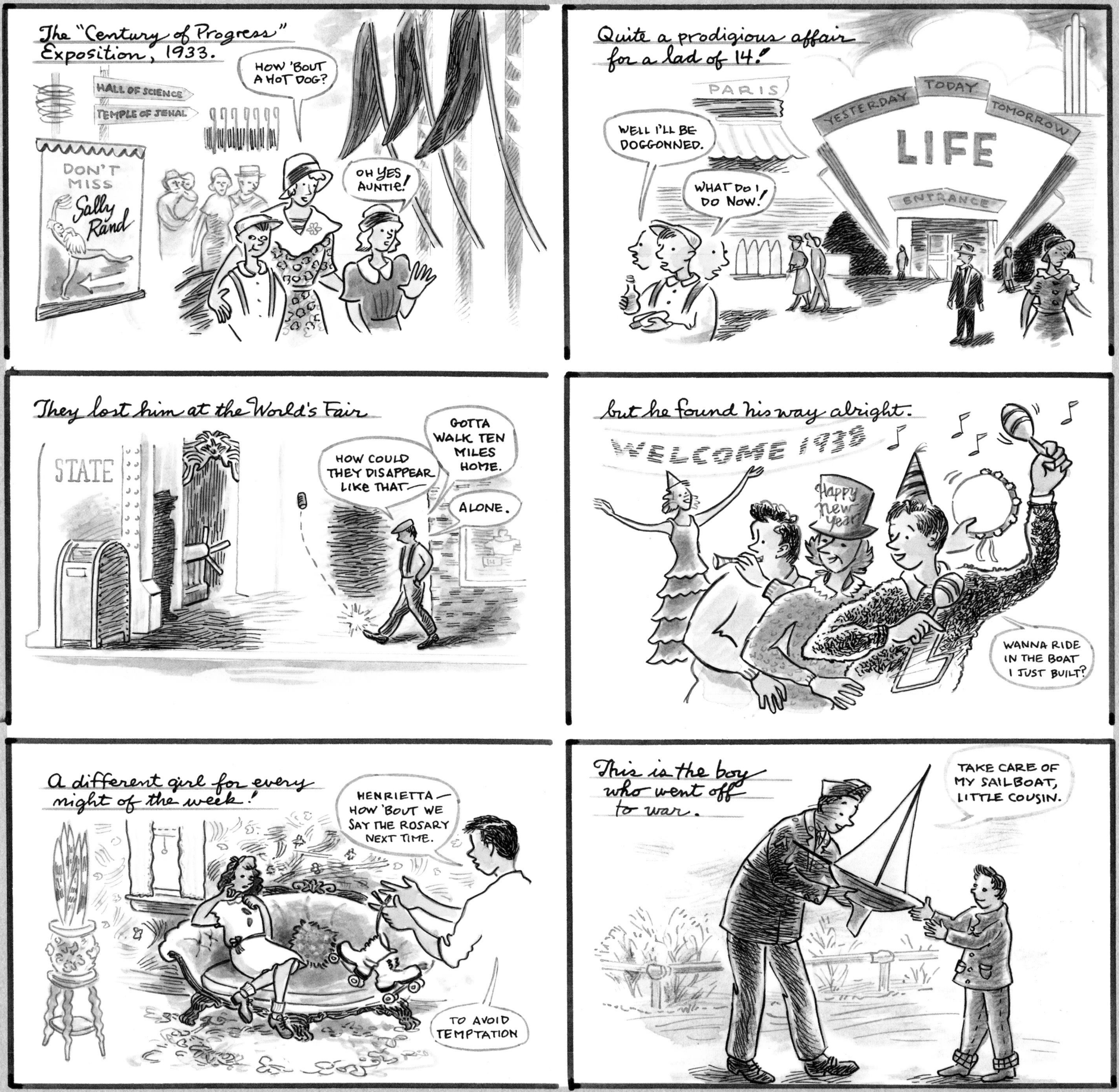
The "Century of Progress" Exposition, 1933.
HALL OF SCIENCE
TEMPLE OF JEHAL
DON'T MISS Sally Rand
HOW 'BOUT A HOT DOG?
OH YES AUNTIE!
Quite a prodigious affair for a lad of 14!
PARIS
YESTERDAY TODAY TOMORROW
LIFE
ENTRANCE
WELL I'LL BE DOGGONNED.
WHAT DO I DO NOW!
They lost him at the World's Fair
STATE
HOW COULD THEY DISAPPEAR LIKE THAT—
GOTTA WALK TEN MILES HOME.
ALONE.
but he found his way alright.
WELCOME 1938
Happy New Year
WANNA RIDE IN THE BOAT I JUST BUILT?
A different girl for every night of the week!
HENRIETTA— HOW 'BOUT WE SAY THE ROSARY NEXT TIME.
TO AVOID TEMPTATION
This is the boy who went off to war.
TAKE CARE OF MY SAILBOAT, LITTLE COUSIN.

Lane Tech High School

4/18,38   Chuck Tyler

"Me, Myself and I"

On March 13,1918 there
was born a song to the family
of Alfred M. Tyler
On March the 13, 1918 there
was a son born to Mrs Stella
Tyler, whose name was later
decided on to be Charles William. With him came joy and hap-
piness to the family, it has remained
here ever since. As he grew he
changed in shape, size, look, and
his will power became stronger
for which he was sorry many
times. At the age of three being
able to get around by myself
I inherited a rather large scar
on my forehead from the bottom
end of a milk bottle which was
thrown at me by my loving
sister.

this is the first of my experiences
that I remember of this life.
Since then I have received
many cuts and scars, too.

In Grammar school I was
not a very good student especially
for studies which required a lot of
memorizing. It was here in
grammar school where I first
started on the mechanic side
of the field of choice. For my high school
for my high school education
I picked Lane Tech because it
gave me a fair opportunity to
try out my field mechanics. In
my first year I decided that
I would not like a mechanical
occupation where I would be
always working under some body
else and besides getting all dirty
so I thought of Engineering, it
had mechanics and also It was
not a dirty profession after I
made up my mind to that I set
out to find a field best suited
for my thoughts which

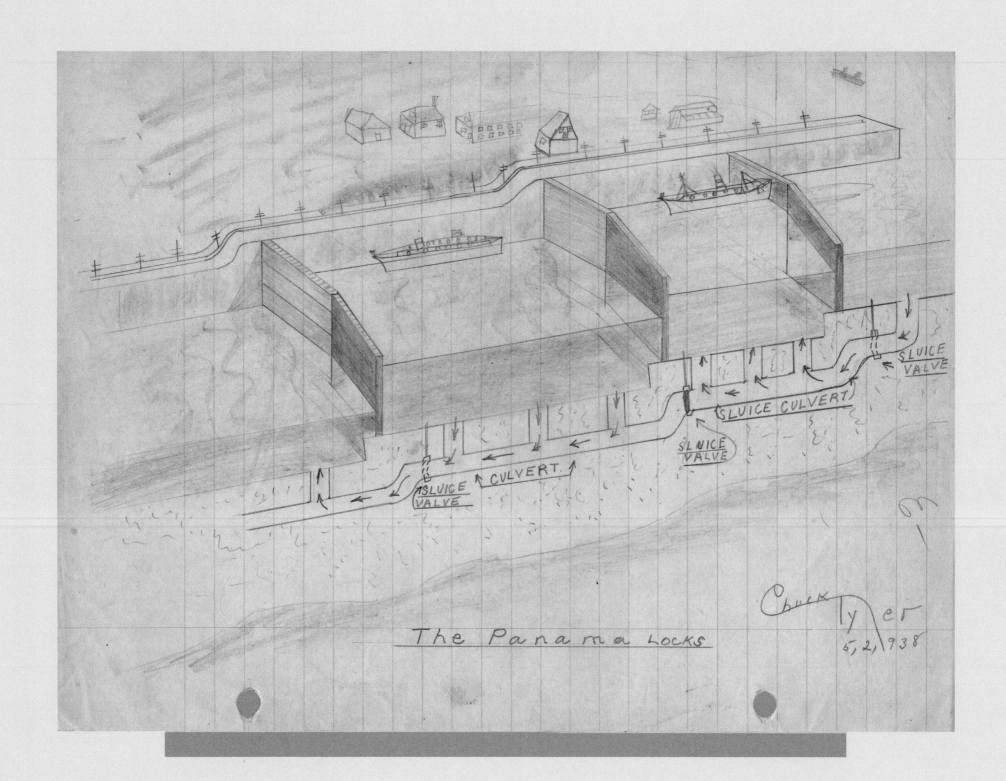

SLUICE VALVE

SLUICE CULVERT

SLUICE VALVE

SLUICE CULVERT

SLUICE VALVE

The Panama Locks

Chuck Tyler
5, 21, 1938

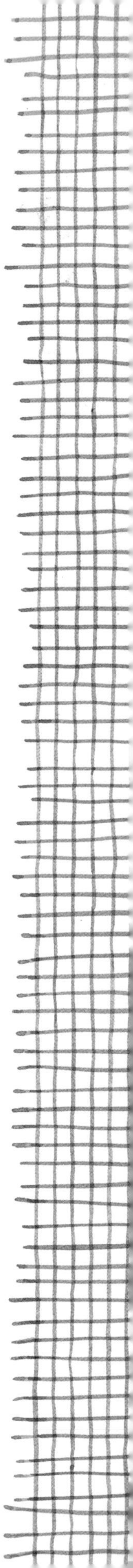

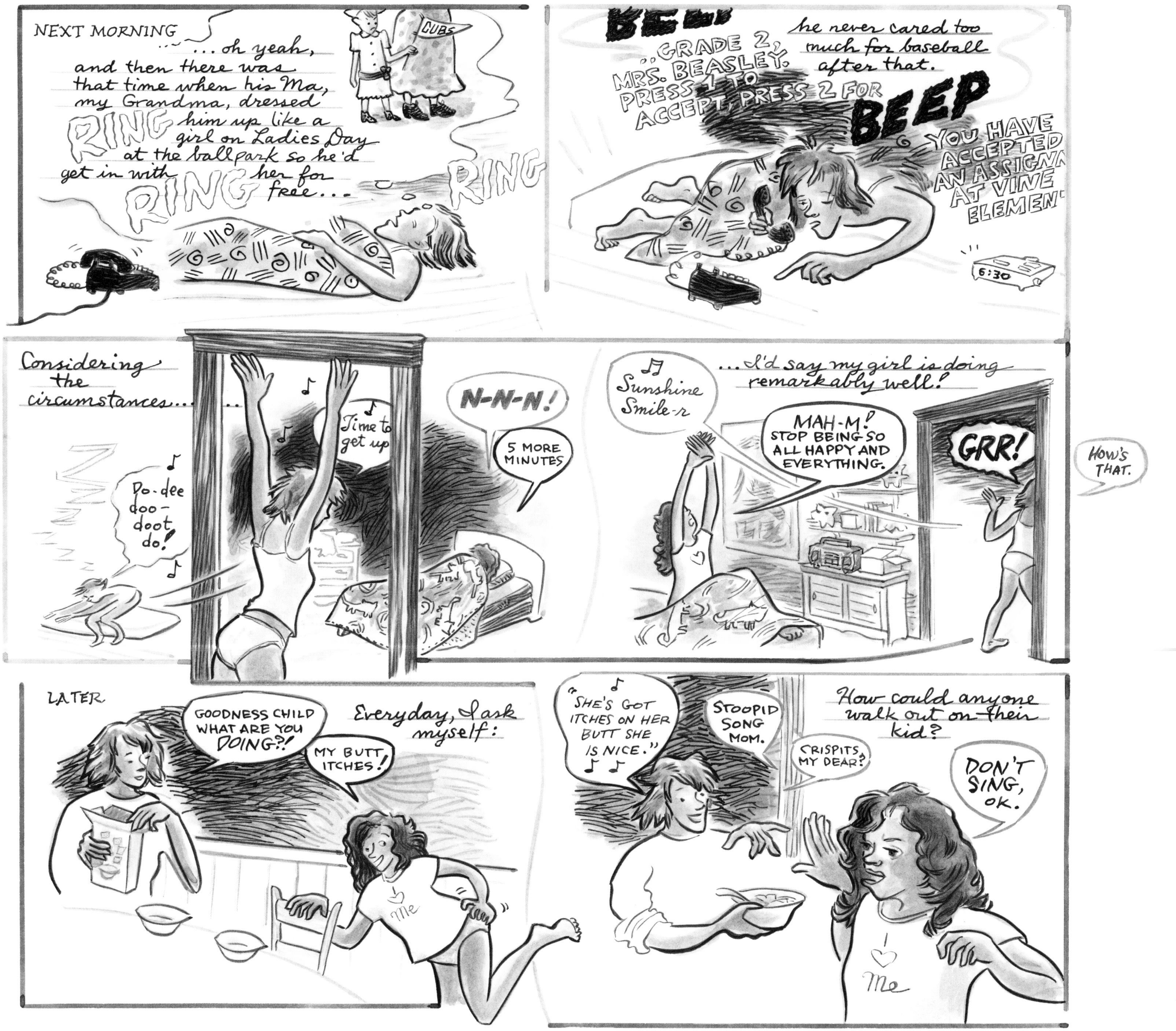
NEXT MORNING
... oh yeah, and then there was that time when his Ma, my Grandma, dressed him up like a girl on Ladies Day at the ballpark so he'd get in with her for free...
CUBS
RING
RING
RING
BEEP
..GRADE 2, MRS. BEASLEY. PRESS 1 TO ACCEPT, PRESS 2 FOR
he never cared too much for baseball after that.
BEEP
YOU HAVE ACCEPTED AN ASSIGN AT VINE ELEMEN
6:30
Considering the circumstances...
Do-dee doo-doot do!
Time to get up
N-N-N!
5 MORE MINUTES
Sunshine Smile-r
...I'd say my girl is doing remarkably well!
MAH-M! STOP BEING SO ALL HAPPY AND EVERYTHING.
GRR!
HOW'S THAT.
LATER
GOODNESS CHILD WHAT ARE YOU DOING?!
MY BUTT ITCHES!
Everyday, I ask myself:
Me
"SHE'S GOT ITCHES ON HER BUTT SHE IS NICE."
STOOPID SONG MOM.
CRISPITS, MY DEAR?
How could anyone walk out on their kid?
DON'T SING, OK.
Me

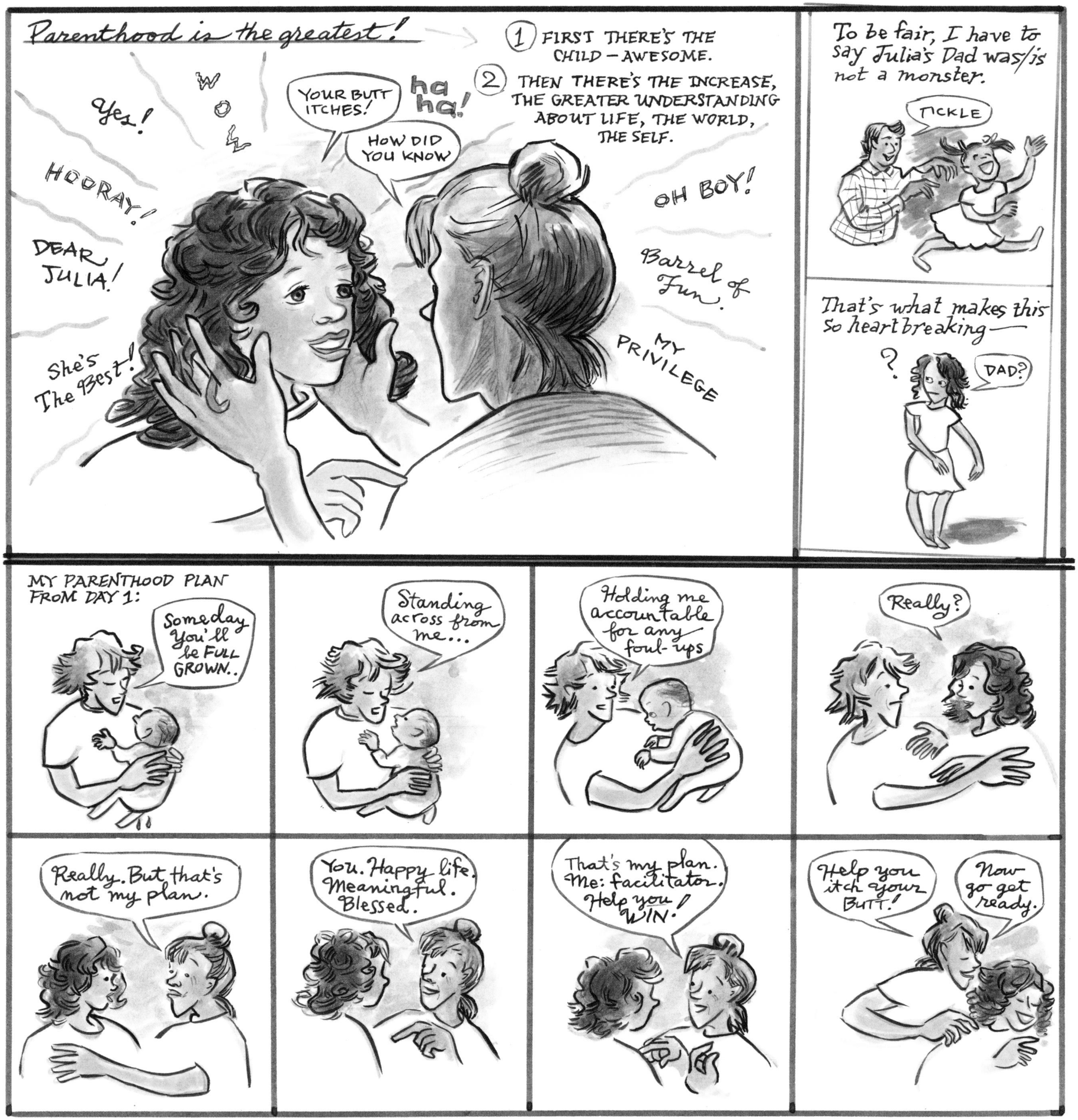
Parenthood is the greatest!
1 FIRST THERE'S THE CHILD — AWESOME.
2 THEN THERE'S THE INCREASE, THE GREATER UNDERSTANDING ABOUT LIFE, THE WORLD, THE SELF.
Yes!
WOW
HOORAY!
DEAR JULIA!
She's The Best!
YOUR BUTT ITCHES!
ha ha!
HOW DID YOU KNOW
OH BOY!
Barrel of Fun.
MY PRIVILEGE
To be fair, I have to say Julia's Dad was/is not a monster.
TICKLE
That's what makes this so heartbreaking—
?
DAD?
MY PARENTHOOD PLAN FROM DAY 1:
Someday you'll be FULL GROWN..
Standing across from me...
Holding me accountable for any foul-ups
Really?
Really. But that's not my plan.
You. Happy life. Meaningful. Blessed.
That's my plan. Me: facilitator. Help you WIN!
Help you itch your BUTT!
Now go get ready.

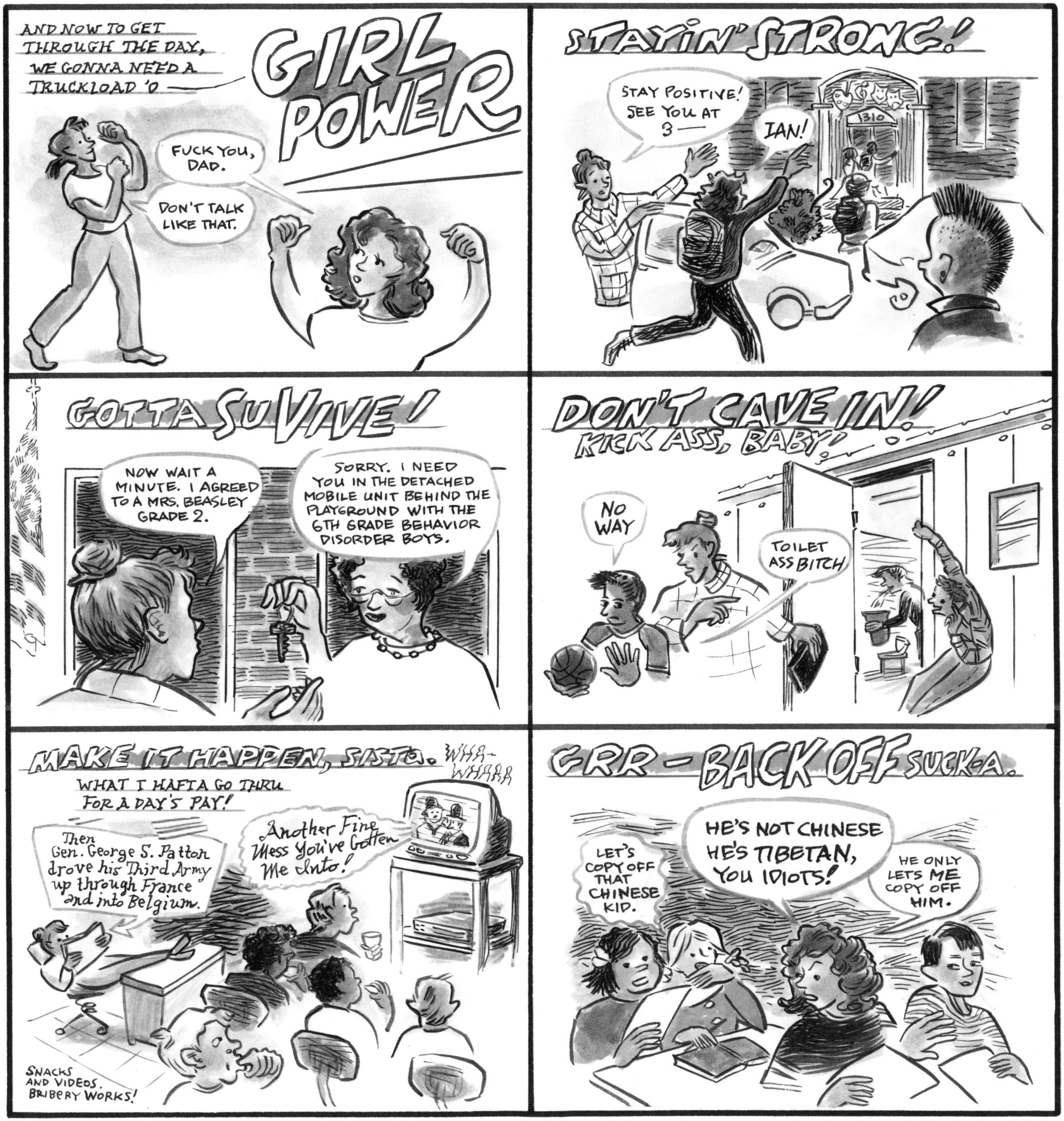
AND NOW TO GET THROUGH THE DAY, WE GONNA NEED A TRUCKLOAD 'O —
GIRL POWER
FUCK YOU, DAD.
DON'T TALK LIKE THAT.
STAYIN' STRONG!
STAY POSITIVE! SEE YOU AT 3 —
IAN!
1310
GOTTA SUVIVE!
NOW WAIT A MINUTE. I AGREED TO A MRS. BEASLEY GRADE 2.
SORRY. I NEED YOU IN THE DETACHED MOBILE UNIT BEHIND THE PLAYGROUND WITH THE 6TH GRADE BEHAVIOR DISORDER BOYS.
DON'T CAVE IN!
KICK ASS, BABY!
NO WAY
TOILET ASS BITCH
MAKE IT HAPPEN, SISTA.
WHA-WHARRA
WHAT I HAFTA GO THRU FOR A DAY'S PAY!
Then Gen. George S. Patton drove his Third Army up through France and into Belgium.
Another Fine Mess You've Gotten Me Into!
SNACKS AND VIDEOS. BRIBERY WORKS!
GRR - BACK OFF SUCKA.
LET'S COPY OFF THAT CHINESE KID.
HE'S NOT CHINESE HE'S TIBETAN, YOU IDIOTS!
HE ONLY LETS ME COPY OFF HIM.

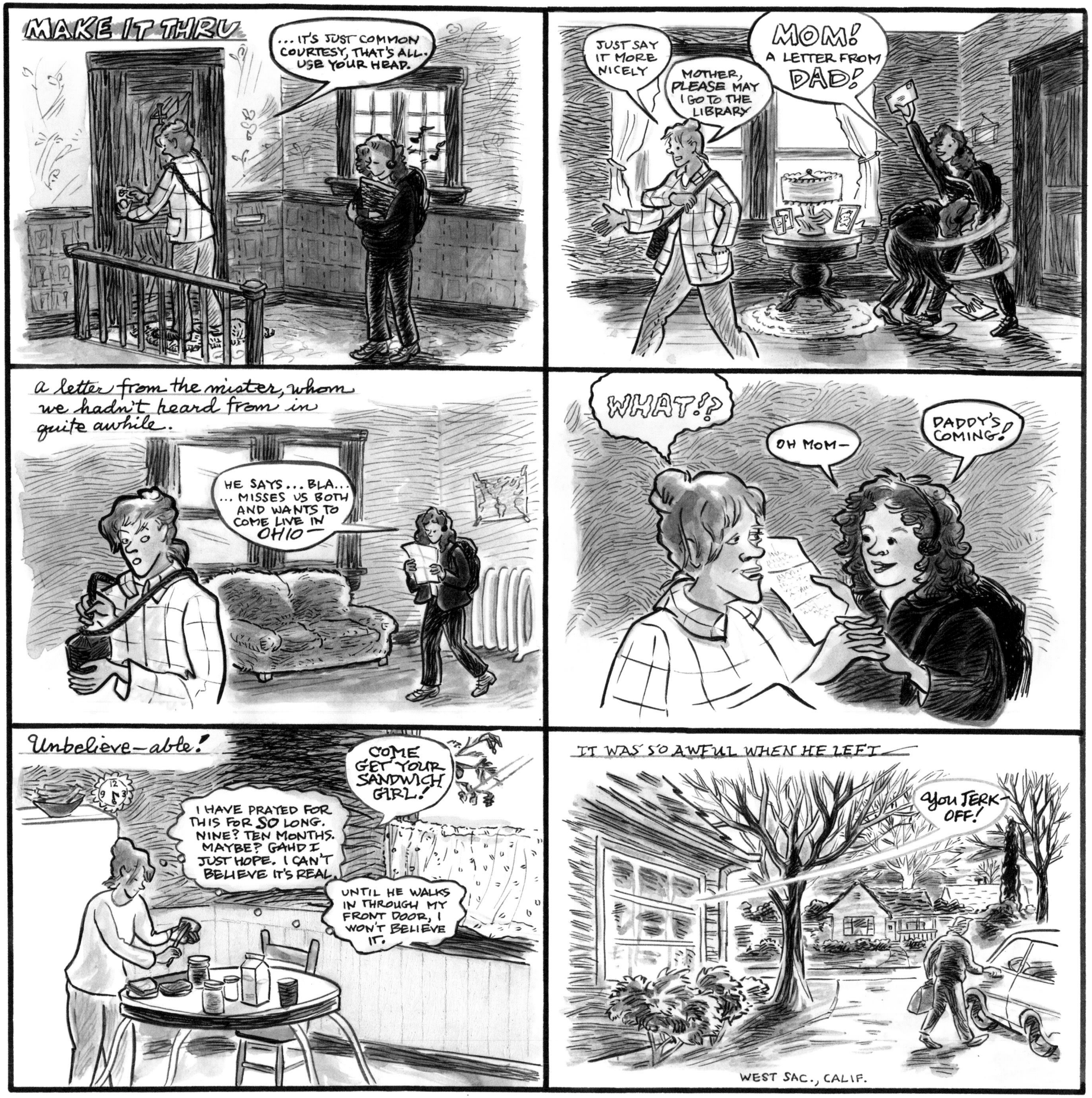
MAKE IT THRU
... IT'S JUST COMMON COURTESY, THAT'S ALL. USE YOUR HEAD.
JUST SAY IT MORE NICELY
MOTHER, PLEASE MAY I GO TO THE LIBRARY
MOM! A LETTER FROM DAD!
a letter from the mister, whom we hadn't heard from in quite awhile.
HE SAYS... BLA... ... MISSES US BOTH AND WANTS TO COME LIVE IN OHIO—
WHAT!?
OH MOM—
DADDY'S COMING!
Unbelieve-able!
COME GET YOUR SANDWICH GIRL!
I HAVE PRAYED FOR THIS FOR SO LONG. NINE? TEN MONTHS. MAYBE? GAHD I JUST HOPE. I CAN'T BELIEVE IT'S REAL
UNTIL HE WALKS IN THROUGH MY FRONT DOOR, I WON'T BELIEVE IT.
IT WAS SO AWFUL WHEN HE LEFT
You JERK-OFF!
WEST SAC., CALIF.

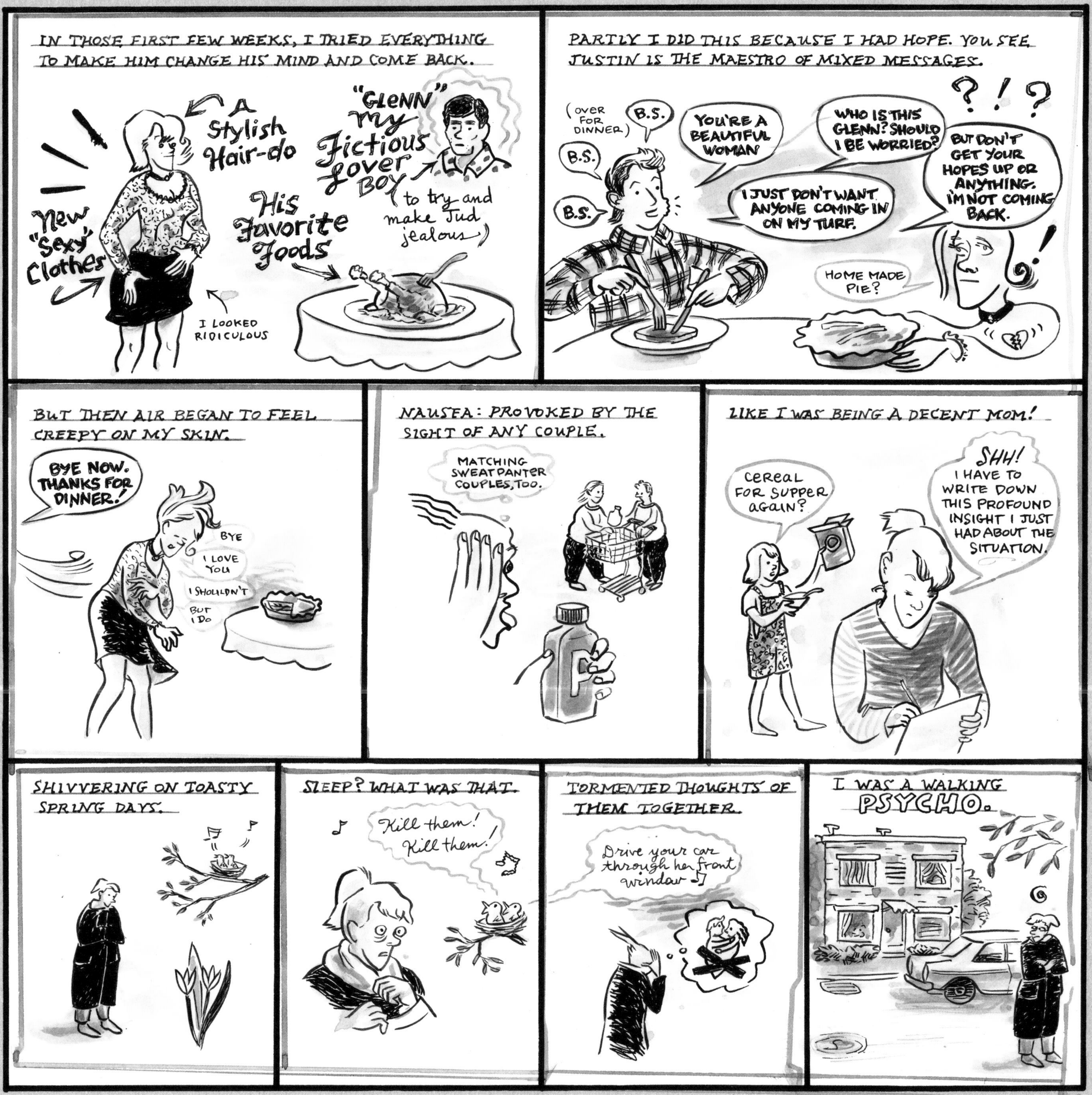
IN THOSE FIRST FEW WEEKS, I TRIED EVERYTHING TO MAKE HIM CHANGE HIS MIND AND COME BACK.
A Stylish Hair-do
"GLENN" my Fictious Lover Boy
(to try and make Jud jealous)
New "Sexy" Clothes
His Favorite Foods
I LOOKED RIDICULOUS
PARTLY I DID THIS BECAUSE I HAD HOPE. YOU SEE, JUSTIN IS THE MAESTRO OF MIXED MESSAGES.
(OVER FOR DINNER)
B.S.
B.S.
B.S.
YOU'RE A BEAUTIFUL WOMAN
WHO IS THIS GLENN? SHOULD I BE WORRIED?
I JUST DON'T WANT ANYONE COMING IN ON MY TURF.
BUT DON'T GET YOUR HOPES UP OR ANYTHING. I'M NOT COMING BACK.
? ! ?
HOME MADE PIE?
BUT THEN AIR BEGAN TO FEEL CREEPY ON MY SKIN.
BYE NOW. THANKS FOR DINNER!
BYE
I LOVE YOU
I SHOULDN'T
BUT I DO
NAUSEA: PROVOKED BY THE SIGHT OF ANY COUPLE.
MATCHING SWEATPANTER COUPLES, TOO.
LIKE I WAS BEING A DECENT MOM!
Cereal for supper again?
SHH! I HAVE TO WRITE DOWN THIS PROFOUND INSIGHT I JUST HAD ABOUT THE SITUATION.
SHIVVERING ON TOASTY SPRING DAYS.
SLEEP? WHAT WAS THAT.
Kill them! Kill them!
TORMENTED THOUGHTS OF THEM TOGETHER.
Drive your car through her front window
I WAS A WALKING PSYCHO.

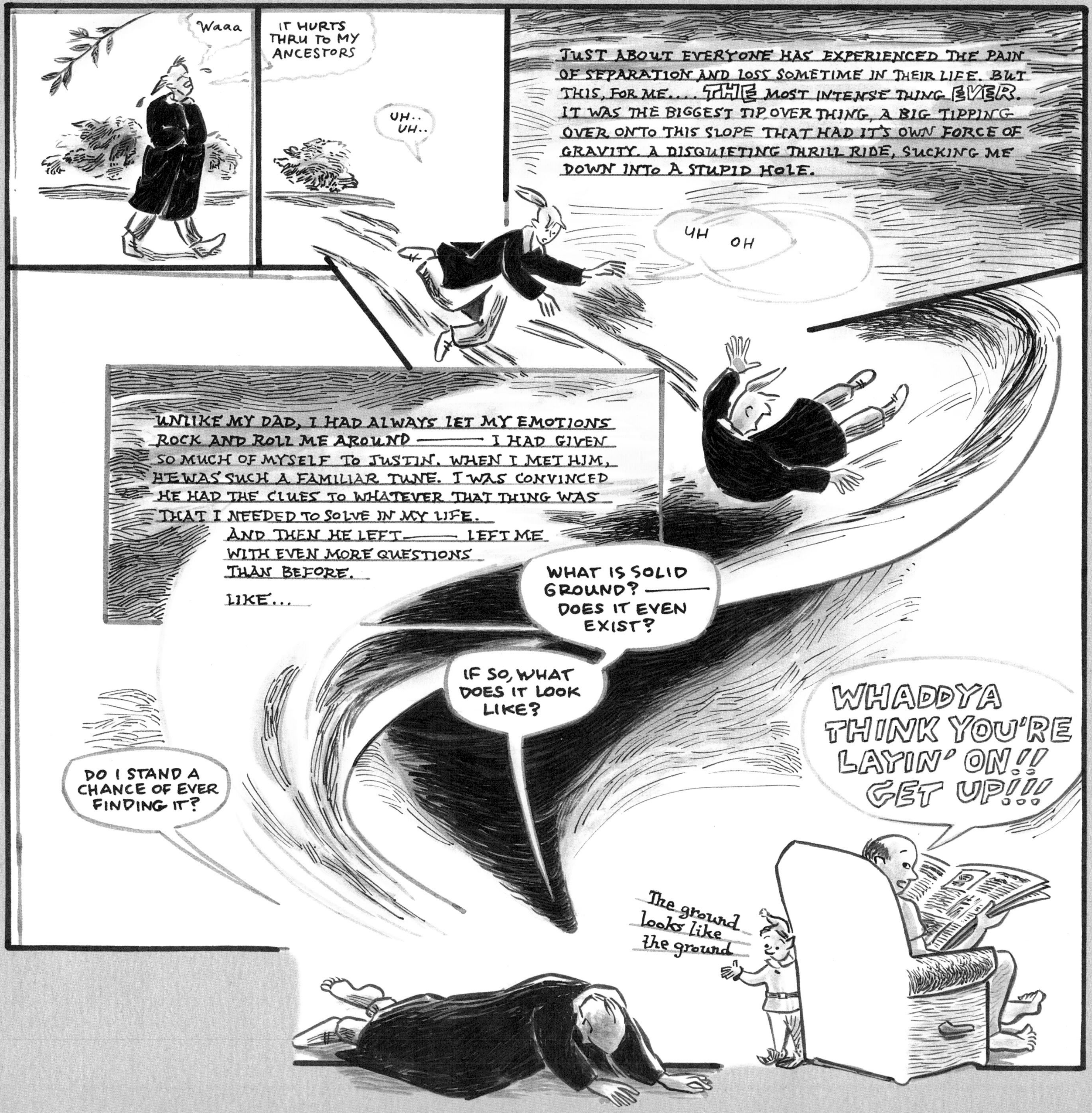
Waaa
IT HURTS THRU TO MY ANCESTORS
UH.. UH..
JUST ABOUT EVERYONE HAS EXPERIENCED THE PAIN OF SEPARATION AND LOSS SOMETIME IN THEIR LIFE. BUT THIS, FOR ME.... THE MOST INTENSE THING EVER. IT WAS THE BIGGEST TIP OVER THING, A BIG TIPPING OVER ONTO THIS SLOPE THAT HAD IT'S OWN FORCE OF GRAVITY. A DISQUIETING THRILL RIDE, SUCKING ME DOWN INTO A STUPID HOLE.
UH OH
UNLIKE MY DAD, I HAD ALWAYS LET MY EMOTIONS ROCK AND ROLL ME AROUND — I HAD GIVEN SO MUCH OF MYSELF TO JUSTIN. WHEN I MET HIM, HE WAS SUCH A FAMILIAR TUNE. I WAS CONVINCED HE HAD THE CLUES TO WHATEVER THAT THING WAS THAT I NEEDED TO SOLVE IN MY LIFE.
AND THEN HE LEFT — LEFT ME WITH EVEN MORE QUESTIONS THAN BEFORE.
LIKE...
WHAT IS SOLID GROUND? — DOES IT EVEN EXIST?
IF SO, WHAT DOES IT LOOK LIKE?
DO I STAND A CHANCE OF EVER FINDING IT?
WHADDYA THINK YOU'RE LAYIN' ON!! GET UP!!!
The ground looks like the ground

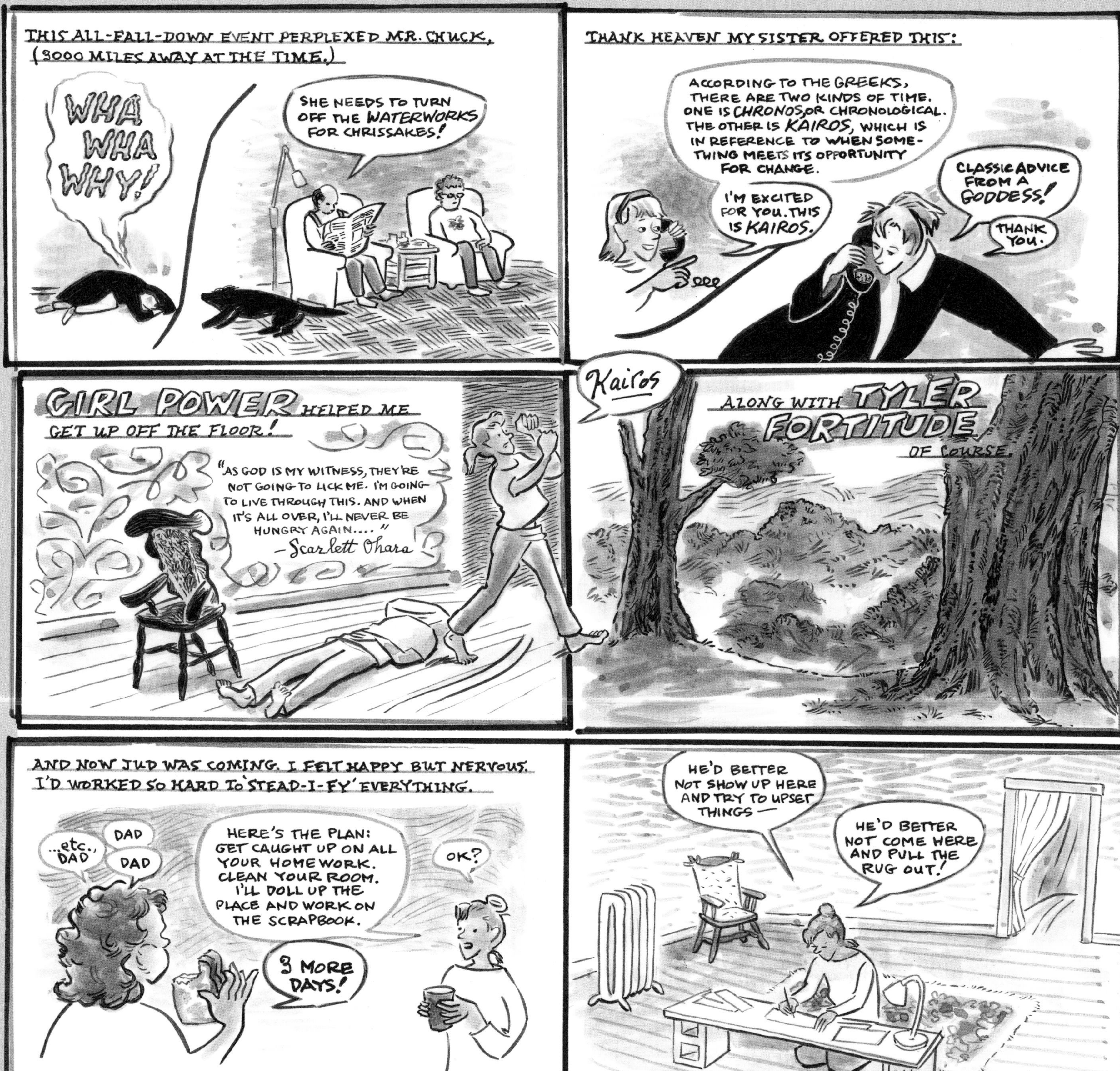
THIS ALL-FALL-DOWN EVENT PERPLEXED MR. CHUCK. (3000 MILES AWAY AT THE TIME.)
WHA WHA WHY!
SHE NEEDS TO TURN OFF THE WATERWORKS FOR CHRISSAKES!
THANK HEAVEN MY SISTER OFFERED THIS:
ACCORDING TO THE GREEKS, THERE ARE TWO KINDS OF TIME. ONE IS CHRONOS, OR CHRONOLOGICAL. THE OTHER IS KAIROS, WHICH IS IN REFERENCE TO WHEN SOMETHING MEETS ITS OPPORTUNITY FOR CHANGE.
I'M EXCITED FOR YOU. THIS IS KAIROS.
CLASSIC ADVICE FROM A GODDESS!
THANK YOU.
GIRL POWER HELPED ME GET UP OFF THE FLOOR!
"AS GOD IS MY WITNESS, THEY'RE NOT GOING TO LICK ME. I'M GOING TO LIVE THROUGH THIS. AND WHEN IT'S ALL OVER, I'LL NEVER BE HUNGRY AGAIN...." —Scarlett Ohara
Kairos
ALONG WITH TYLER FORTITUDE OF COURSE.
AND NOW JUD WAS COMING. I FELT HAPPY BUT NERVOUS. I'D WORKED SO HARD TO 'STEAD-I-FY' EVERYTHING.
...etc., DAD
DAD
DAD
HERE'S THE PLAN: GET CAUGHT UP ON ALL YOUR HOMEWORK. CLEAN YOUR ROOM. I'LL DOLL UP THE PLACE AND WORK ON THE SCRAPBOOK.
OK?
3 MORE DAYS!
HE'D BETTER NOT SHOW UP HERE AND TRY TO UPSET THINGS—
HE'D BETTER NOT COME HERE AND PULL THE RUG OUT!

DAD'S ARMY SCRAPBOOK
AND
TOUR OF DUTY HIGHLIGHTS

PART II

NORTH AFRICA

JUNE 1944 — JULY 1944

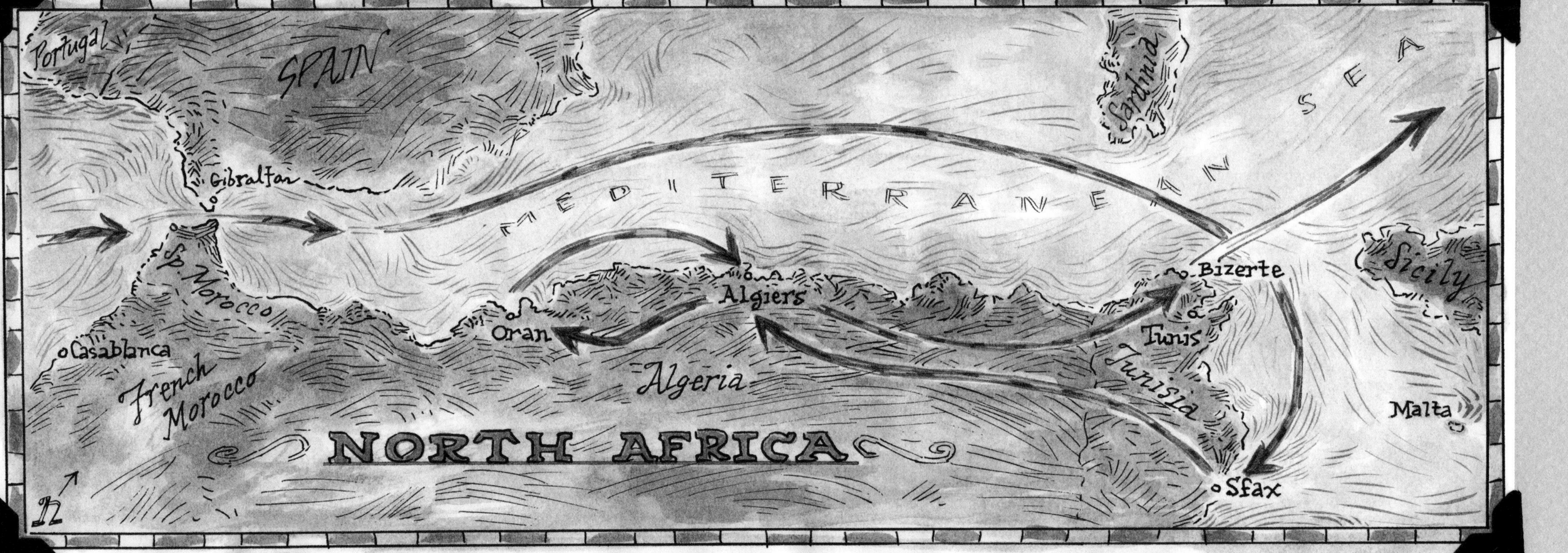
Portugal
SPAIN
Sardinia
MEDITERRANEAN SEA
Gibraltar
Sp. Morocco
Casablanca
French Morocco
Oran
Algiers
Algeria
Bizerte
Tunis
Tunisia
Sicily
Malta
Sfax
NORTH AFRICA

The Sandbox 22

"Disembarkment from Shenango, Pennsylvania. 'Par-tee and never return' we used to say. I shipped out with the 8TH Air Force. Anyone who volunteered to be a 'ship's fitter' got special eats. So I said 'yeah' and they gave me a mop, 'cause everyone was seasick. Not me.

"When we hit Africa, the captain didn't want to run a-ground... ordered guys to start jumping off. An airman swapped me his pistol for my rifle and he gave me his sunglasses, too. That first bunch never came back-up. Him included."

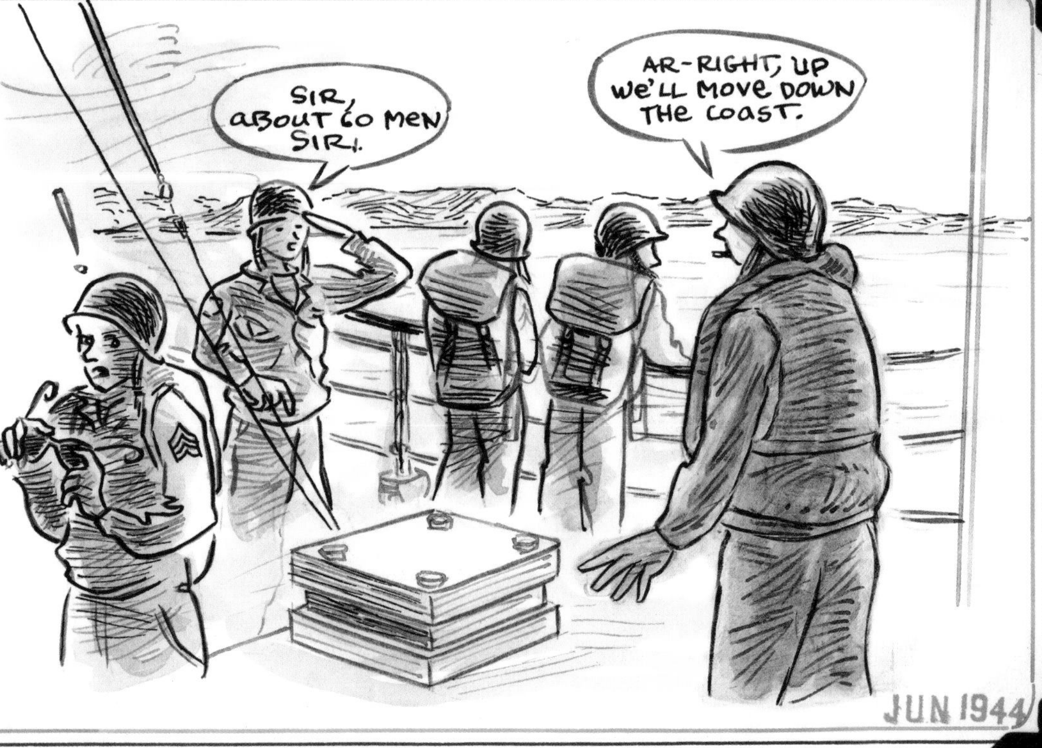
!
SIR, ABOUT 60 MEN SIR.
AR-RIGHT, UP WE'LL MOVE DOWN THE COAST.
JUN 1944

23

"So they decided to go through Gibraltar, where we seen all kinds of stuff floating. We're thinking, 'Boy, we must-a sunk a German ship bigger than hell,' but I didn't find out till we were in France, much later, that it was our records floating."

"My records — what a mess! I'd get with an outfit, then someone else would need my skills and I'd go with them. They'd post a list each morning. I got transferred so many times, I felt like I was AWOL!"

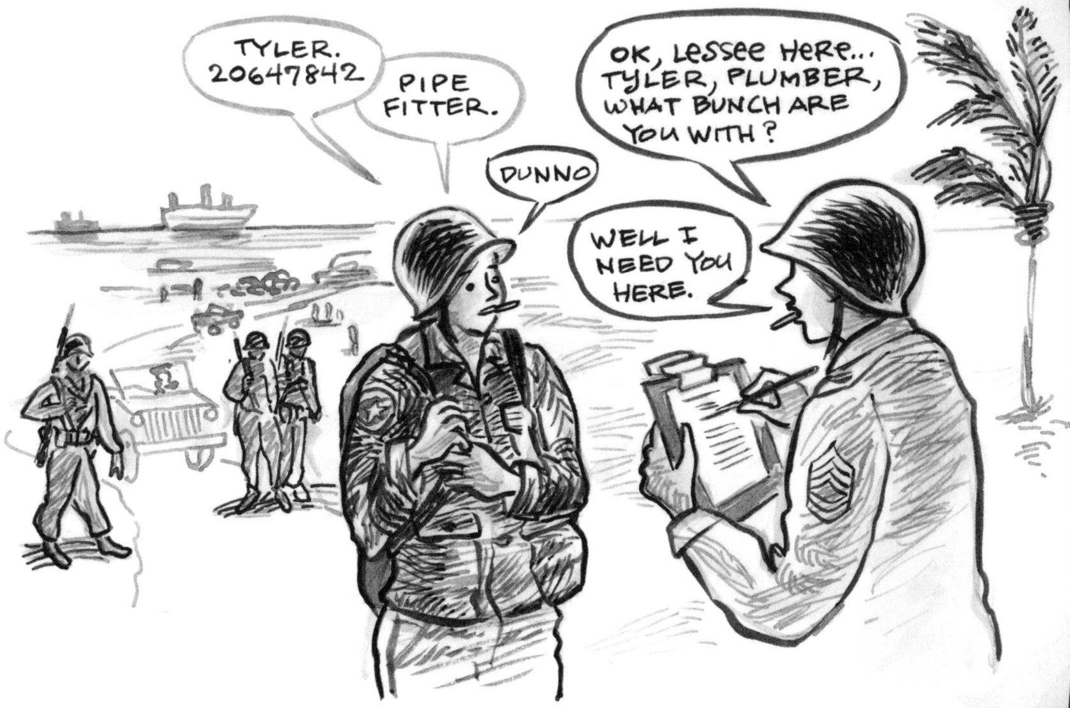
TYLER. 20647842
PIPE FITTER.
DUNNO
OK, LESSEE HERE... TYLER, PLUMBER, WHAT BUNCH ARE YOU WITH?
WELL I NEED YOU HERE.

24

"I think Sfax was the first stop. Right away they sez, 'you engineers and plumbers, go to the tents area.' The Navy ship had a de-salter and they needed us to run a fresh water line to the hospital. 'Here, put these pipes together.' I couldn't. No wonder: they were metric! I'd never seen metric before. Our group, trying to screw on American SAE threads — we're welding it. I made a lead pot with wipe joints, I even used candles — I tried everything and got the job done."

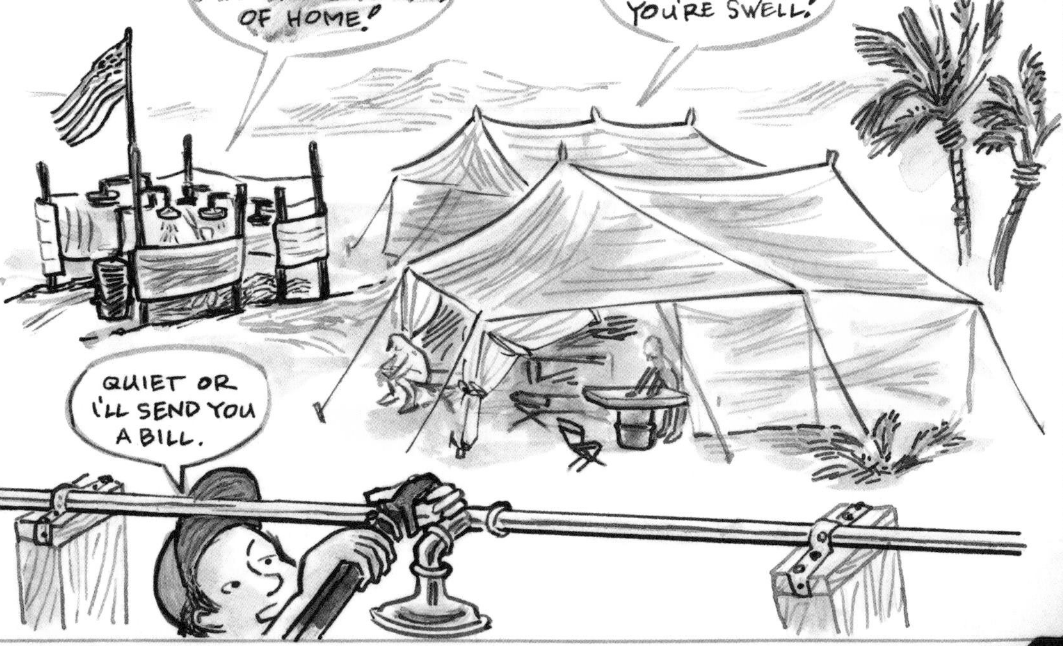
LA-LA-LA! ALL THE COMFORTS OF HOME!
GEE CHARLIE. YOU'RE SWELL!
QUIET OR I'LL SEND YOU A BILL.

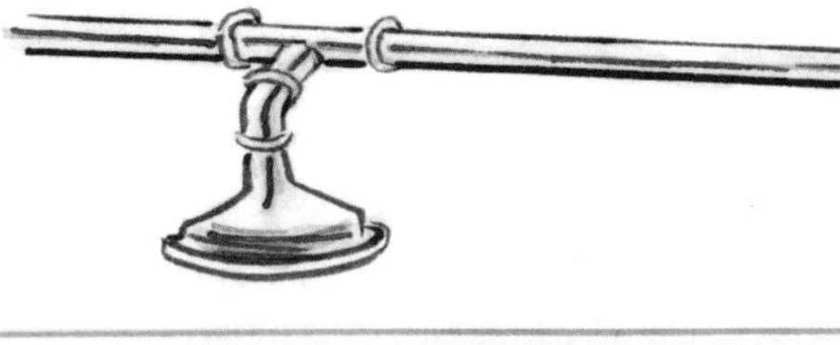

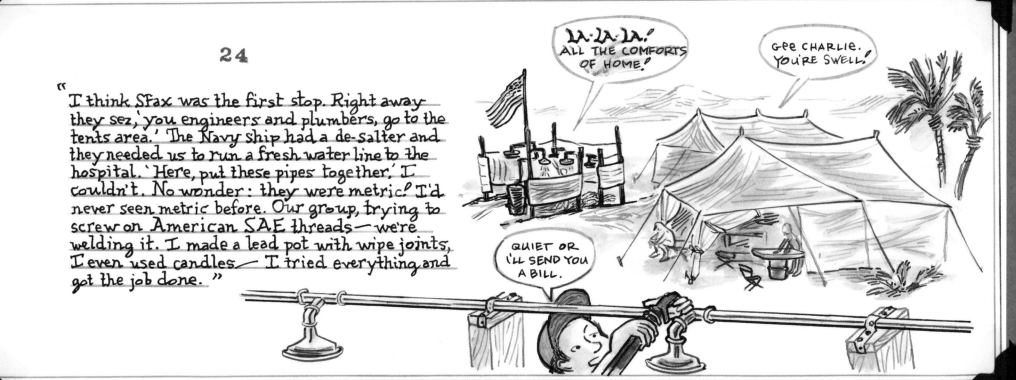

25

"I had a little run-in with the FBI over this— Fort Benning Idiot. This bossy lieutenant was telling me how to join pipes. I told him 'you're full of shit, it don't go like that,' and he said 'Do as I say or I'll have your stripes!' He wanted a court martial. So I told the Judge Advocate, 'My dad's a plumber, my grandpa's a plumber... I've been involved in construction my whole life!' And then the judge points to the lieutenant and says 'Let the professional do his job, fer Chrissakes!' I built a nice shower."

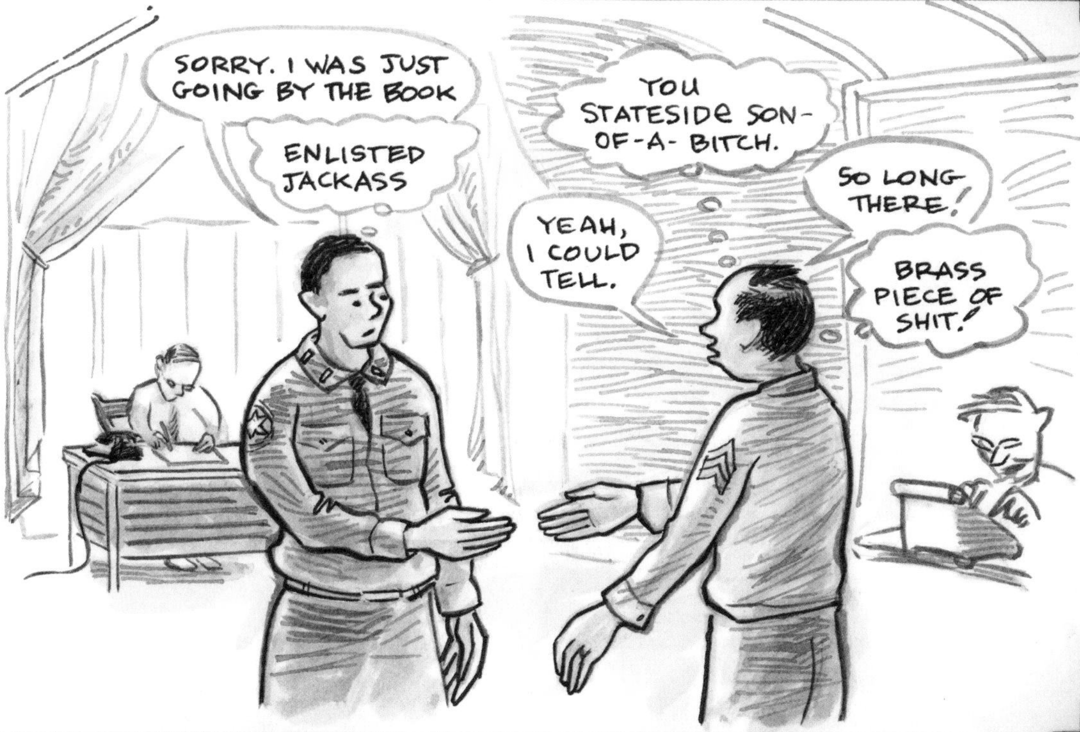
SORRY. I WAS JUST GOING BY THE BOOK
ENLISTED JACKASS
YOU STATESIDE SON-OF-A-BITCH.
YEAH, I COULD TELL.
SO LONG THERE!
BRASS PIECE OF SHIT!

26

"After that, we had so much water, they decided to wash planes, wash trucks— everything. We didn't know the unwritten rules of the desert: that to have water spilt all over like that was a no-no. Lo and behold, everyday our water line would get a new hole in it. And we were losing a soldier, two soldiers a night. When I had night duty, I saw men sneak down to try and shoot or stab our soldiers. They'd tear their clothes off and then cut holes in the lines. Next morning, through special intelligence, we got hold of a Sheik."

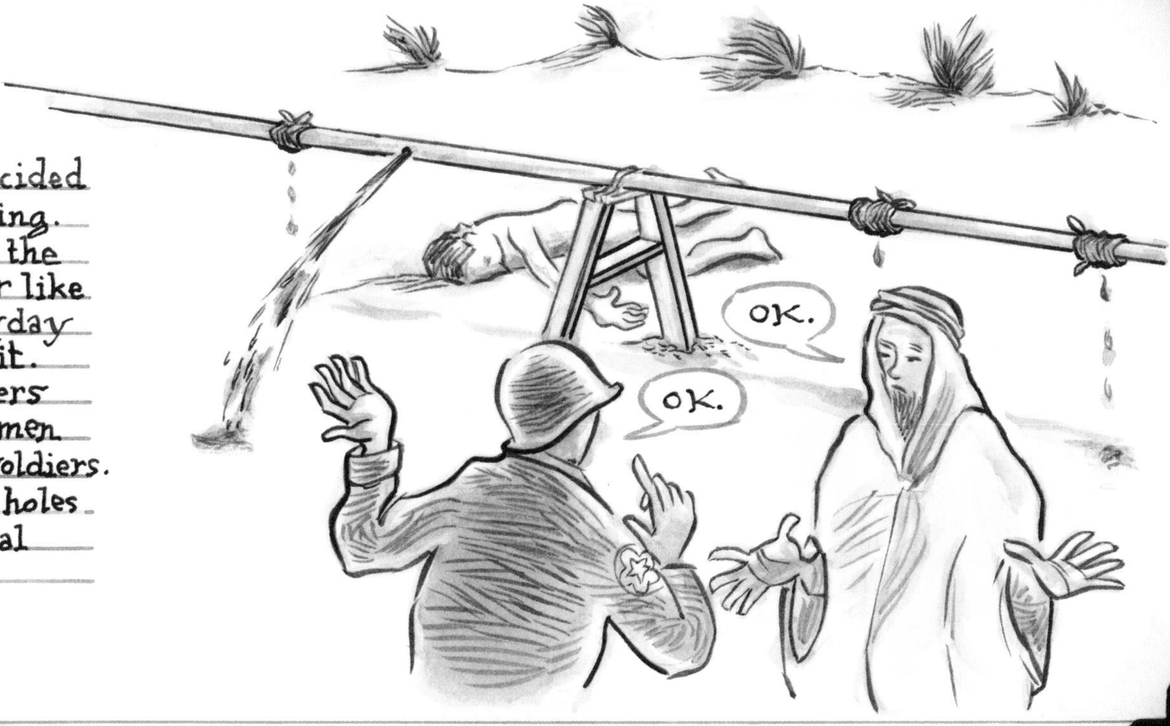
OK.
OK.

27

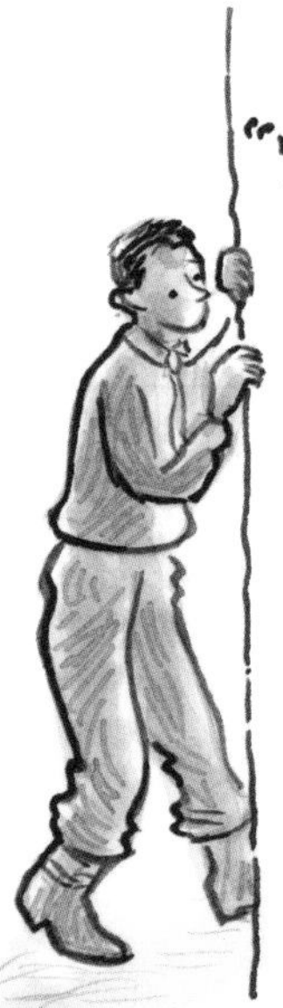

"The deal was, his men would not kill our soldiers if we would let his harum come in and use the shower. Oh boy, did we ever agree to that one! All those girls! Everyone volunteered, but the Sheik brought in his own private security force: French Moroccan soldiers, all cut up, lips bleeding from fights, every guy 6'6" or better, each one wearing a fez and a sword, and holding a long rifle. They stood sentry at the shower tent, the one I built, to keep me and all the other GIs at a distance."

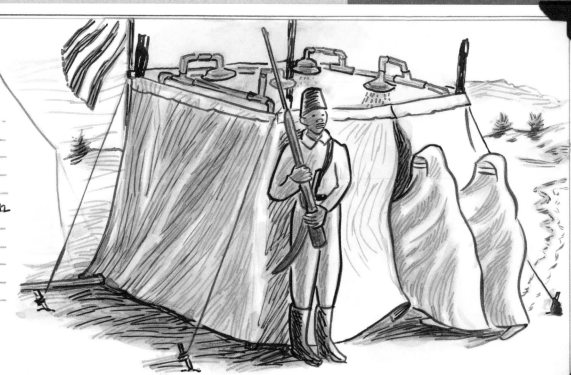

28

"After that, they didn't know what to do with me. I completed every task they assigned right away. I even rebuilt the latrines, but that was nothing—dig a trench and put down a wooden board with holes in it. There just wasn't any plumbing left to do. So they gave me busy work and that's when the drinking began in earnest, to ease the boredom. To not miss home. Everybody drank. That was just the way it was. To forget where we were."

Uncle Sam can't keep up with me. Tell Dad I put in a shower for a harum.
don't know what they'll do with me next.
I miss you, Red. Great news we've got a stork coming
'The wife's a Redhead
Yer wife's a doll, Charlie.

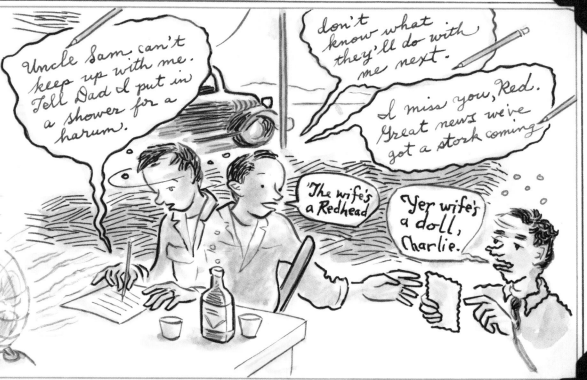

29

"Enlisted had beer, but the officers had booze. The Navy always had booze on the ships. And since I had to work with the Navy on water projects, I had access. Once, I was working out in the heat and this guy hands me a little bottle of Anisette. I drank it down. 'This is nothing,' I thought. So I went over to the Navy ship and got 3-4 more bottles. Swilled it all down, clean like water. Boy, the next morning, I couldn't scratch my head with both hands. Oh, that was awful!"

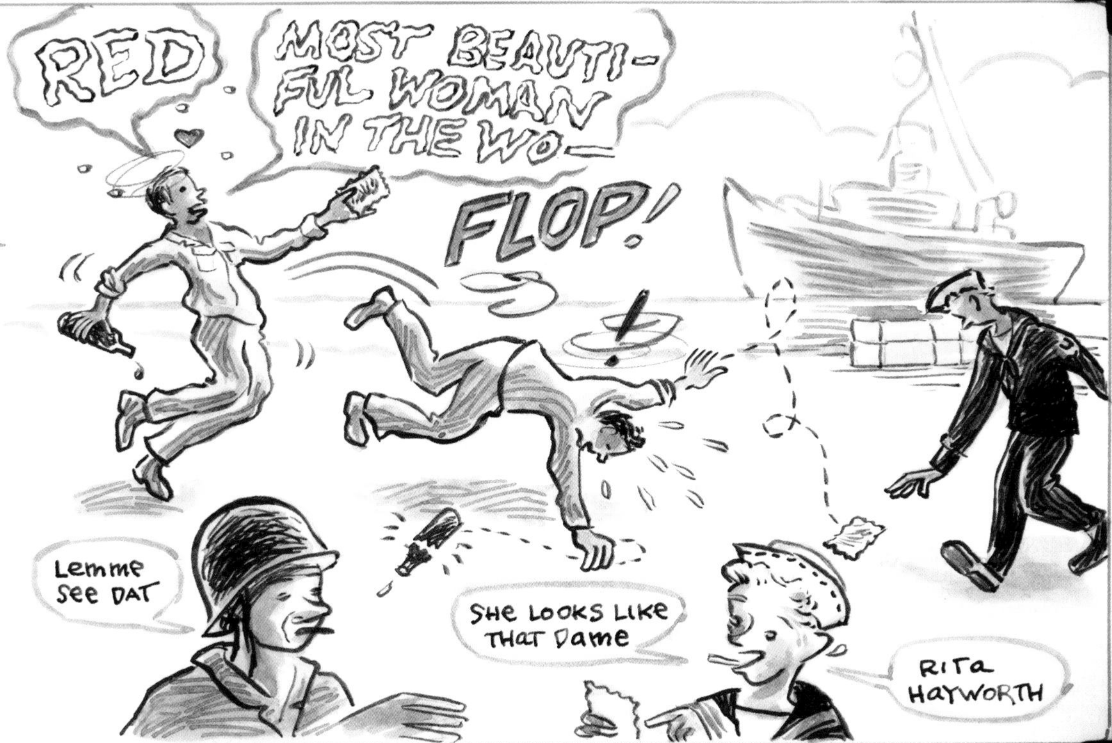
RED
MOST BEAUTI-FUL WOMAN IN THE WO—
FLOP!
LEMME SEE DAT
SHE LOOKS LIKE THAT DAME
RITA HAYWORTH

30

"Bad times the next morning, too. My head was pounding and I was never so thirsty. So I stumbled over to the middle of the base to get me a drink of water. They had this triangular bag hanging there with these nipple spouts below. I drew myself a long, cool drink of water, but AWGH! — Quinine water for malaria. On top of my Anisette hang-over. P.U.! But was the only water available. And then when I realized that I had lost my picture of Red ... this was worst of all. After this incident, I quit foolin' around with shit I didn't know."

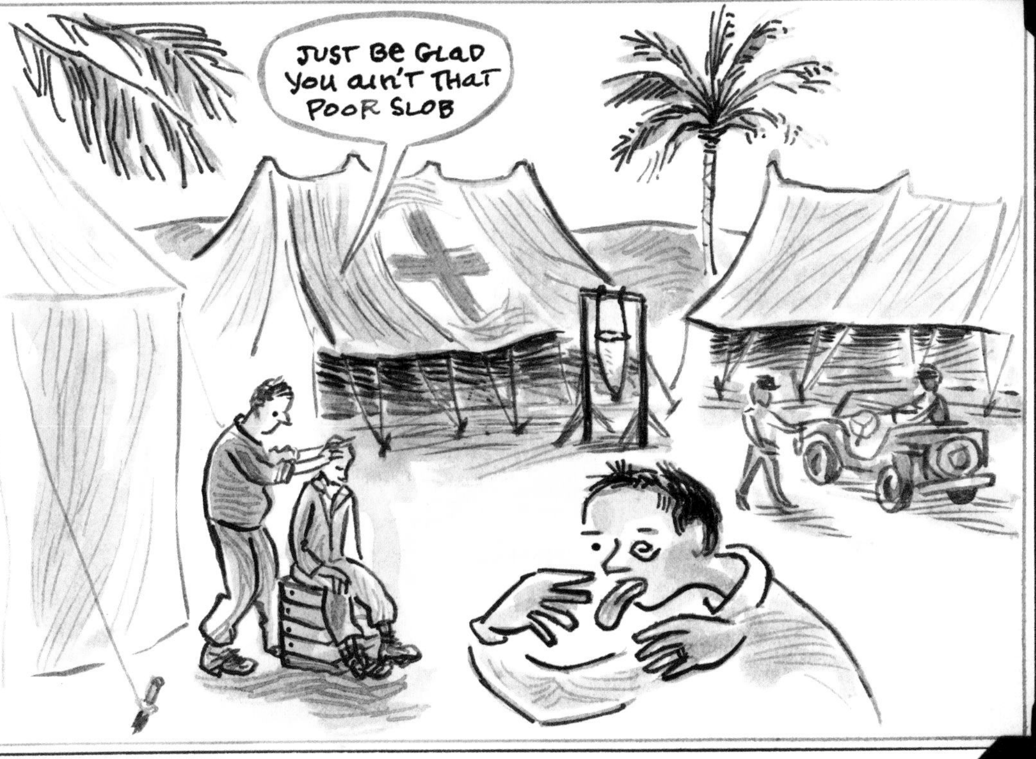
JUST BE GLAD YOU AIN'T THAT POOR SLOB

31

"As a boy, I had a darkroom. Photography was one of my hobbies and I took plenty of pictures of Red before I left. The one I lost that night was my favorite. —— Before I came over here, we decided she'd be better off in Chicago with my parents. War-time, you know. We wrote letters back and forth and every month I'd send her my pay, $60 dollars, (but Ma took $50 for expenses!). Army censors worked over my letters pretty good — they cut out almost everything I wrote!"

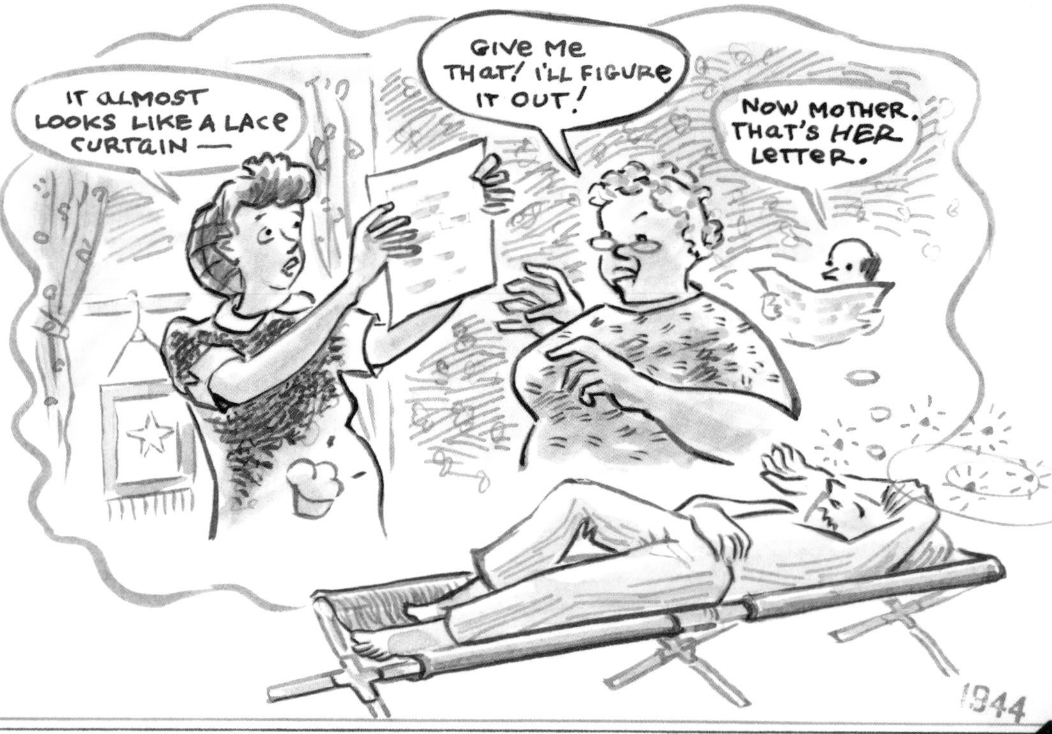
IT ALMOST LOOKS LIKE A LACE CURTAIN —
GIVE ME THAT! I'LL FIGURE IT OUT!
NOW MOTHER. THAT'S HER LETTER.
1944

32

"Goddamn, it was as hot as hell in the daytime. So we made ice cream with gasoline. We got sugar, eggs and cream from the cook, stirred it up nice and put it in a big jar, set the jar in a washtub full of 3/4 hi-octane, then stirred the jar. Ice formed on the sides and bottom and froze the cream inside. —— At night it could get pretty cold in the desert. One of my duties was to crawl up under the tanks with my little camp stove at 3a.m to warm up the oil so that the pistons would move first thing in the morning. Huge 8 cylinder engines."

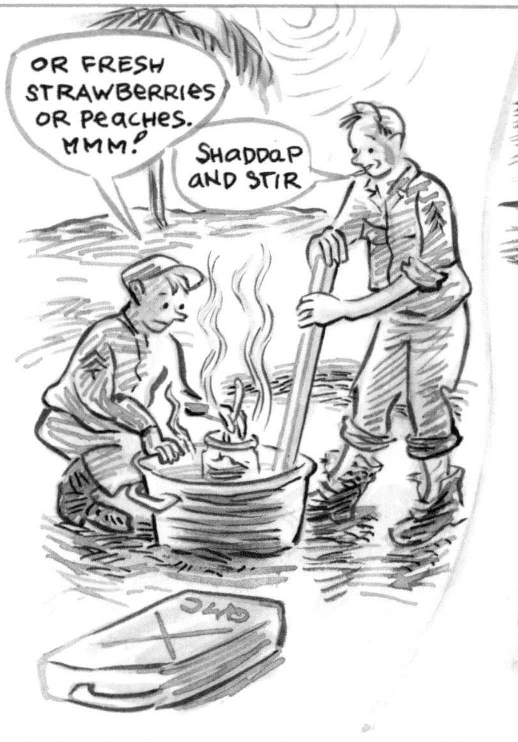
OR FRESH STRAWBERRIES OR PEACHES. MMM!
SHADDAP AND STIR

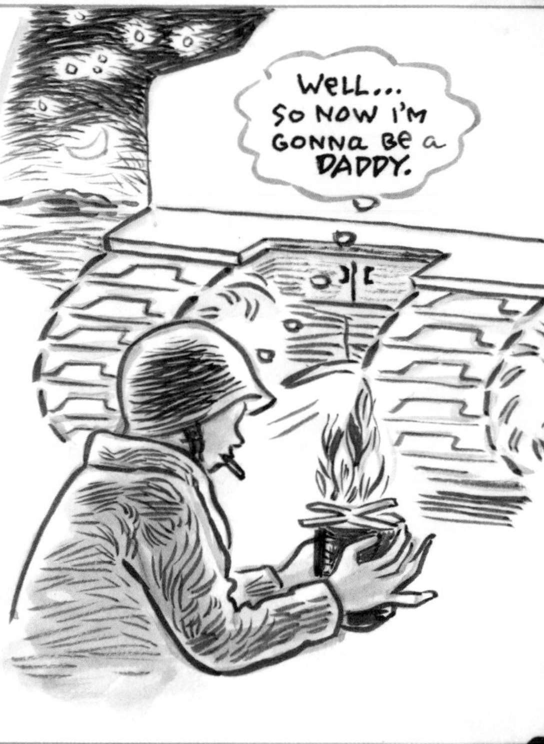
WELL... SO NOW I'M GONNA BE A DADDY.

33

"Binoculars. Nice souvenir. I was with some squad and we went after some tanks with a bottle of gasoline and a rag in it. We got a hold of one tank and burned it up good, burned the two guys out of there and it was the first Germans I helped capture. Some place in North Africa. I don't know where the hell it was.

"That's where I picked up my first souvenir. Spoils of war, I guess you could say. But now I had to be vigilant with my stuff."

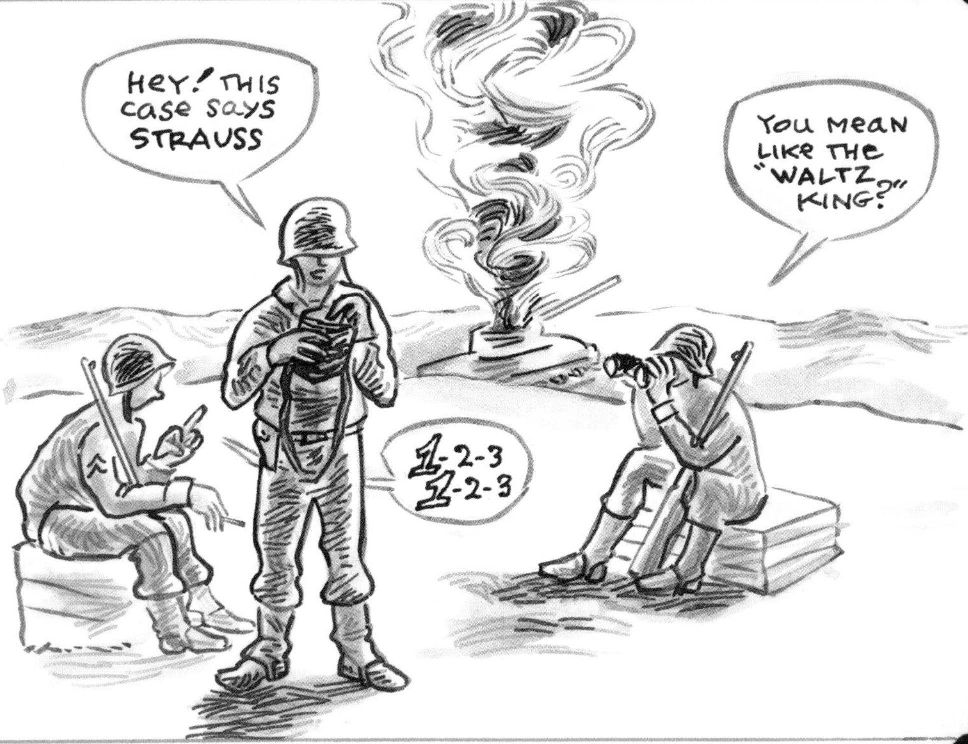
HEY! THIS CASE SAYS STRAUSS
YOU MEAN LIKE THE "WALTZ KING?"
1-2-3 1-2-3

34

"Sons-of-bitches stole things, our own guys! The brass would say, 'Put your dufflebags in a pile..' for somebody to rifle through later on, when we weren't around. I seen this happen, so I always put my bag in the middle, under the others. Maybe some guys didn't get back, they got killed or something. S-O-Bs would take their souvenirs — guys who hadn't seen any action, hadn't earnt the stuff. Once I seen this guy who got caught stealing — the others drug him into the shower, beat the hell out of him then pissed all over him. Taught him a lesson."

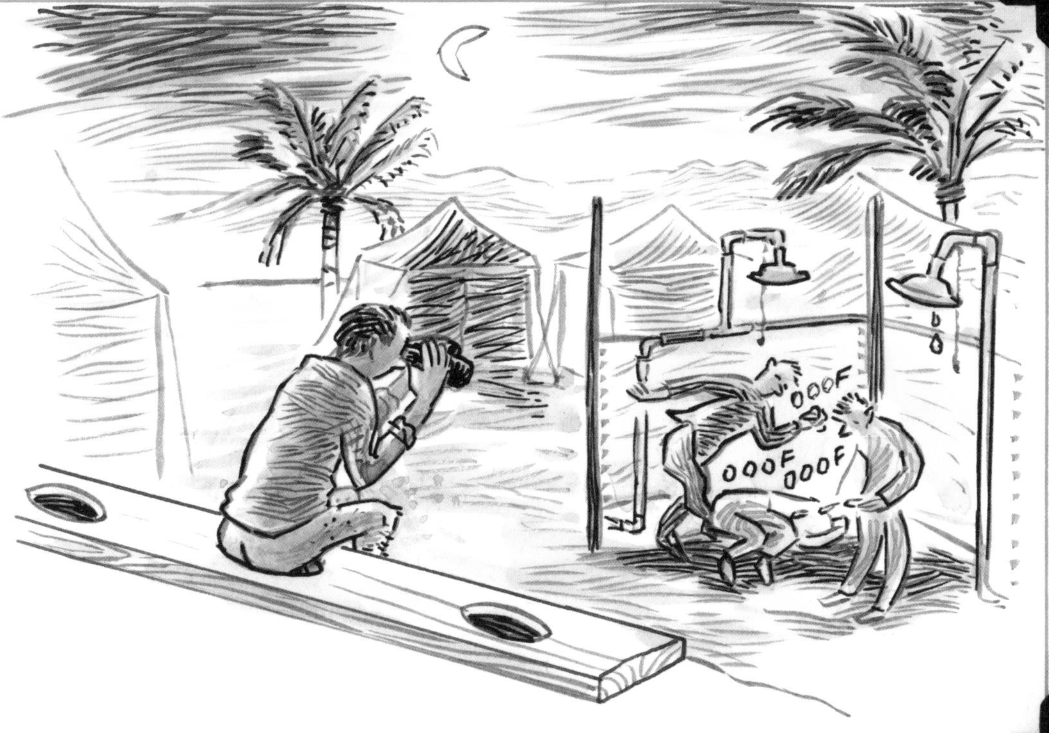
OOOF
OOOF OOOF

35

"Oran to Algiers by train. Stopping every mile or so. These guys would come up to the side of the boxcar interested in our 'mattress covers.' (Body bags. We each had one.) 'Sure, we'll sell 'em to ya.' So we'd tie the cord to the inside of the car door while they inspected the merchandise. They kept their money in a bag that hung between their legs. So then *toot toot* the train started to go. We'd give them the bag and take their money and then the train would *yank* the bag back in. They'd chase us with their pouches flappin'! Woo, every few miles or so we'd play this trick, our gang."

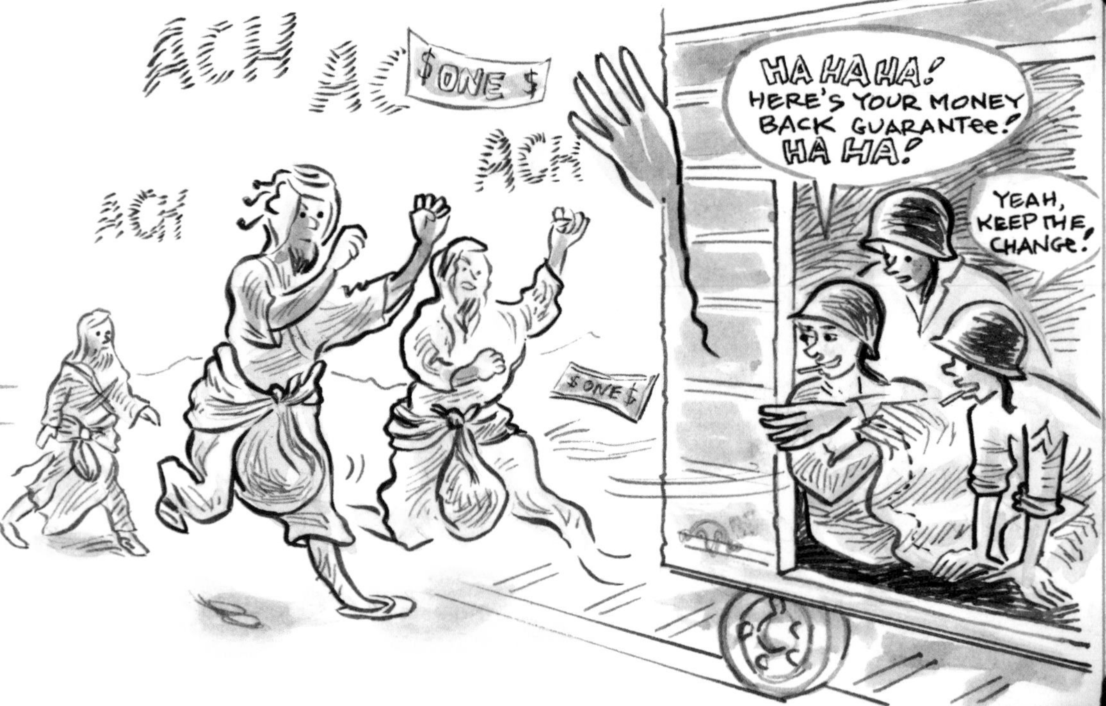
ACH ACH
$ONE $
ACH
ACH
HA HA HA!
HERE'S YOUR MONEY BACK GUARANTEE!
HA HA!
YEAH, KEEP THE CHANGE!
$ONE $

36

"I walked into the Casbah, but found out later I could've had my throat slit. Off limits. — On the train again to Bizerte, a 40 and 8 boxcar (40 men, 8 horses). So I says, 'This 48 is stinky. I'm going to ride on top of the gondola. It had a canvas top, soft as a hammock. I figured I'd get fresh air and nobody would bother my stuff. Me and this other guy in our spanking clean cottons. Next morning, when we got up, we were black top to toe, covered in coal soot. Leaving Africa, headed for Italy on a ship, as black as those French Moroccans.'"

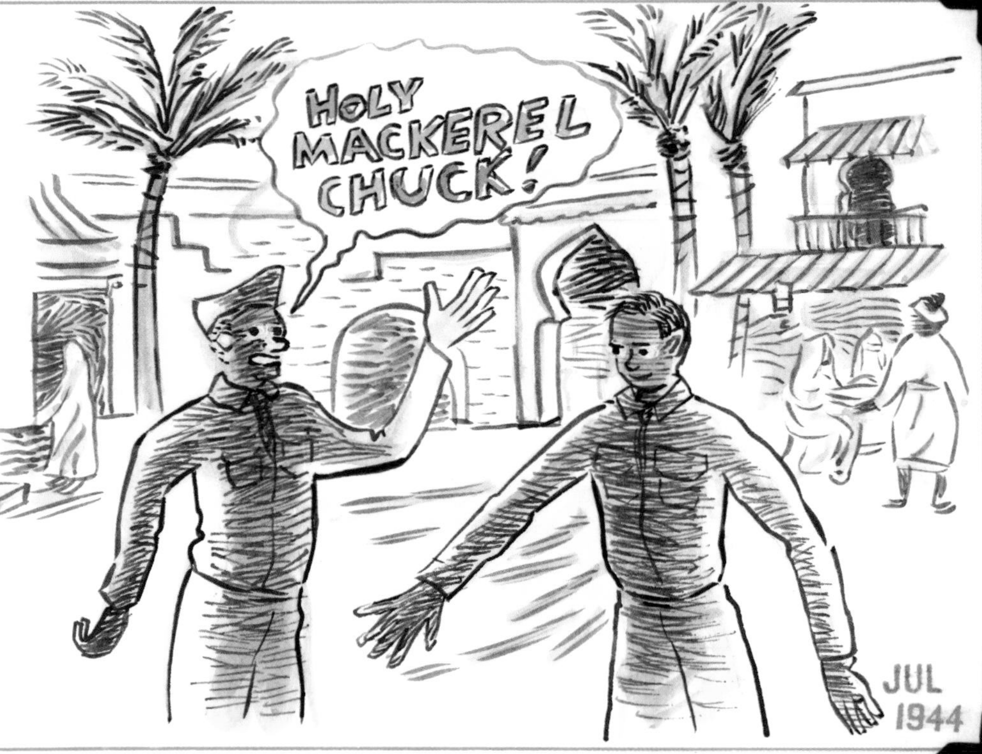
HOLY MACKEREL CHUCK!
JUL 1944

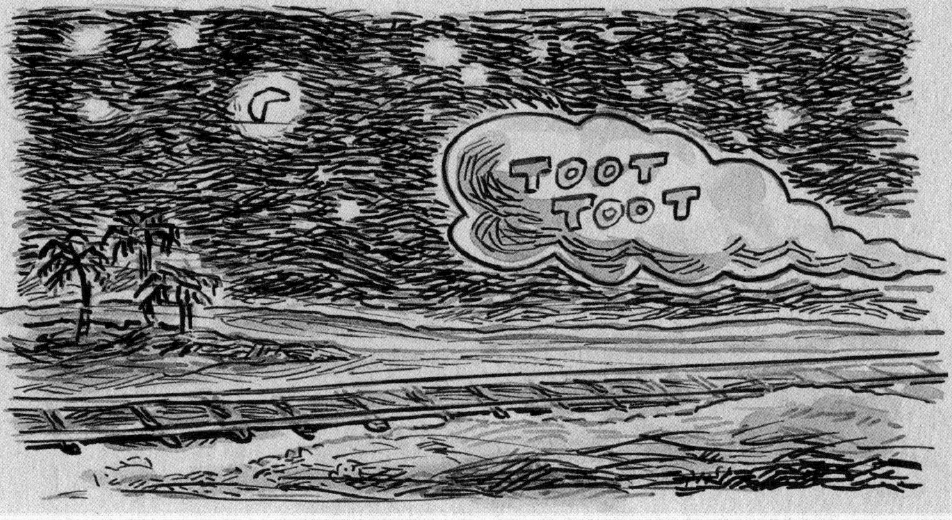
TOOT TOOT

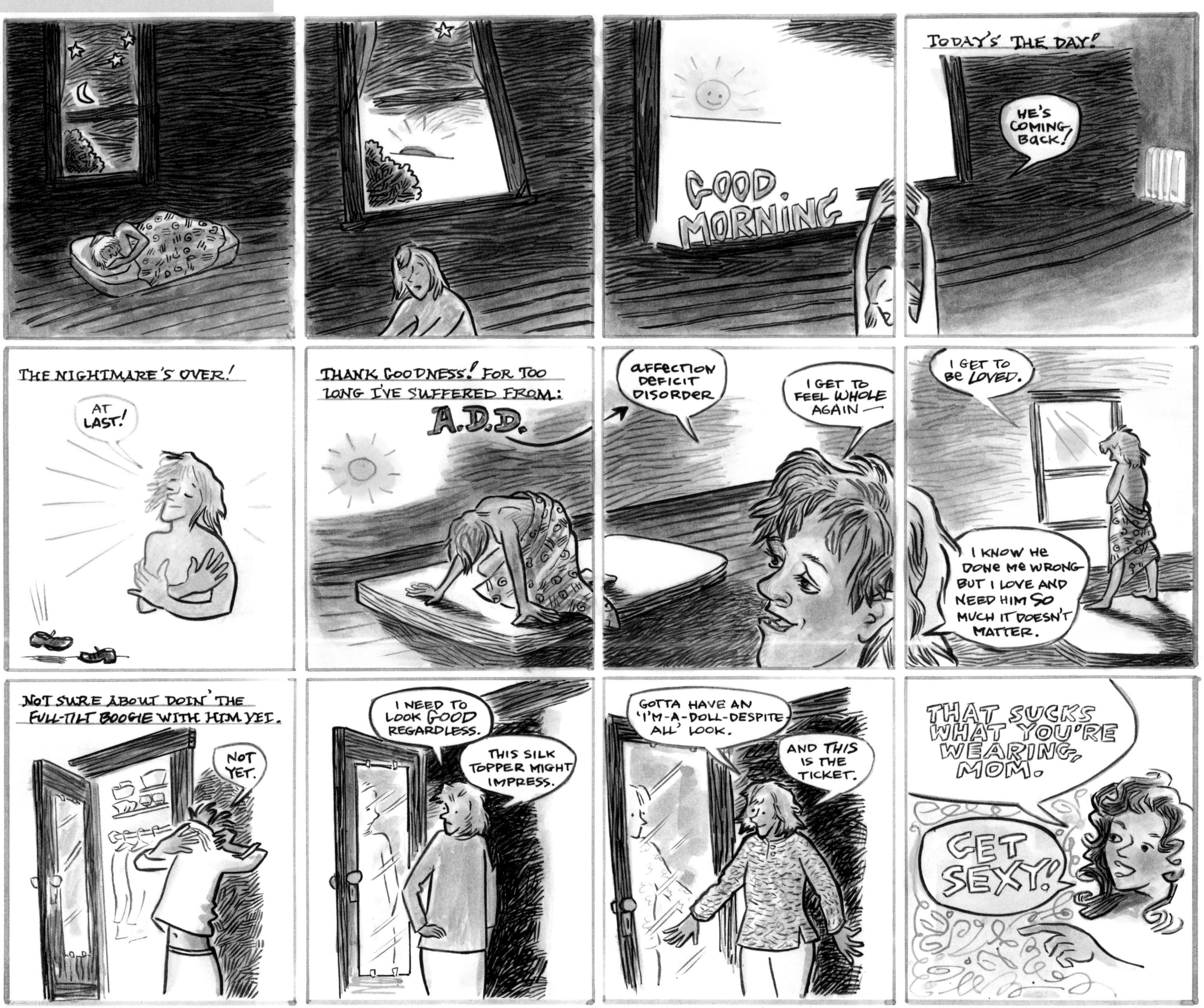
GOOD MORNING
TODAY'S THE DAY!
HE'S COMING BACK!
THE NIGHTMARE'S OVER!
AT LAST!
THANK GOODNESS! FOR TOO LONG I'VE SUFFERED FROM:
A.D.D.
AFFECTION DEFICIT DISORDER
I GET TO FEEL WHOLE AGAIN —
I GET TO BE LOVED.
I KNOW HE DONE ME WRONG BUT I LOVE AND NEED HIM SO MUCH IT DOESN'T MATTER.
NOT SURE ABOUT DOIN' THE FULL-TILT BOOGIE WITH HIM YET.
NOT YET.
I NEED TO LOOK GOOD REGARDLESS.
THIS SILK TOPPER MIGHT IMPRESS.
GOTTA HAVE AN 'I'M-A-DOLL-DESPITE-ALL' LOOK.
AND THIS IS THE TICKET.
THAT SUCKS WHAT YOU'RE WEARING, MOM.
GET SEXY!

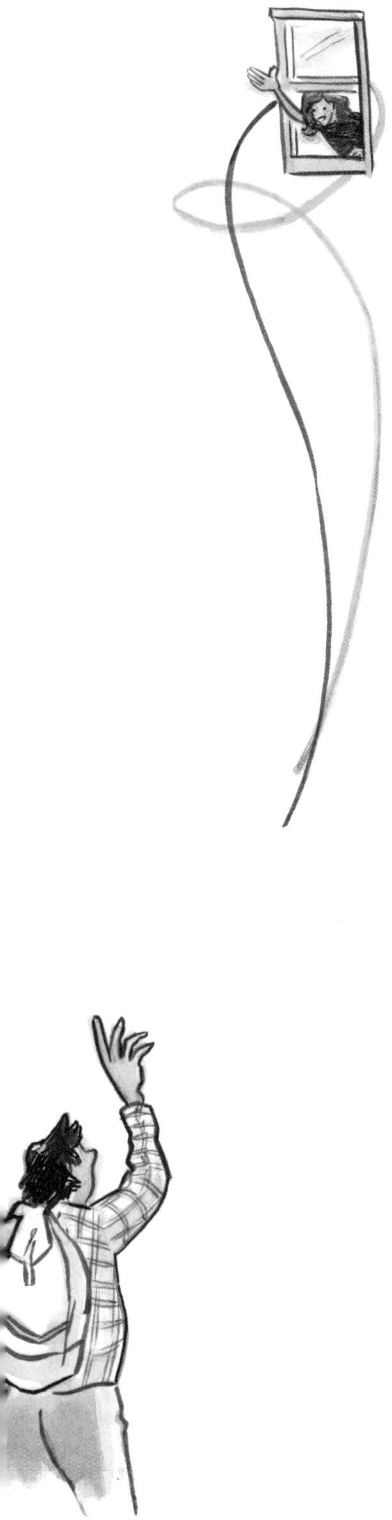

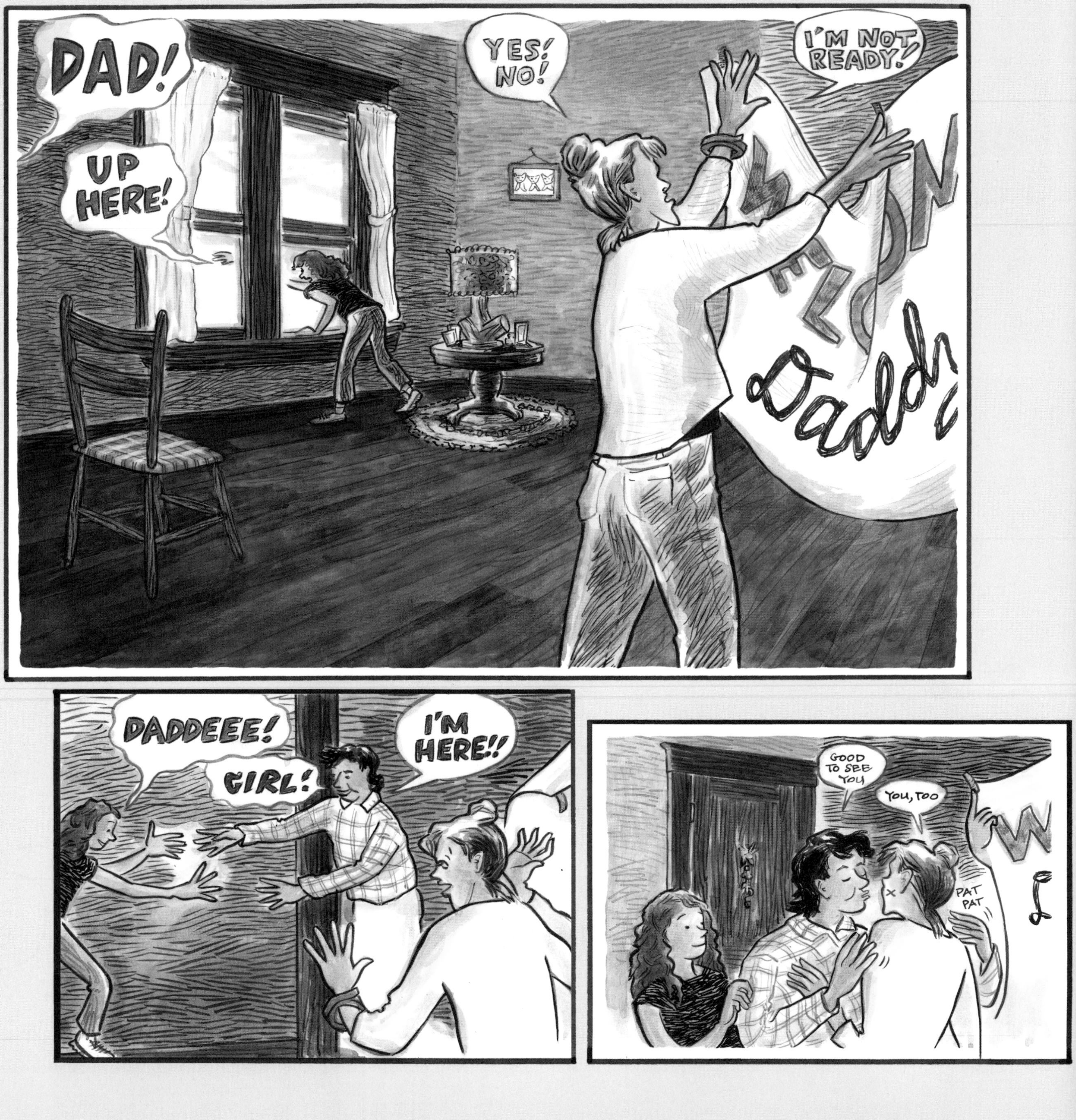
DAD!
UP HERE!
YES! NO!
I'M NOT READY!
DADDEEE!
GIRL!
I'M HERE!!
GOOD TO SEE YOU
YOU, TOO
PAT PAT

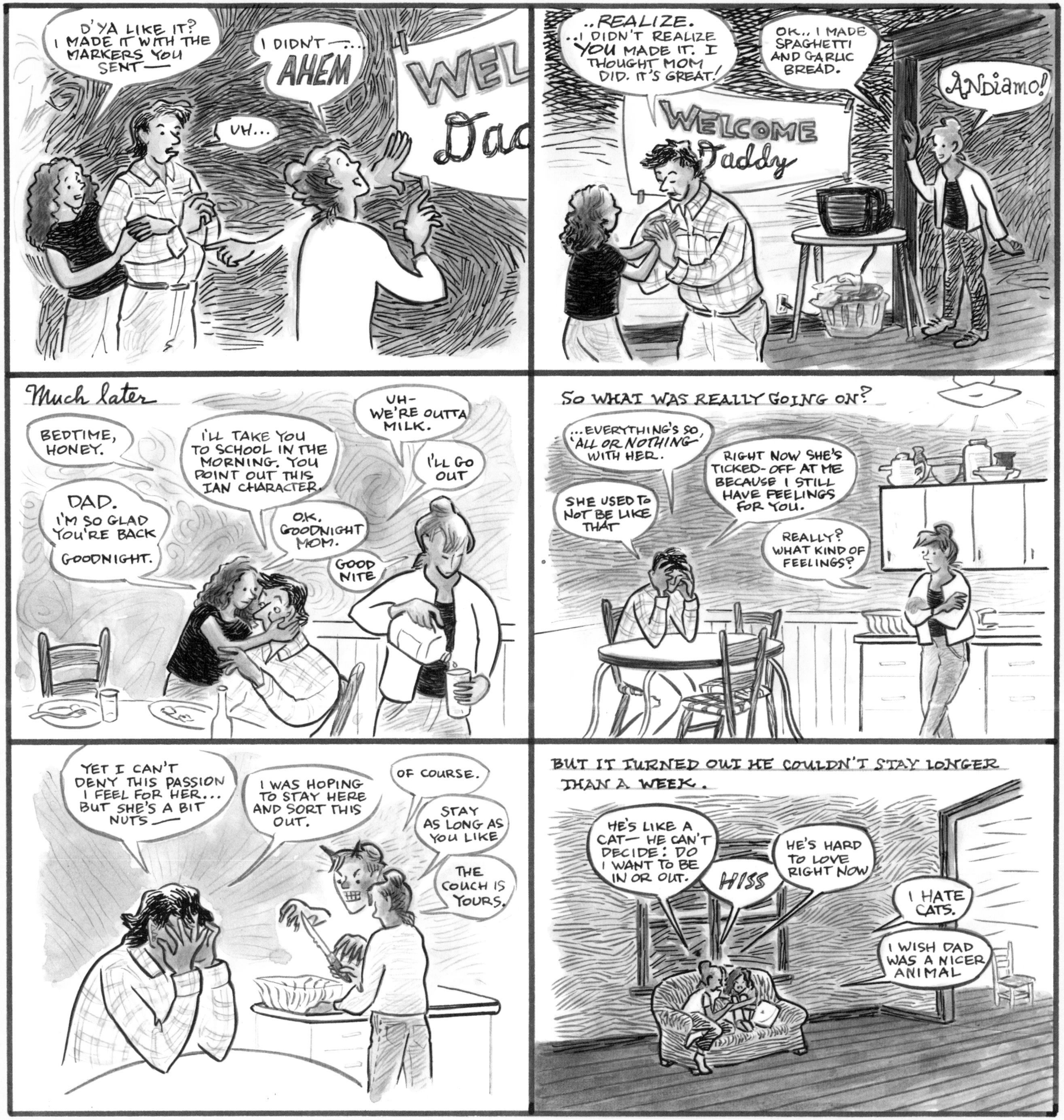
D'YA LIKE IT? I MADE IT WITH THE MARKERS YOU SENT—
I DIDN'T—...
AHEM
UH...
WEL
Dad
..REALIZE. ..I DIDN'T REALIZE YOU MADE IT. I THOUGHT MOM DID. IT'S GREAT!
OK.. I MADE SPAGHETTI AND GARLIC BREAD.
WELCOME Daddy
ANDiamo!
Much later
BEDTIME, HONEY.
I'LL TAKE YOU TO SCHOOL IN THE MORNING. YOU POINT OUT THIS IAN CHARACTER.
UH- WE'RE OUTTA MILK.
I'LL GO OUT
DAD. I'M SO GLAD YOU'RE BACK GOODNIGHT.
OK. GOODNIGHT MOM.
GOOD NITE
SO WHAT WAS REALLY GOING ON?
...EVERYTHING'S SO 'ALL OR NOTHING' WITH HER.
SHE USED TO NOT BE LIKE THAT
RIGHT NOW SHE'S TICKED-OFF AT ME BECAUSE I STILL HAVE FEELINGS FOR YOU.
REALLY? WHAT KIND OF FEELINGS?
YET I CAN'T DENY THIS PASSION I FEEL FOR HER... BUT SHE'S A BIT NUTS—
I WAS HOPING TO STAY HERE AND SORT THIS OUT.
OF COURSE.
STAY AS LONG AS YOU LIKE
THE COUCH IS YOURS.
BUT IT TURNED OUT HE COULDN'T STAY LONGER THAN A WEEK.
HE'S LIKE A CAT— HE CAN'T DECIDE: DO I WANT TO BE IN OR OUT.
HISS
HE'S HARD TO LOVE RIGHT NOW
I HATE CATS.
I WISH DAD WAS A NICER ANIMAL

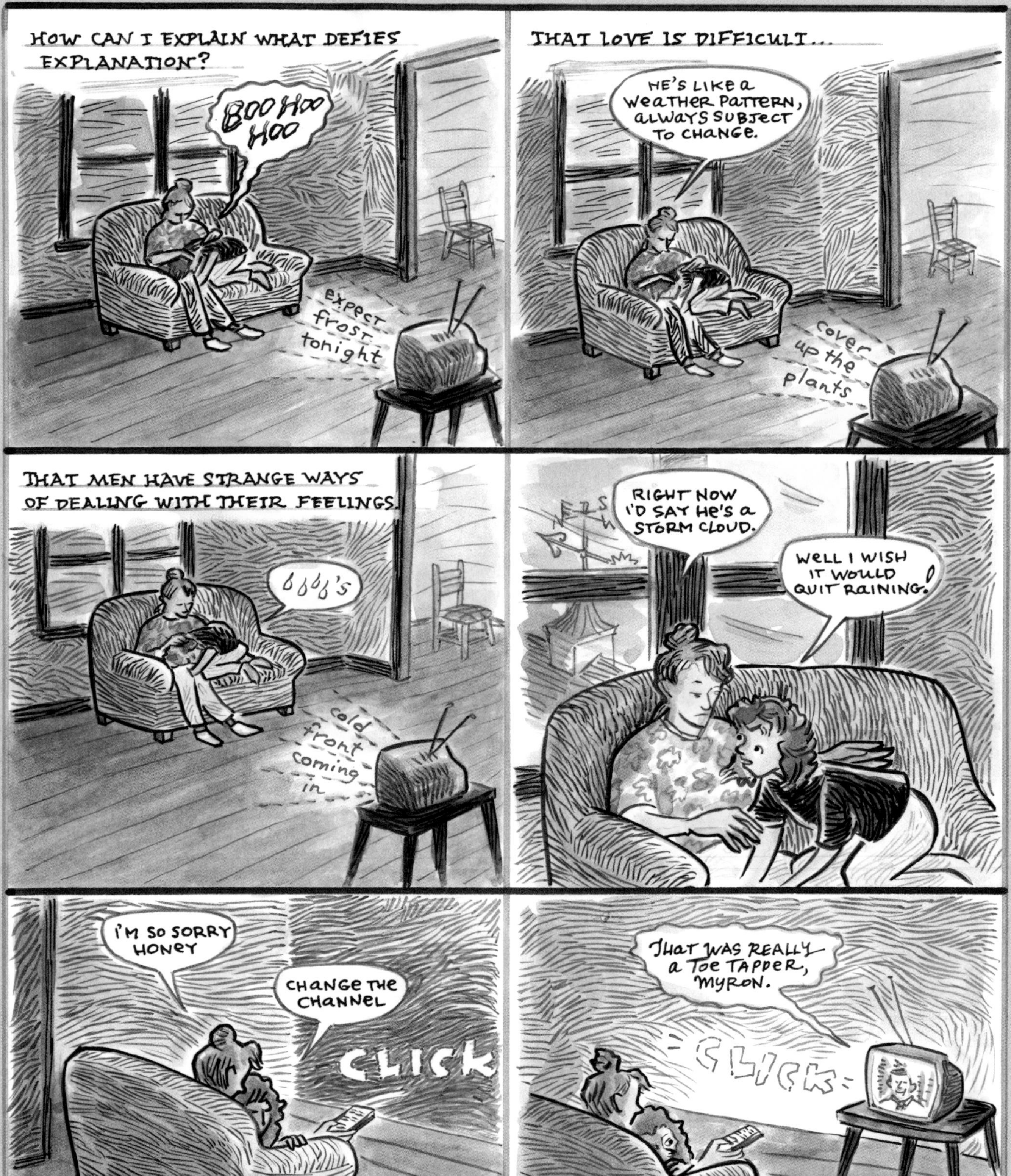
HOW CAN I EXPLAIN WHAT DEFIES EXPLANATION?
BOO HOO HOO
expect frost tonight
THAT LOVE IS DIFFICULT...
HE'S LIKE A WEATHER PATTERN, ALWAYS SUBJECT TO CHANGE.
cover up the plants
THAT MEN HAVE STRANGE WAYS OF DEALING WITH THEIR FEELINGS.
cold front coming in
RIGHT NOW I'D SAY HE'S A STORM CLOUD.
WELL I WISH IT WOULD QUIT RAINING!
I'M SO SORRY HONEY
CHANGE THE CHANNEL
CLICK
CLICK
THAT WAS REALLY A TOE TAPPER, MYRON.

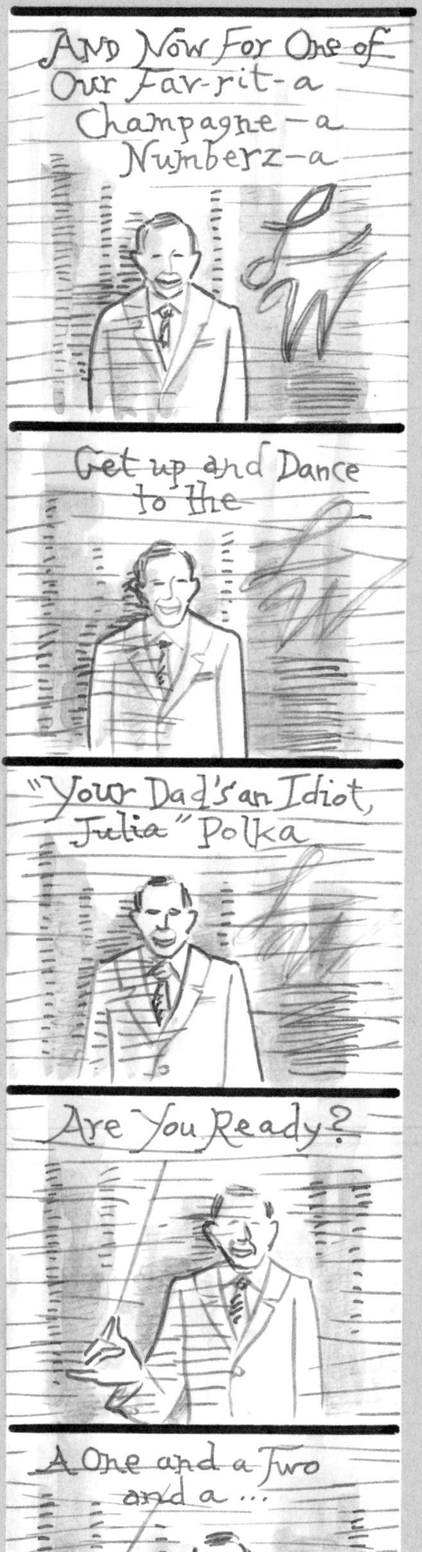
AND Now For One of Our Far-rit-a Champagne-a Numberz-a
LW
Get up and Dance to the
"Your Dad's an Idiot, Julia" Polka
Are You Ready?
A One and a Two and a...

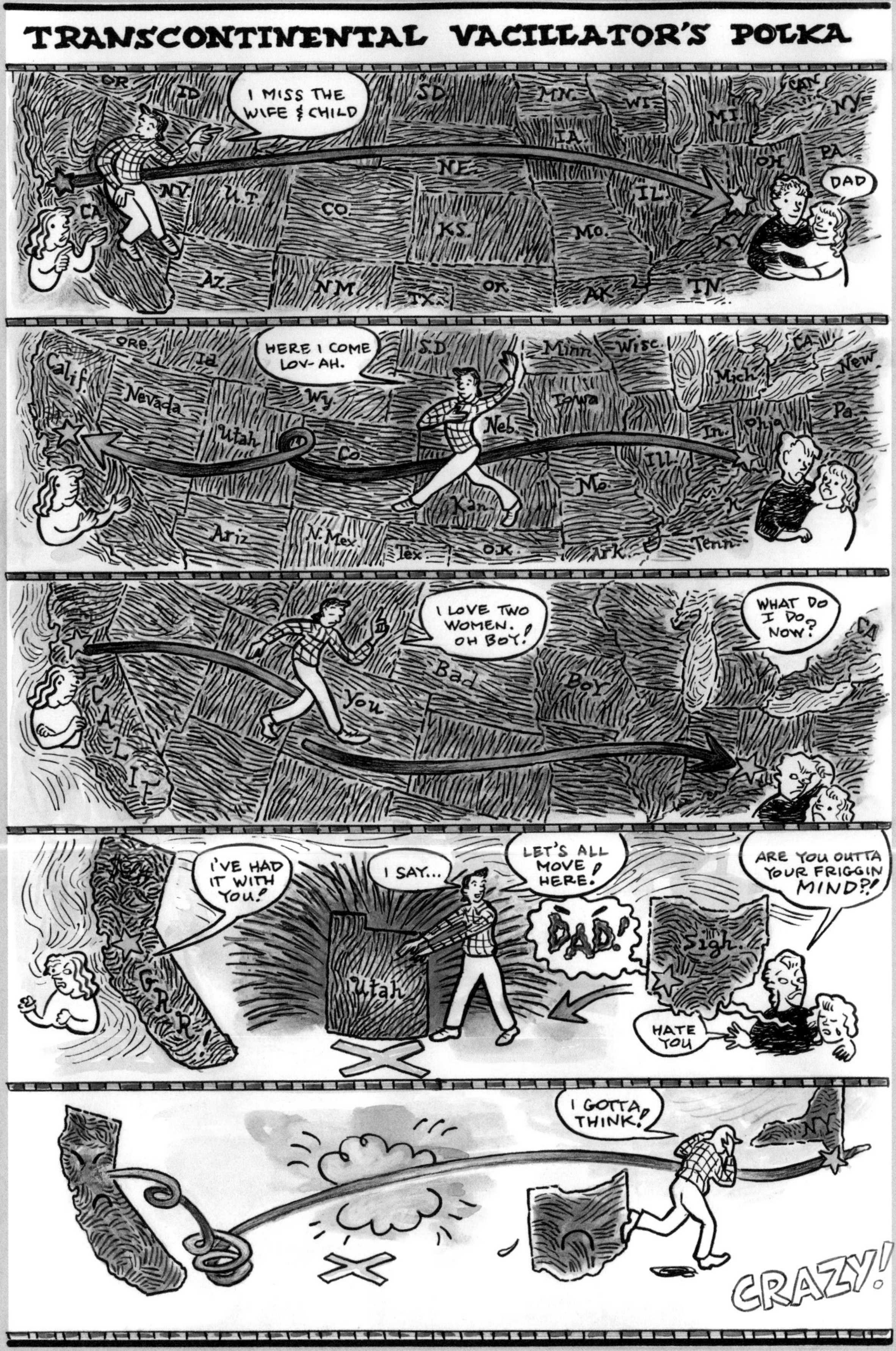
TRANSCONTINENTAL VACILLATOR'S POLKA
I MISS THE WIFE & CHILD
DAD
HERE I COME LOV-AH.
I LOVE TWO WOMEN. OH BOY!
WHAT DO I DO NOW?
Bad
You
Boy
I'VE HAD IT WITH YOU!
I SAY...
LET'S ALL MOVE HERE!
DAD!
ARE YOU OUTTA YOUR FRIGGIN MIND?!
Utah
Sigh.
GRR
HATE YOU
I GOTTA THINK!
CRAZY!

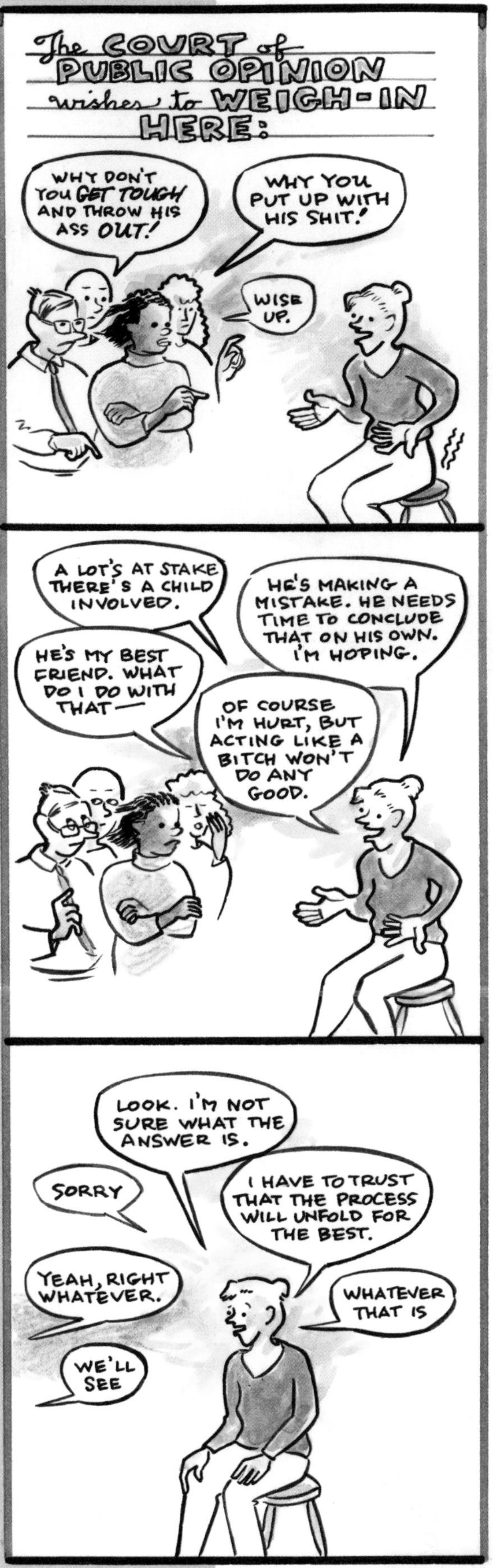
The COURT of PUBLIC OPINION wishes to WEIGH-IN HERE:
WHY DON'T YOU GET TOUGH AND THROW HIS ASS OUT!
WHY YOU PUT UP WITH HIS SHIT!
WISE UP.
A LOT'S AT STAKE THERE'S A CHILD INVOLVED.
HE'S MAKING A MISTAKE. HE NEEDS TIME TO CONCLUDE THAT ON HIS OWN. I'M HOPING.
HE'S MY BEST FRIEND. WHAT DO I DO WITH THAT—
OF COURSE I'M HURT, BUT ACTING LIKE A BITCH WON'T DO ANY GOOD.
LOOK. I'M NOT SURE WHAT THE ANSWER IS.
SORRY
I HAVE TO TRUST THAT THE PROCESS WILL UNFOLD FOR THE BEST.
YEAH, RIGHT WHATEVER.
WHATEVER THAT IS
WE'LL SEE

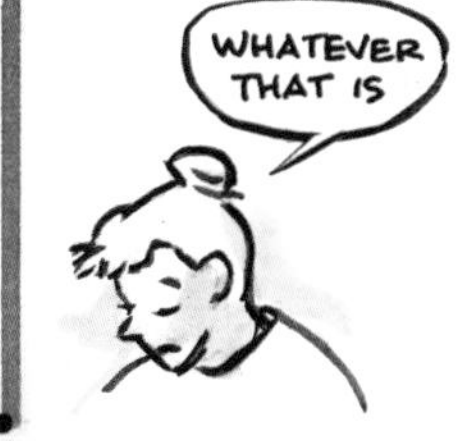
WHATEVER THAT IS

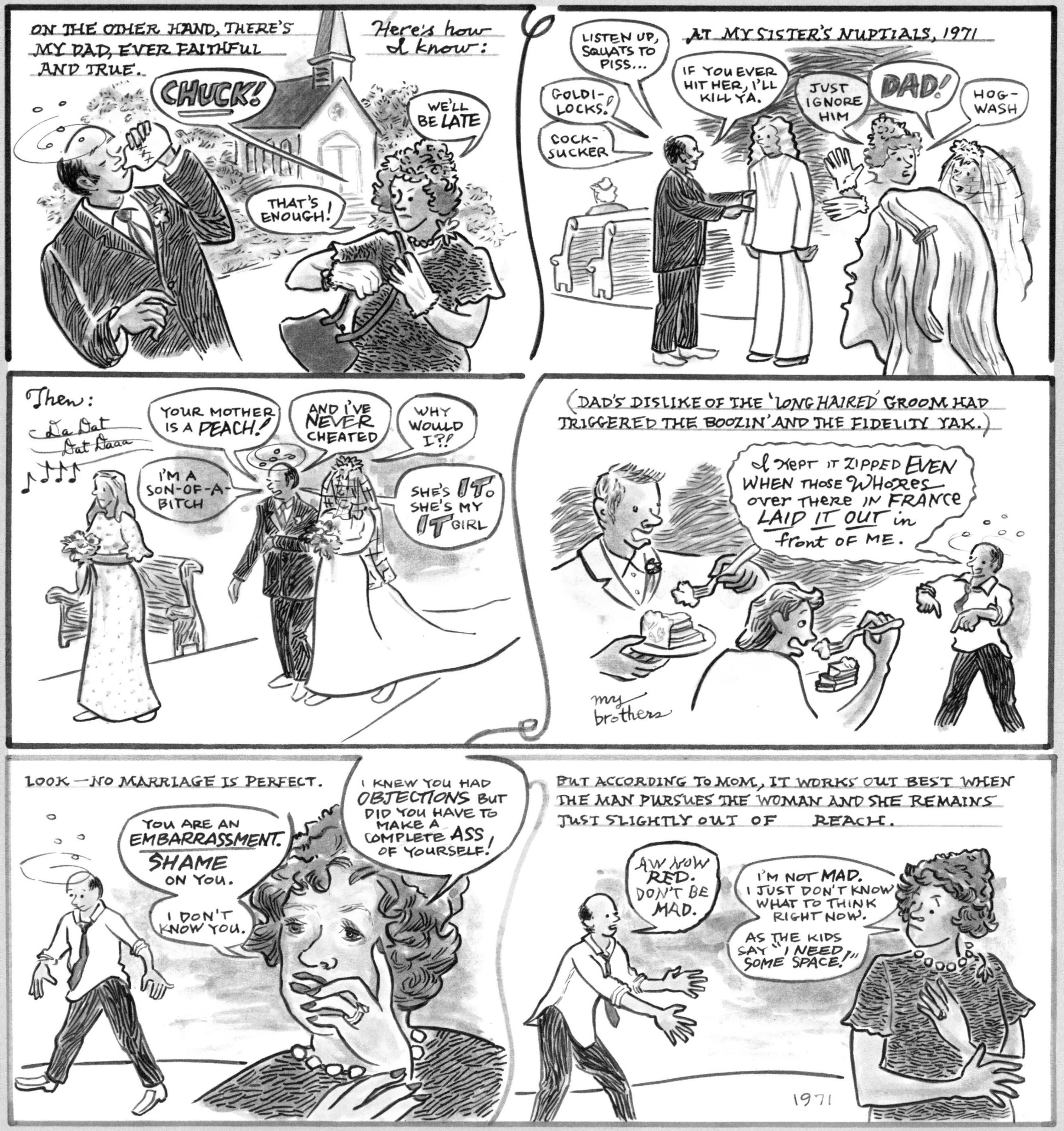
ON THE OTHER HAND, THERE'S MY DAD, EVER FAITHFUL AND TRUE.
Here's how I know:
CHUCK!
WE'LL BE LATE
THAT'S ENOUGH!
AT MY SISTER'S NUPTIALS, 1971
LISTEN UP, SQUATS TO PISS...
GOLDI-LOCKS!
COCK-SUCKER
IF YOU EVER HIT HER, I'LL KILL YA.
JUST IGNORE HIM
DAD!
HOG-WASH
Then:
Da Dat Dat Daaa
YOUR MOTHER IS A PEACH!
AND I'VE NEVER CHEATED
WHY WOULD I?!
I'M A SON-OF-A-BITCH
SHE'S IT. SHE'S MY IT GIRL
(DAD'S DISLIKE OF THE 'LONG HAIRED' GROOM HAD TRIGGERED THE BOOZIN' AND THE FIDELITY YAK.)
I kept it zipped EVEN WHEN THOSE WHORES over there in FRANCE LAID IT OUT in front of ME.
my brothers
LOOK—NO MARRIAGE IS PERFECT.
YOU ARE AN EMBARRASSMENT. SHAME ON YOU.
I DON'T KNOW YOU.
I KNEW YOU HAD OBJECTIONS BUT DID YOU HAVE TO MAKE A COMPLETE ASS OF YOURSELF!
BUT ACCORDING TO MOM, IT WORKS OUT BEST WHEN THE MAN PURSUES THE WOMAN AND SHE REMAINS JUST SLIGHTLY OUT OF REACH.
AW NOW RED. DON'T BE MAD.
I'M NOT MAD. I JUST DON'T KNOW WHAT TO THINK RIGHT NOW.
AS THE KIDS SAY "I NEED SOME SPACE!"
1971

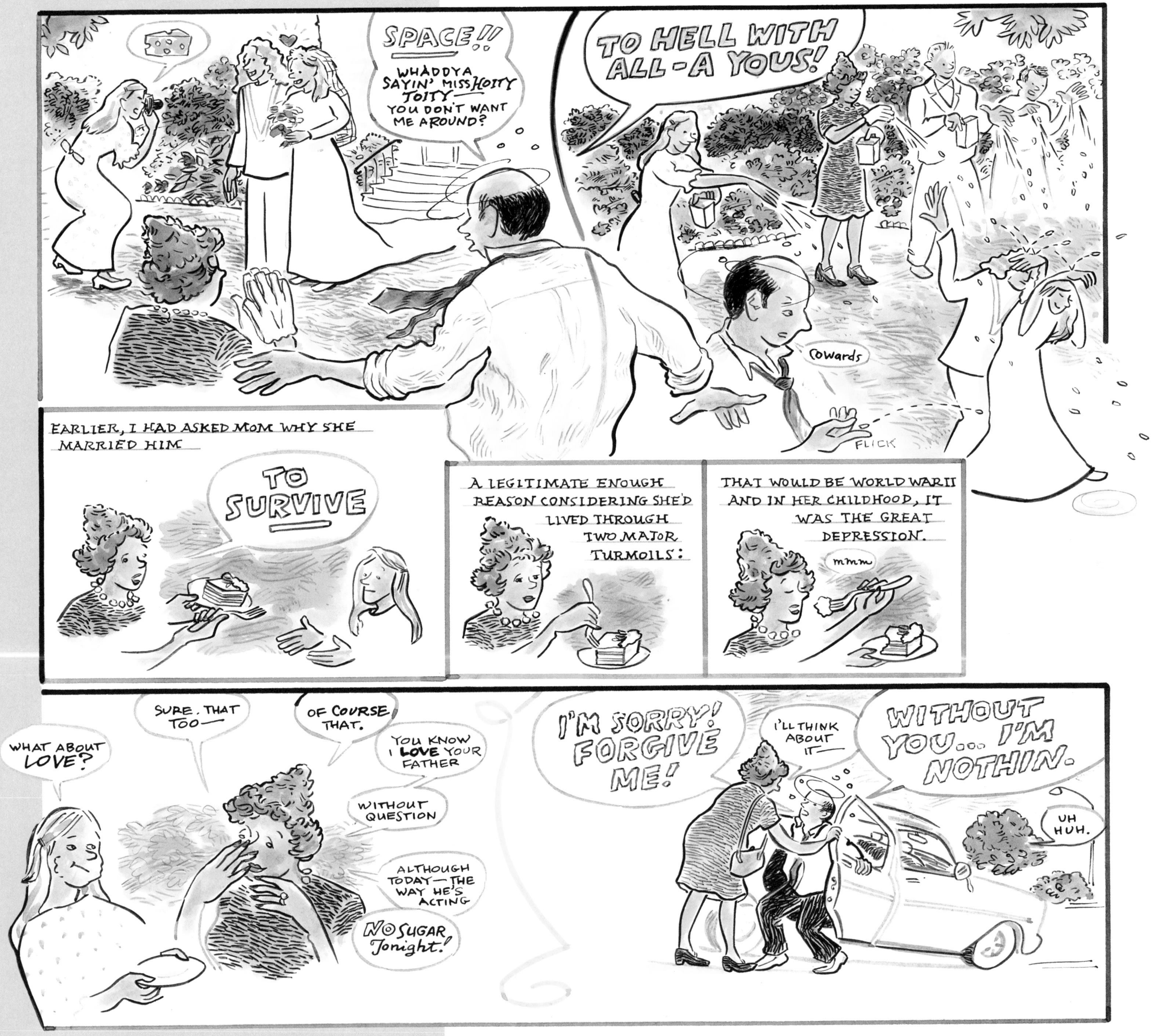
SPACE!!
WHADDYA SAYIN' MISS HOITY TOITY— YOU DON'T WANT ME AROUND?
TO HELL WITH ALL-A YOUS!
COWARDS
FLICK
EARLIER, I HAD ASKED MOM WHY SHE MARRIED HIM
TO SURVIVE
A LEGITIMATE ENOUGH REASON CONSIDERING SHE'D LIVED THROUGH TWO MAJOR TURMOILS:
THAT WOULD BE WORLD WAR II AND IN HER CHILDHOOD, IT WAS THE GREAT DEPRESSION.
mmm
WHAT ABOUT LOVE?
SURE. THAT TOO—
OF COURSE THAT.
YOU KNOW I LOVE YOUR FATHER
WITHOUT QUESTION
ALTHOUGH TODAY—THE WAY HE'S ACTING
NO SUGAR Tonight!
I'M SORRY! FORGIVE ME!
I'LL THINK ABOUT IT—
WITHOUT YOU... I'M NOTHIN.
UH HUH.

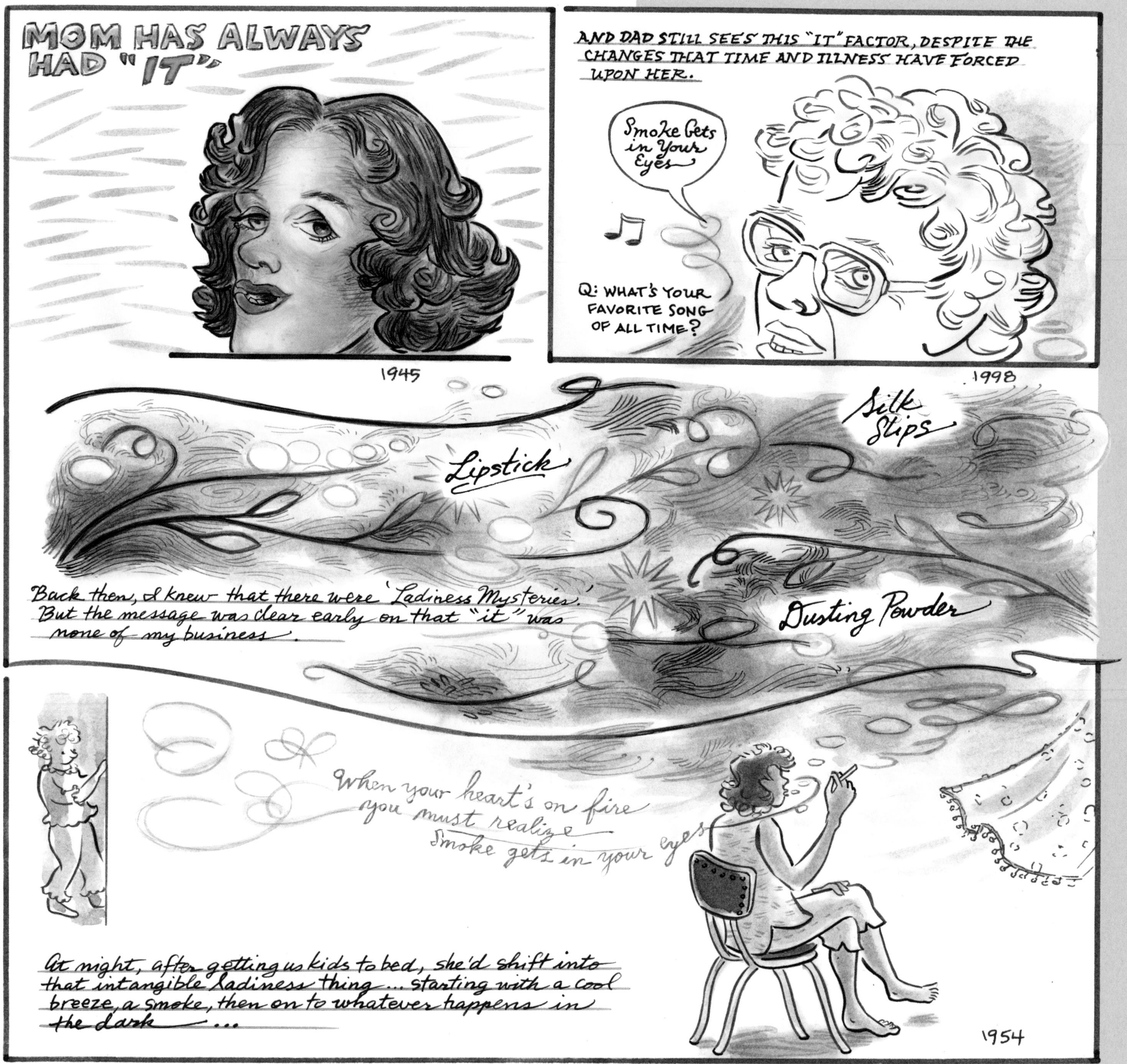
MOM HAS ALWAYS HAD "IT"
1945
AND DAD STILL SEES THIS "IT" FACTOR, DESPITE THE CHANGES THAT TIME AND ILLNESS HAVE FORCED UPON HER.
Smoke Gets in Your Eyes
Q: WHAT'S YOUR FAVORITE SONG OF ALL TIME?
1998
Silk Slips
Lipstick
Dusting Powder
Back then, I knew that there were 'Ladiness Mysteries'. But the message was clear early on that "it" was none of my business.
When your heart's on fire you must realize Smoke gets in your eyes
At night, after getting us kids to bed, she'd shift into that intangible ladiness thing... starting with a cool breeze, a smoke, then on to whatever happens in the dark...
1954

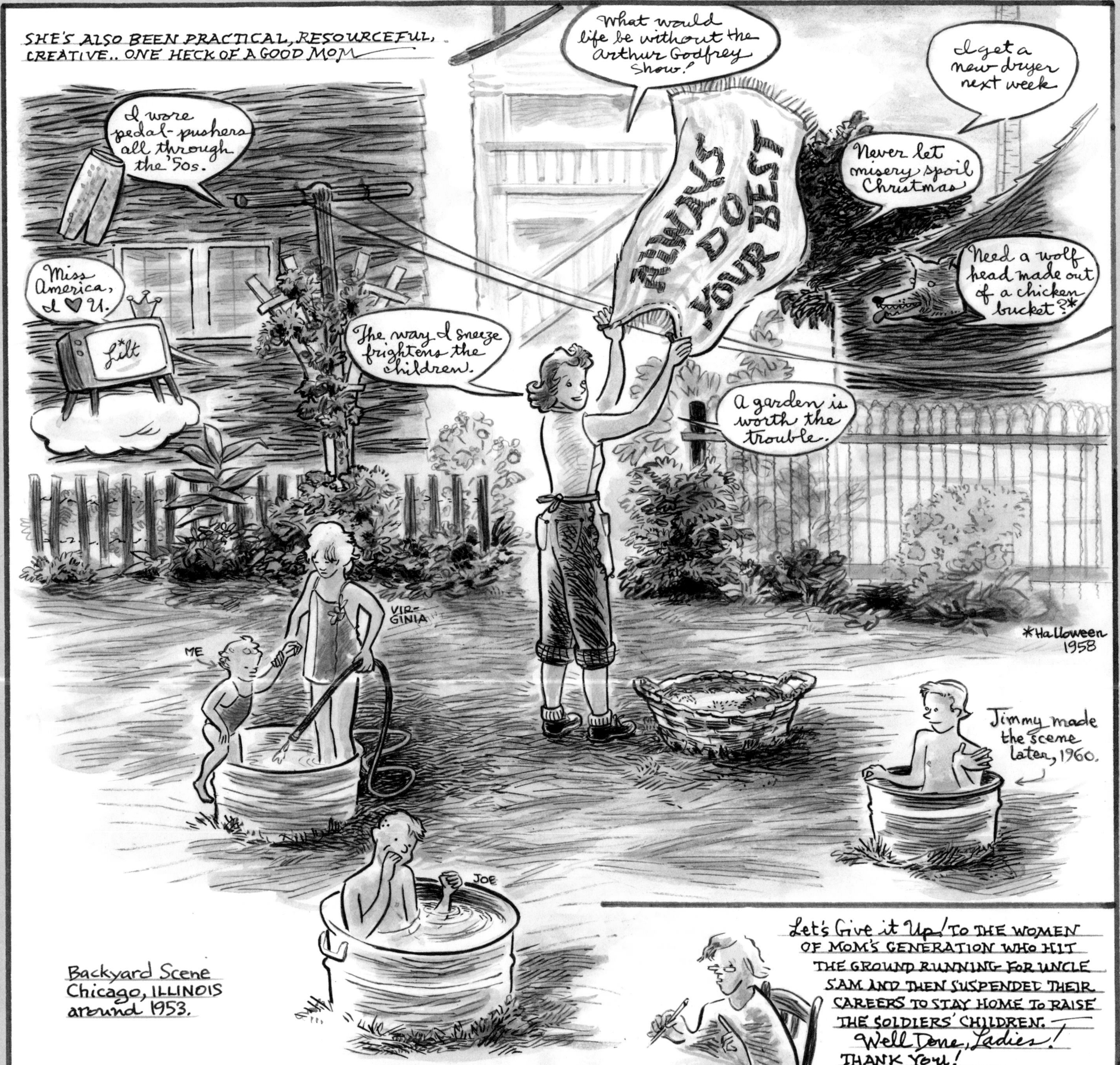
SHE'S ALSO BEEN PRACTICAL, RESOURCEFUL, CREATIVE.. ONE HECK OF A GOOD MOM
What would life be without the Arthur Godfrey Show!
I get a new dryer next week
I wore pedal-pushers all through the '50s.
ALWAYS DO YOUR BEST
Never let misery spoil Christmas
Miss America, I ♥ U.
Lilt*
Need a wolf head made out of a chicken bucket?*
The way I sneeze frightens the children.
A garden is worth the trouble.
VIR-GINIA
ME
*Halloween 1958
Jimmy made the scene later, 1960.
JOE
Backyard Scene Chicago, ILLINOIS around 1953.
Let's Give it Up! TO THE WOMEN OF MOM'S GENERATION WHO HIT THE GROUND RUNNING FOR UNCLE SAM AND THEN SUSPENDED THEIR CAREERS TO STAY HOME TO RAISE THE SOLDIERS' CHILDREN.
Well Done, Ladies!
THANK YOU!

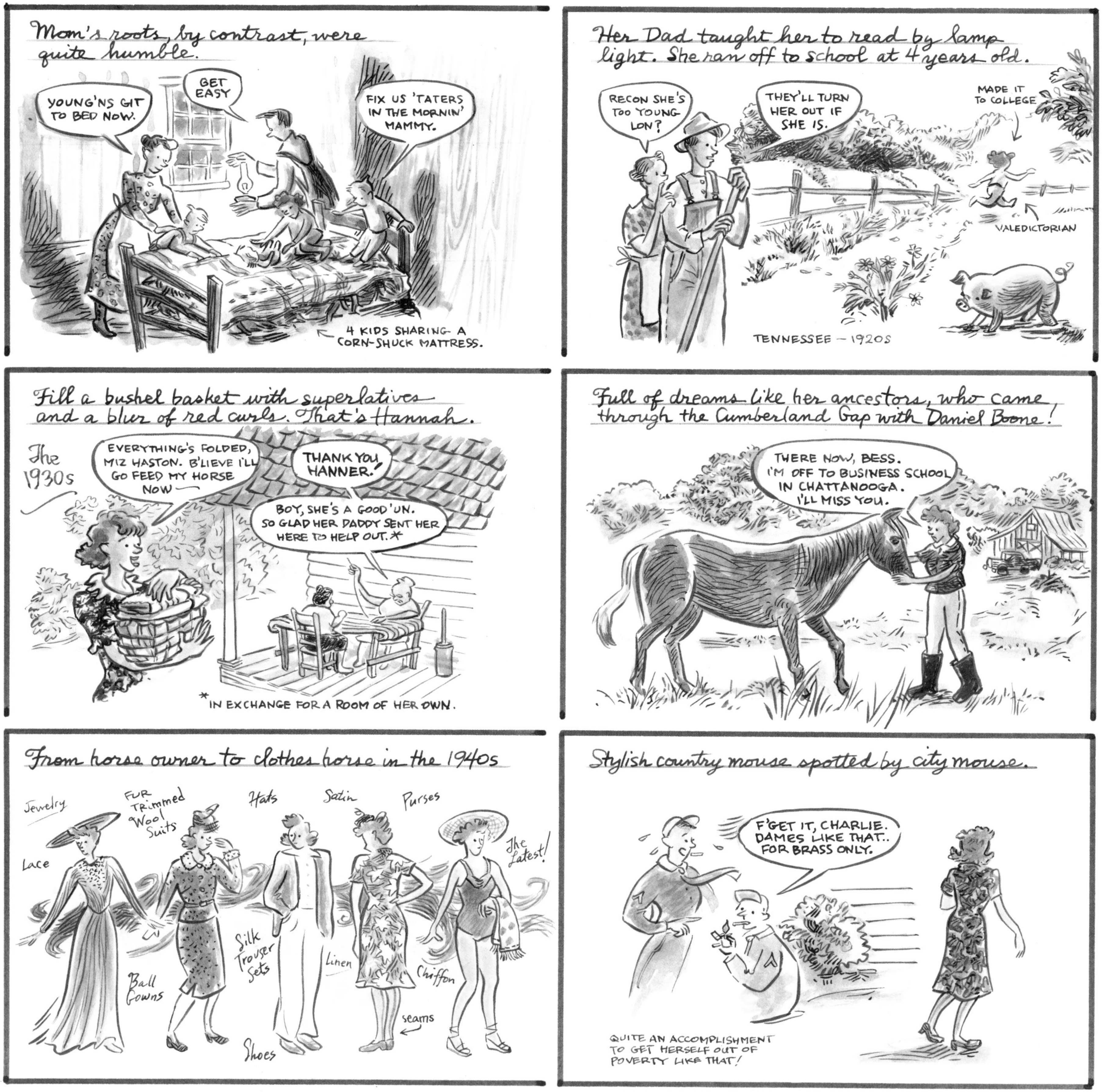
Mom's roots, by contrast, were quite humble.
YOUNG'NS GIT TO BED NOW.
GET EASY
FIX US 'TATERS IN THE MORNIN' MAMMY.
4 KIDS SHARING A CORN-SHUCK MATTRESS.
Her Dad taught her to read by lamp light. She ran off to school at 4 years old.
RECON SHE'S TOO YOUNG LON?
THEY'LL TURN HER OUT IF SHE IS.
MADE IT TO COLLEGE
VALEDICTORIAN
TENNESSEE – 1920S
Fill a bushel basket with superlatives and a blur of red curls. That's Hannah.
The 1930s
EVERYTHING'S FOLDED, MIZ HASTON. B'LIEVE I'LL GO FEED MY HORSE NOW
THANK YOU, HANNER!
BOY, SHE'S A GOOD 'UN. SO GLAD HER DADDY SENT HER HERE TO HELP OUT.*
*IN EXCHANGE FOR A ROOM OF HER OWN.
Full of dreams like her ancestors, who came through the Cumberland Gap with Daniel Boone!
THERE NOW, BESS. I'M OFF TO BUSINESS SCHOOL IN CHATTANOOGA. I'LL MISS YOU.
From horse owner to clothes horse in the 1940s
Jewelry
FUR Trimmed Wool Suits
Hats
Satin
Purses
The Latest!
Lace
Ball Gowns
Silk Trouser Sets
Linen
Chiffon
seams
Shoes
Stylish country mouse spotted by city mouse.
F'GET IT, CHARLIE. DAMES LIKE THAT.. FOR BRASS ONLY.
QUITE AN ACCOMPLISHMENT TO GET HERSELF OUT OF POVERTY LIKE THAT!

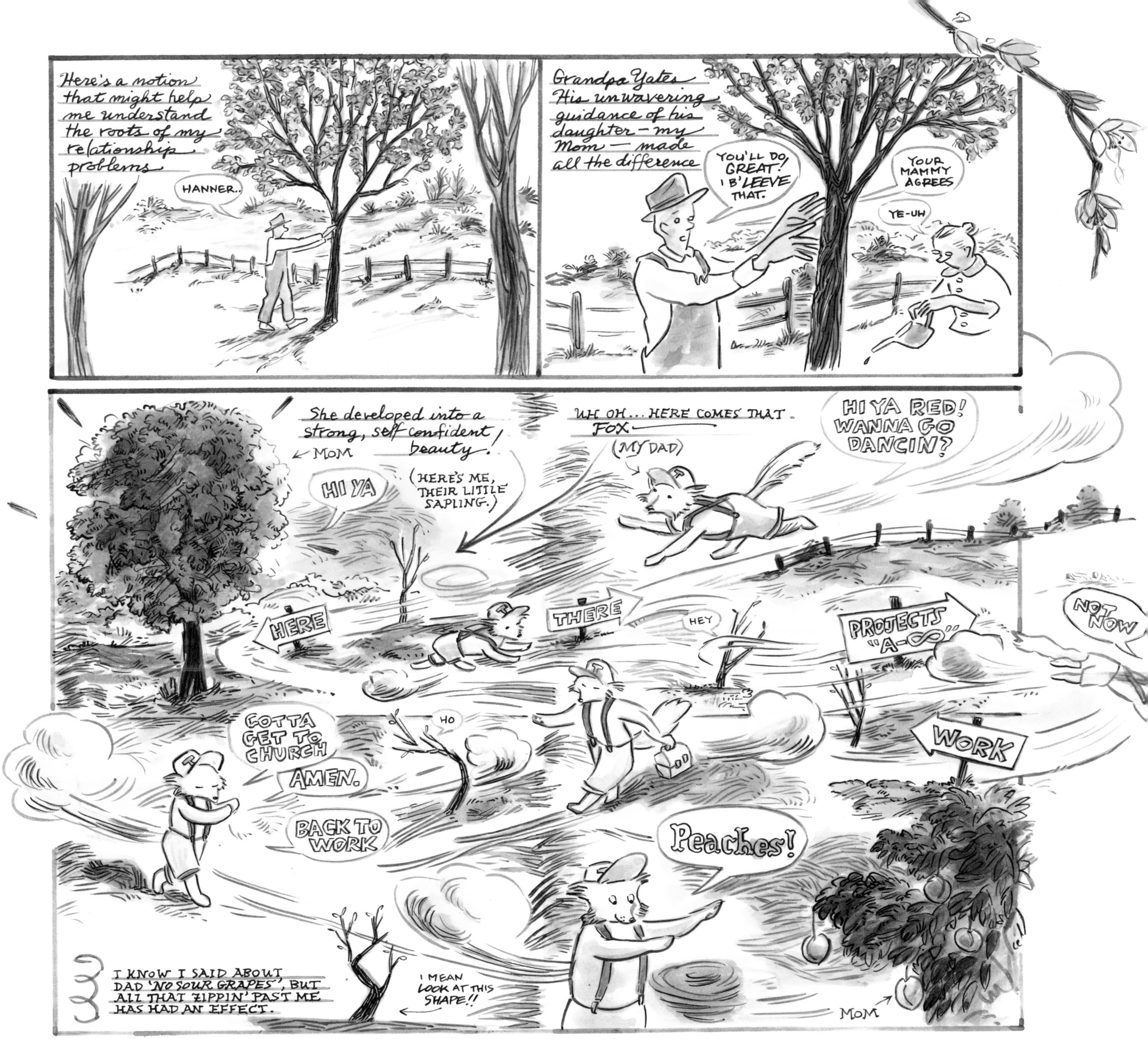

Here's a notion that might help me understand the roots of my relationship problems
HANNER..
Grandpa Yates. His unwavering guidance of his daughter — my Mom — made all the difference
YOU'LL DO GREAT! I B'LEEVE THAT.
YOUR MAMMY AGREES
YE-UH
She developed into a strong, self confident beauty!
MOM
HI YA
(HERE'S ME, THEIR LITTLE SAPLING.)
UH OH... HERE COMES THAT FOX
(MY DAD)
HI YA RED! WANNA GO DANCIN?
HERE
THERE
HEY
PROJECTS "A-∞"
NOT NOW
WORK
GOTTA GET TO CHURCH
HO
AMEN.
BACK TO WORK
Peaches!
I KNOW I SAID ABOUT DAD 'NO SOUR GRAPES', BUT ALL THAT ZIPPIN' PAST ME HAS HAD AN EFFECT.
I MEAN LOOK AT THIS SHAPE!!
MOM

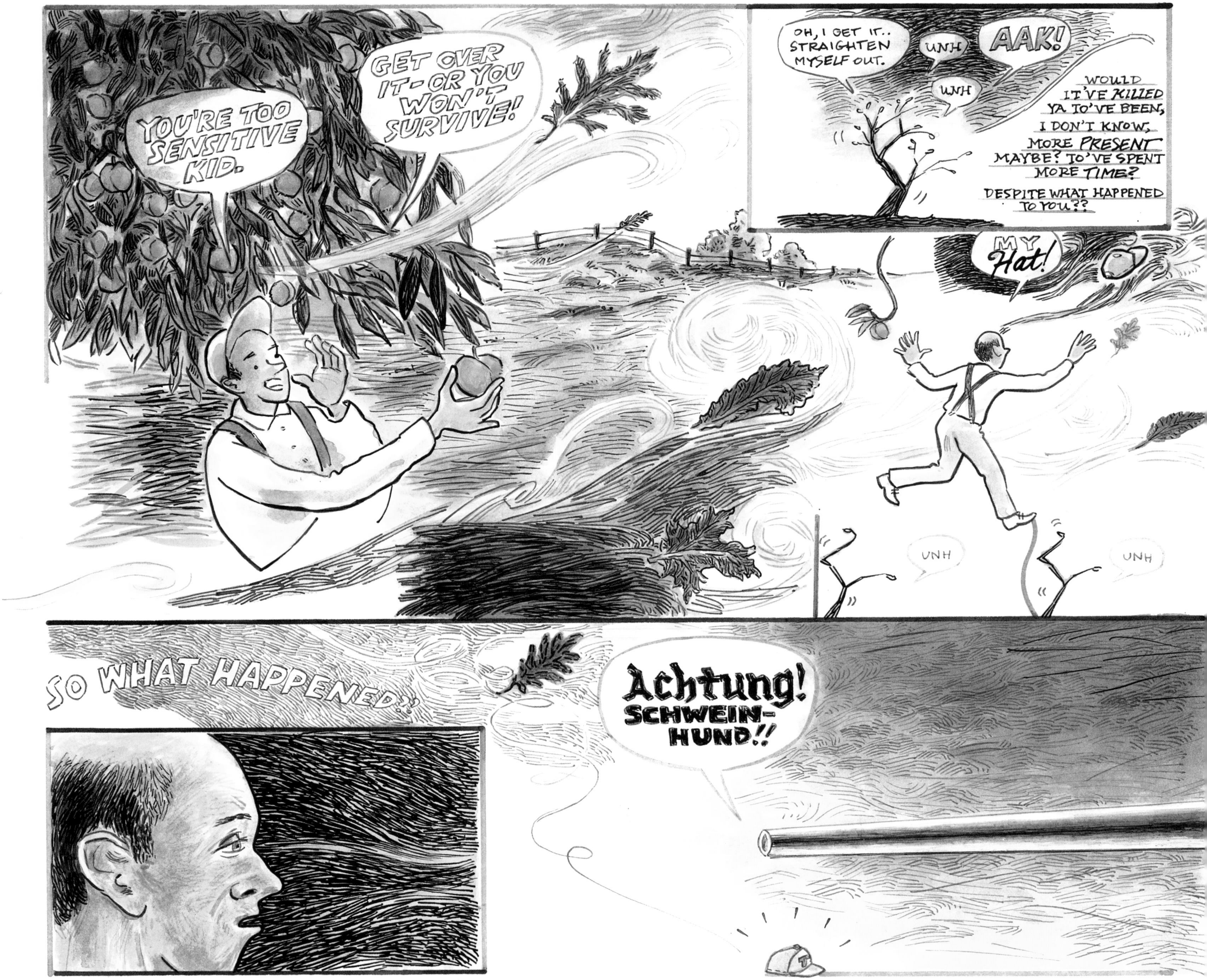
YOU'RE TOO SENSITIVE KID.
GET OVER IT- OR YOU WON'T SURVIVE!
OH, I GET IT.. STRAIGHTEN MYSELF OUT.
UNH
AAK!
UNH
WOULD IT'VE KILLED YA TO'VE BEEN, I DON'T KNOW, MORE PRESENT MAYBE? TO'VE SPENT MORE TIME? DESPITE WHAT HAPPENED TO YOU??
MY Hat!
UNH
UNH
SO WHAT HAPPENED?!
Achtung! SCHWEIN-HUND!!

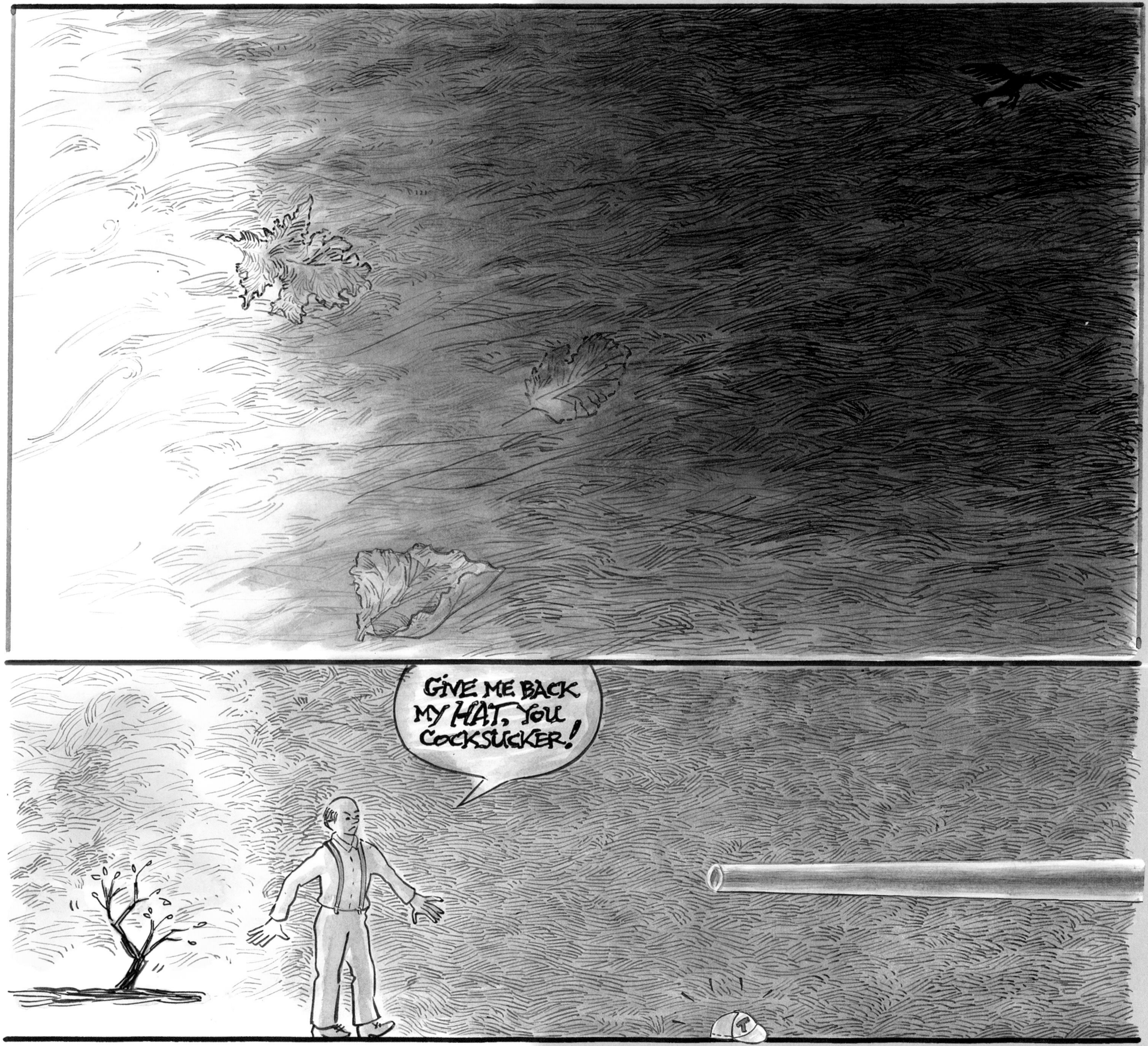
GIVE ME BACK MY HAT, YOU COCKSUCKER!

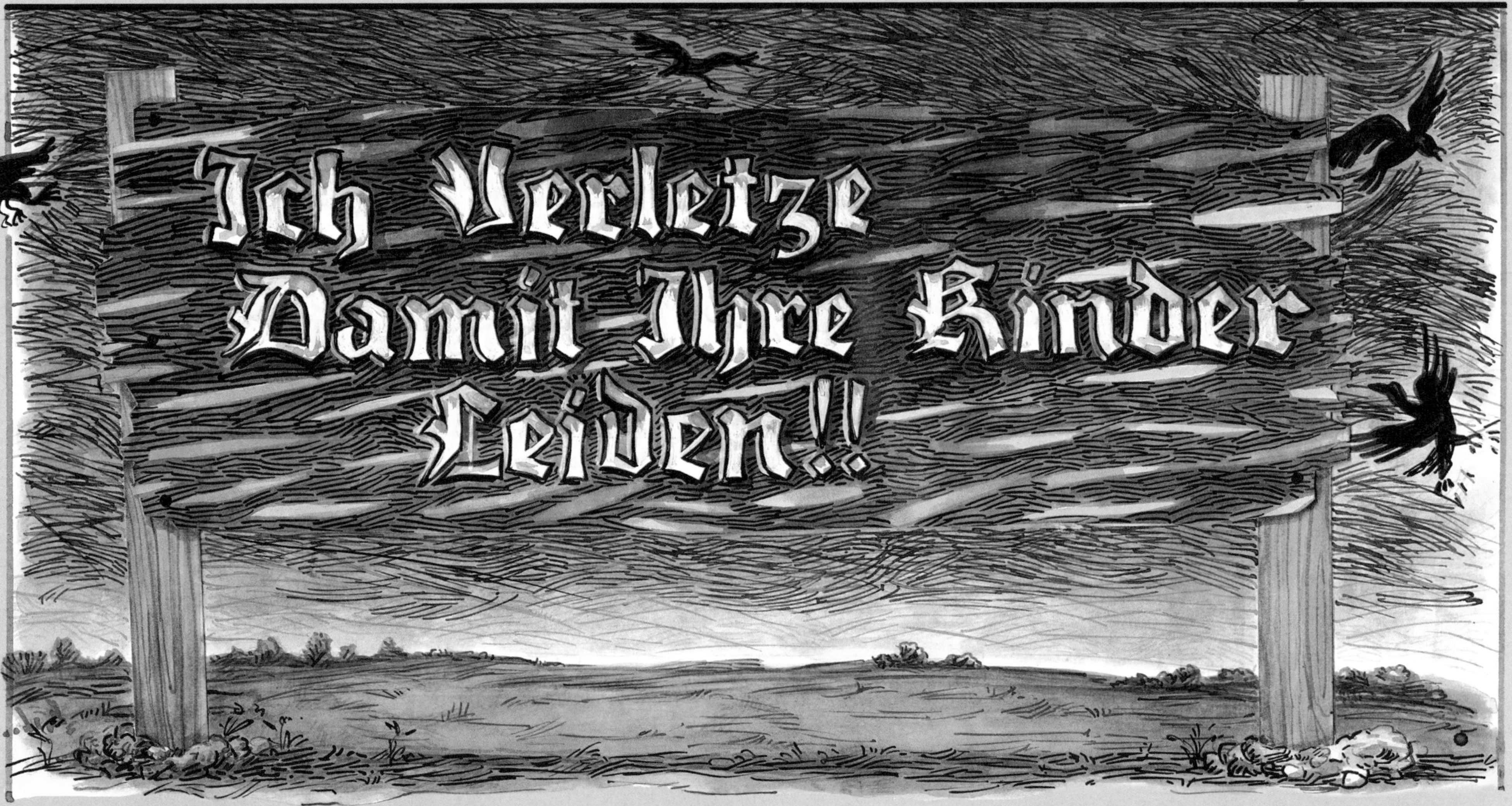
Ich Verletze
Damit Ihre Kinder
Leiden!!

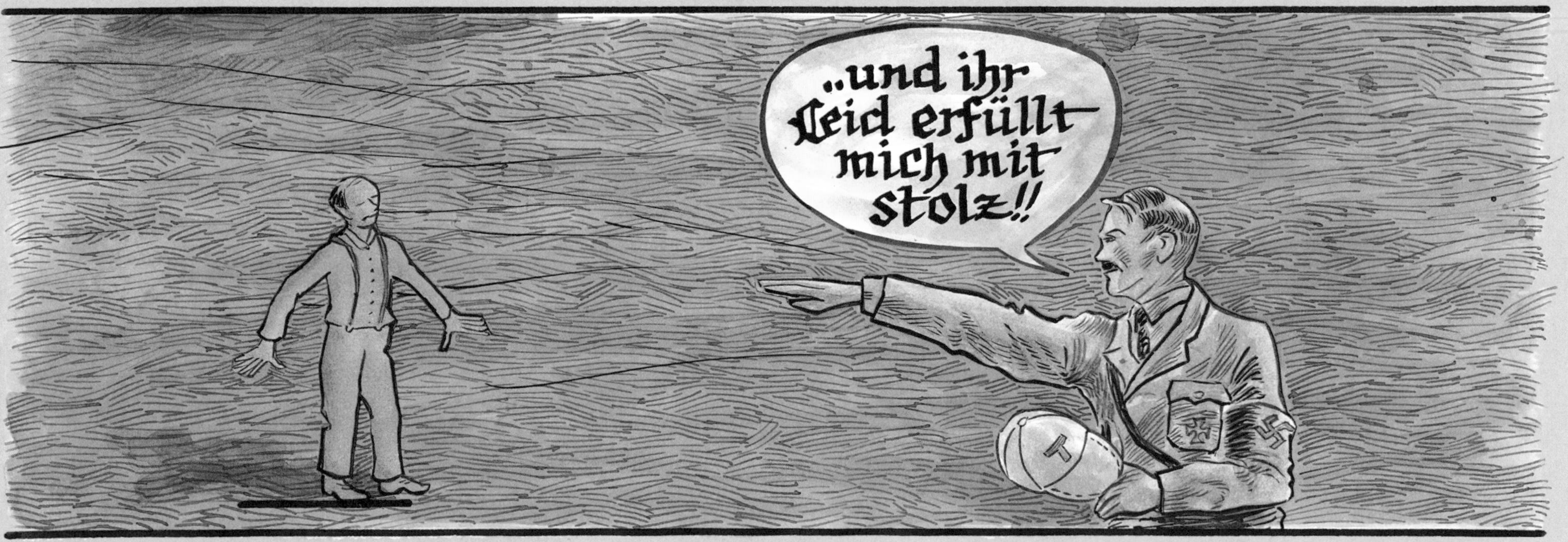
..und ihr Leid erfüllt mich mit stolz!!

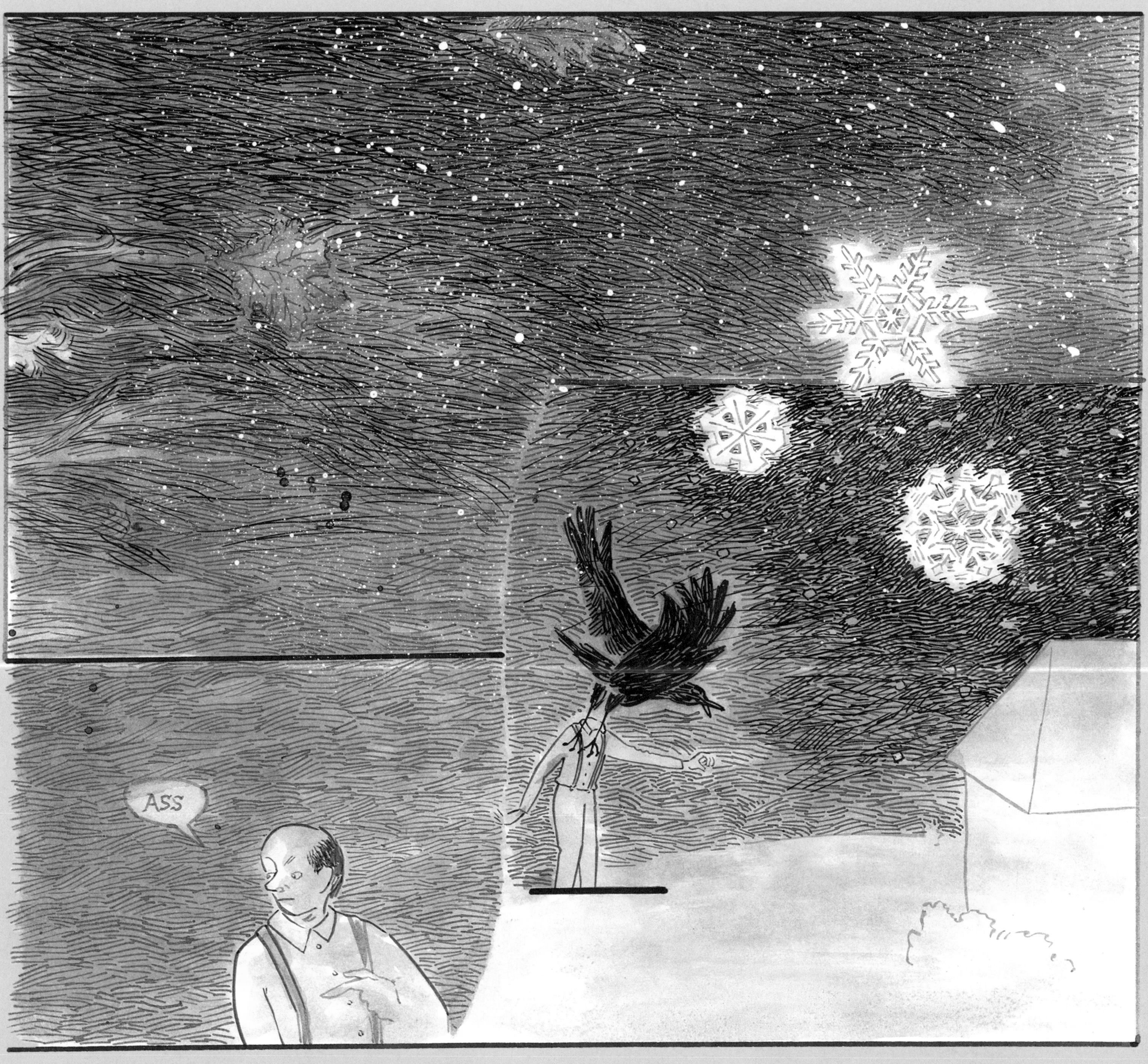
ASS

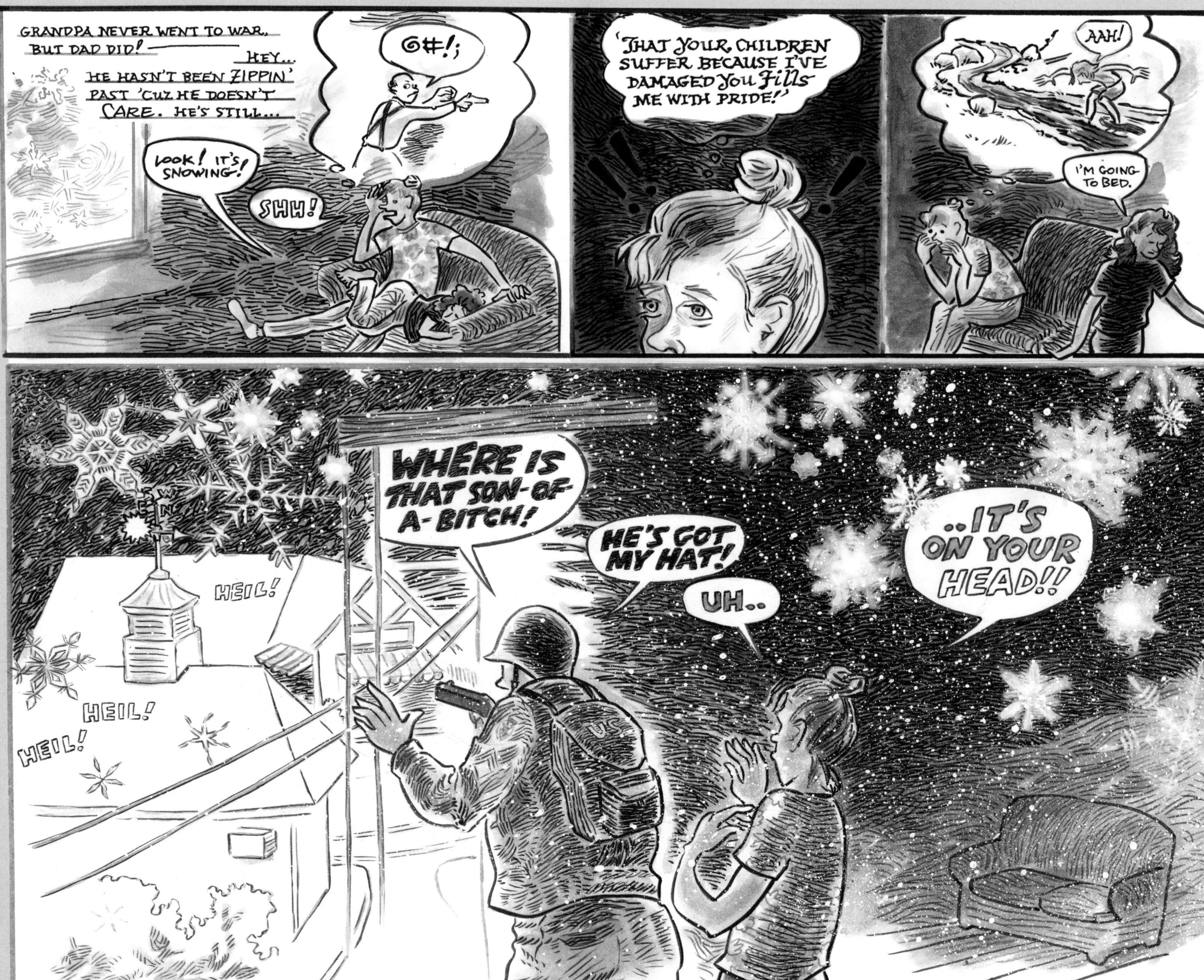
GRANDPA NEVER WENT TO WAR, BUT DAD DID!
HEY... HE HASN'T BEEN ZIPPIN' PAST 'CUZ HE DOESN'T CARE. HE'S STILL...
@#!;
LOOK! IT'S SNOWING!
SHH!
'THAT YOUR CHILDREN SUFFER BECAUSE I'VE DAMAGED YOU FILLS ME WITH PRIDE!'
AAH!
I'M GOING TO BED.
HEIL!
HEIL!
HEIL!
WHERE IS THAT SON-OF-A-BITCH!
HE'S GOT MY HAT!
UH..
..IT'S ON YOUR HEAD!!

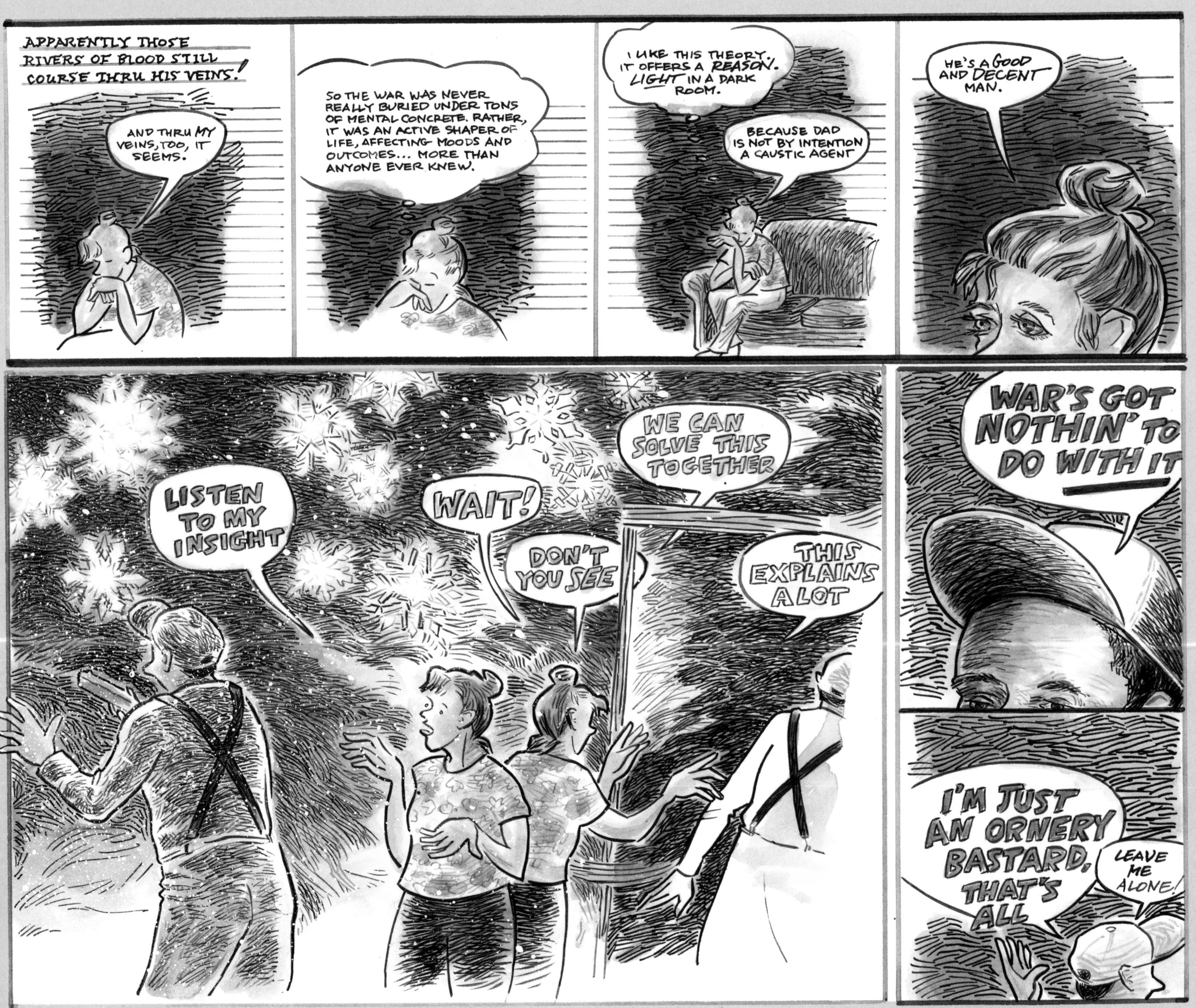
APPARENTLY THOSE RIVERS OF BLOOD STILL COURSE THRU HIS VEINS!
AND THRU MY VEINS, TOO, IT SEEMS.
SO THE WAR WAS NEVER REALLY BURIED UNDER TONS OF MENTAL CONCRETE. RATHER, IT WAS AN ACTIVE SHAPER OF LIFE, AFFECTING MOODS AND OUTCOMES... MORE THAN ANYONE EVER KNEW.
I LIKE THIS THEORY. IT OFFERS A REASON. LIGHT IN A DARK ROOM.
BECAUSE DAD IS NOT BY INTENTION A CAUSTIC AGENT
HE'S A GOOD AND DECENT MAN.
LISTEN TO MY INSIGHT
WAIT!
DON'T YOU SEE
WE CAN SOLVE THIS TOGETHER
THIS EXPLAINS ALOT
WAR'S GOT NOTHIN' TO DO WITH IT
I'M JUST AN ORNERY BASTARD, THAT'S ALL
LEAVE ME ALONE!

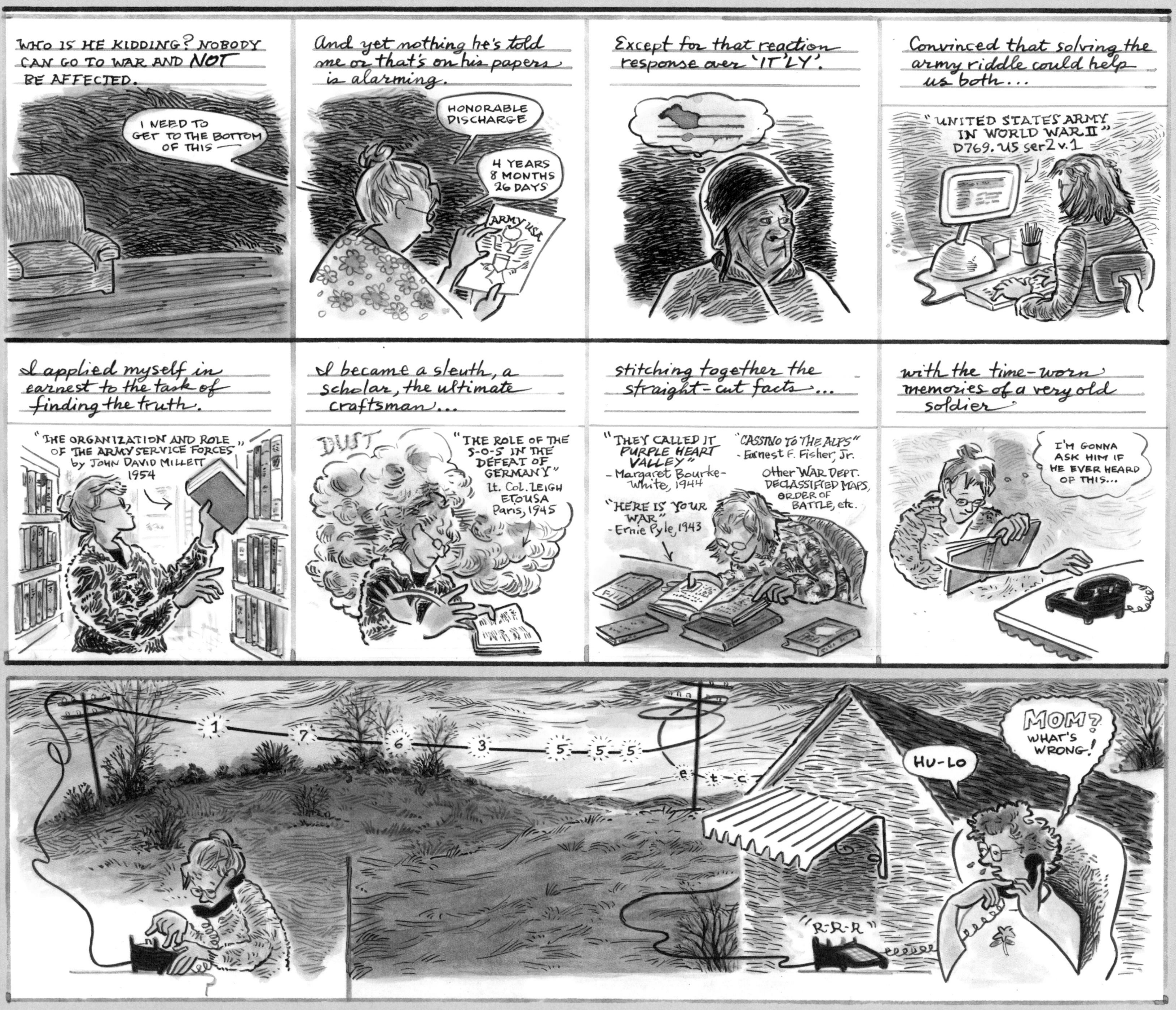
WHO IS HE KIDDING? NOBODY CAN GO TO WAR AND NOT BE AFFECTED.
I NEED TO GET TO THE BOTTOM OF THIS —
And yet nothing he's told me or that's on his papers is alarming.
HONORABLE DISCHARGE
4 YEARS 8 MONTHS 26 DAYS
ARMY USA
Except for that reaction response over 'IT'LY'.
Convinced that solving the army riddle could help us both...
"UNITED STATES ARMY IN WORLD WAR II" D769. US ser2 v.1
I applied myself in earnest to the task of finding the truth.
"THE ORGANIZATION AND ROLE OF THE ARMY SERVICE FORCES" by JOHN DAVID MILLETT 1954
I became a sleuth, a scholar, the ultimate craftsman...
DUST
"THE ROLE OF THE S-O-S IN THE DEFEAT OF GERMANY" Lt. Col. LEIGH ETOUSA Paris, 1945
stitching together the straight-cut facts...
"THEY CALLED IT PURPLE HEART VALLEY" - Margaret Bourke-White, 1944
"CASSINO TO THE ALPS" - Ernest F. Fisher, Jr.
"HERE IS YOUR WAR" - Ernie Pyle, 1943
Other WAR DEPT. DECLASSIFIED MAPS, ORDER OF BATTLE, etc.
with the time-worn memories of a very old soldier
I'M GONNA ASK HIM IF HE EVER HEARD OF THIS...
1 7 6 3 5 5 5
e t c
HU-LO
MOM? WHAT'S WRONG!
R-R-R

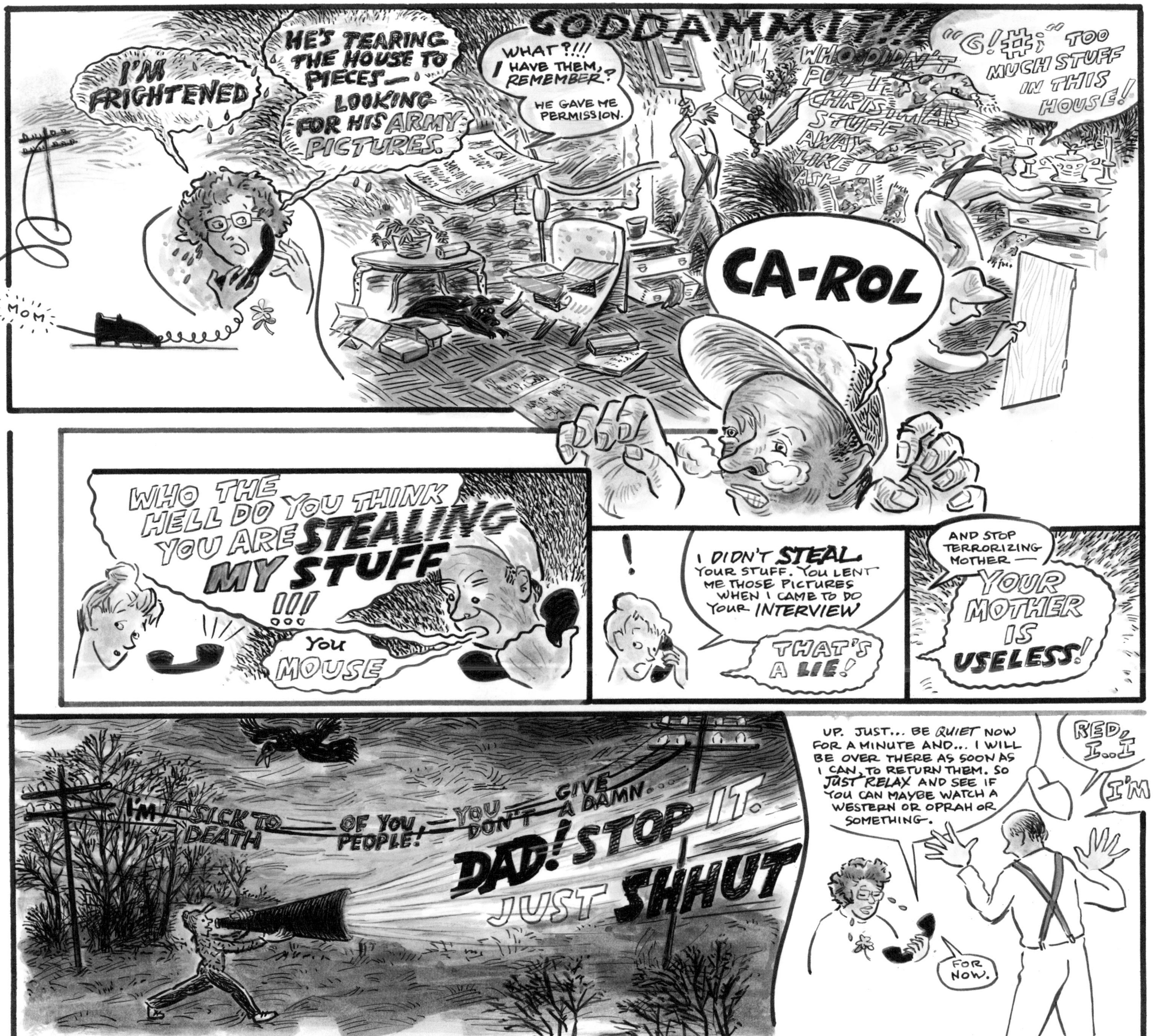

I'M FRIGHTENED
HE'S TEARING THE HOUSE TO PIECES— LOOKING FOR HIS ARMY PICTURES.
MOM
WHAT?!!! I HAVE THEM, REMEMBER?
HE GAVE ME PERMISSION.
GODDAMMIT!!!
WHO DIDN'T PUT THE CHRISTMAS STUFF AWAY LIKE I ASK—
"G!#;" TOO MUCH STUFF IN THIS HOUSE!
CA-ROL
WHO THE HELL DO YOU THINK YOU ARE STEALING MY STUFF !!! ???
YOU MOUSE
!
I DIDN'T STEAL YOUR STUFF. YOU LENT ME THOSE PICTURES WHEN I CAME TO DO YOUR INTERVIEW
THAT'S A LIE!
AND STOP TERRORIZING MOTHER—
YOUR MOTHER IS USELESS!
I'M SICK TO DEATH OF YOU PEOPLE! YOU DON'T GIVE A DAMN...
DAD! STOP IT. JUST SHHUT
UP. JUST... BE QUIET NOW FOR A MINUTE AND... I WILL BE OVER THERE AS SOON AS I CAN, TO RETURN THEM. SO JUST RELAX AND SEE IF YOU CAN MAYBE WATCH A WESTERN OR OPRAH OR SOMETHING.
RED, I...I
I'M...
FOR NOW.

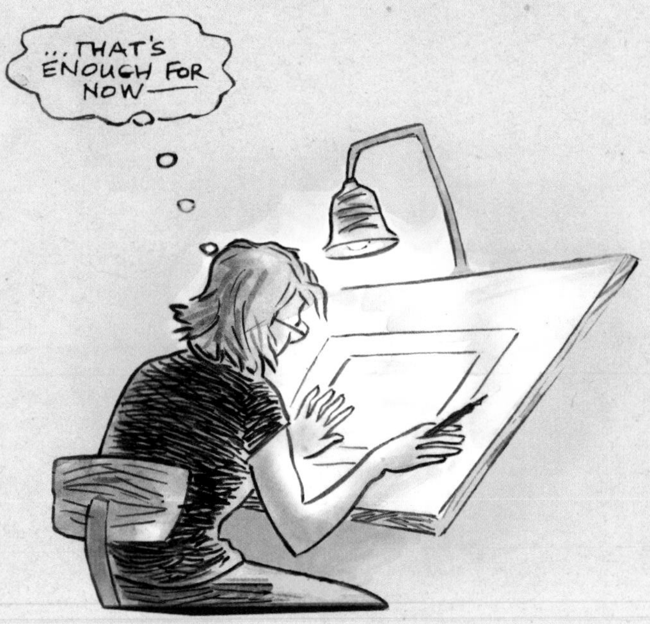
...THAT'S ENOUGH FOR NOW—

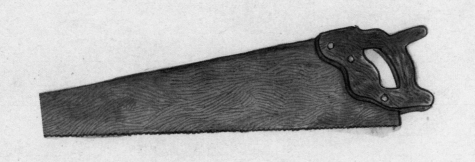